Twinkle twinkle little star,
the world is at your feet.

(Encouragement from my days teaching computers in an adult literacy classroom — a reminder that learning is always possible, and the world is full of opportunity.)

Mastering Excel
for Home Budgeting

A practical guide to create a home budget with Microsoft Excel and LibreOffice Calc, using formulas, VBA, and advanced techniques.

It's all about the budget

Thomas W. Pettit

PetiteKat
Press

Mastering Excel for Home Budgeting
© 2025 Thomas W. Pettit. All rights reserved.

No part of this publication may be reproduced, stored in a retrieval system, or transmitted in any form or by any means — electronic, mechanical, photocopying, recording,
or otherwise — without the prior written permission of the publisher, except for brief quotations used in critical reviews or articles.

Published by PetiteKat Press

Paperback ISBN: 978-1-7638642-0-7
eBook ISBN: 978-1-7638642-1-4
https://*www.petitekatpress.com.au*

This book is intended for educational purposes only.
The author and publisher have made every effort to ensure the accuracy of the information herein, but assume no responsibility for any errors, omissions, or outcomes resulting from its use.
Readers are advised to consult relevant professionals when applying concepts to real-world situations.

First Edition: 2025

Trademark Acknowledgements

Microsoft Excel and **Microsoft Windows** are trademarks of **Microsoft Corporation**.

LibreOffice is a trademark of **The Document Foundation**.
This book is not endorsed by, sponsored by, or affiliated with Microsoft Corporation or The Document Foundation.

Contributors

Publishing Product Manager: Thomas W. Pettit

Editorial Team: Thomas W. Pettit,
Michelle Pettit-Rupuha

Design and Production: Thomas W. Pettit

Marketing Coordination: Michelle Pettit-Rupuha

Proofreading Team: Thomas W. Pettit
Michelle Pettit-Rupuha

Support and Motivation: Elizabeth Diane Cliffe

Publication Details:

Title: Mastering Excel for Home Budgeting

First Edition: June 2025

Production Reference: 0004

Publisher: PetiteKat Press

ISBN: 978-1-7638642-0-7

To my partner in life, Elizabeth Diane Cliffe,
for your invaluable contributions and unwavering support in bringing this book to life.

Your constant encouragement, the countless cups of coffee, and your patience with the back of my head during those long, quiet hours of concentration have been nothing short of inspiring.

Thank you for believing in me, supporting my vision, and creating the space I needed to make this project possible.

– *Thomas W. Pettit*

Preface

Welcome to "Mastering Excel for Home Budgeting." This book is a labor of love, born out of my passion for helping individuals take control of their finances using the powerful tools available in Microsoft Excel. Over the years, I have seen many people struggle with managing their budgets, and I wanted to create a resource that would make this process easier and more accessible.

My journey with Excel began many years ago when I first started teaching computer classes in Melbourne, Australia. Since then, I have had the privilege of working with various organizations, including the Royal Agricultural Society (RAS), New South Wales Police Force, the Royal Australian Air Force (RAAF), Transport NSW, and Grosvenor Engineering. These experiences have given me a deep understanding of the practical applications of Excel and the challenges people face when using it.

This book is designed to guide you through the process of creating a comprehensive home budget using Excel. Whether you are a complete beginner or have some experience with spreadsheets, you will find valuable tips and techniques to help you manage your finances more effectively.

I hope you find this book helpful and that it empowers you to take control of your financial future. Thank you for joining me on this journey.

Let's get started building your budgeting system — one step at a time!

About the author

Thomas W. Pettit is a multi-faceted Senior Software Developer, educator, and

author with an extensive career spanning over four decades. After completing his studies in software development, he initially taught computer classes in Melbourne, Australia, before pursuing his true calling in software and database development. His professional journey has included key roles at organizations such as the Royal Agricultural Society (RAS), New South Wales Police Force, Royal Australian Air Force (RAAF), Transport NSW, and Grosvenor Engineering, among others.

Thomas is skilled in a wide range of platforms, including MS Access, MS Excel, SQL Server, MySQL, .NET, and VBA. He co-authored *The MySQL Workshop: A Practical Guide to Working with Data and Managing Databases with MySQL*, a valuable resource for professionals in database management. *Mastering Excel for Home Budgeting* is the second course he has written, designed to demystify Excel through practical, everyday applications.

With a passion for teaching and extensive experience across both public and private sectors, Thomas is dedicated to empowering others to make the most of today's technologies.

A Note from the Author

There are many training books available for Excel, but the author noticed that most of those aimed at total beginners did not provide extensive, real-world, and useful results at the end. This book attempts to address this by guiding beginners through a useful and comprehensive real-world budget application they can continue to use in real life and expand on.

This training course is designed for individuals who want to learn how to create their own spreadsheet applications, specifically for personal budgeting. The author believes that the content should be interesting, relevant, and useful for the learner, which is why the course focuses on creating a Home-Budget application.

The course is structured to provide targeted exercises and activities that will teach the necessary skills for creating spreadsheet applications and includes tips and tricks the author has learned over many years of experience.

By the end of the course, participants will have gained the skills and confidence to create their own spreadsheet applications for personal and professional use.

Using LibreOffice Calc with This Book

While this book is based on Microsoft Excel, you can also successfully complete all lessons using LibreOffice Calc — a free, open-source spreadsheet application.

LibreOffice Calc supports nearly all the features used in this book, including formulas, formatting, charts, and macros (with some minor differences, which are noted throughout).

If you don't already have LibreOffice installed, you can download and install it for free here: https://www.libreoffice.org/download/download-libreoffice/
or Scan or click the QRCode.

> **Note:**
> LibreOffice is available for Windows, macOS, and Linux.
> This book focuses on Windows-based usage, but LibreOffice users on any platform should be able to follow along with only minor interface differences.

Recommended Setup for LibreOffice Users

To make following the instructions easier, you can adjust LibreOffice Calc to look more like Microsoft Excel:

1. Enable the **Tabbed (Ribbon) Interface**:
    a. Go to **View** → **User Interface**.
    b. Select **Tabbed** and (optional) click Apply to All.
2. Set the **Icon Theme** to **Colibre**:
    a. Go to Tools → Options → LibreOffice → View.
    b. Under **Icon Theme**, select **Colibre**.
    c. Click OK to apply.

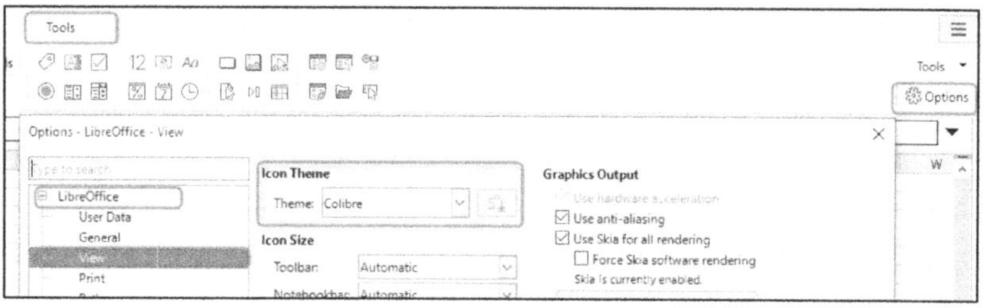

With these quick settings, LibreOffice will closely match the screenshots and instructions shown in this book.

Important

Throughout the chapters:

- Special tips will be provided when LibreOffice users need to take a slightly different step.
- Macros are provided in both Excel VBA and LibreOffice BASIC formats for your convenience.
- After you change to Ribbon view, several of the options that were available under the View menu will now be available from here. When View menu is referenced, you can use either method as shown below.

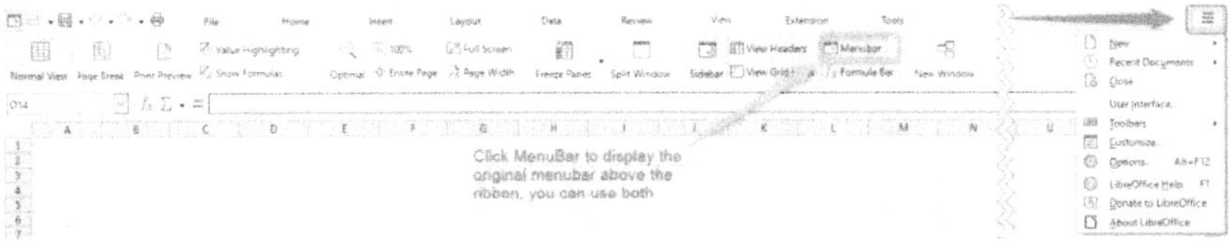

GitHub

Accessing the Support Files (GitHub)

Throughout this book, you will be guided to create your own budgeting workbook step-by-step.
However, if you prefer, you can also download ready-to-use files, templates, and macros to support your learning.

The companion files for this book are available on GitHub, a secure online repository.
Even if you have never used GitHub before, don't worry — simple links and QR codes are provided to take you directly to the files you need.

The GitHub repository contains:

- Sample completed budget workbooks (Excel and LibreOffice versions).
- Pre-written macros (Excel VBA and LibreOffice BASIC).
- Templates to help you get started faster.
- Additional resources and updates if corrections are ever needed.

> **Note:**
> You do not need a GitHub account to access or download the files.
> All downloads are publicly available for your convenience.

In the following section, and throughout the book, you will find QR Codes that can be scanned to access additional resources and content for both the eBook and paperback versions of this book. Use a QR Code scanner on your smartphone or tablet to quickly navigate to the relevant online materials or click on them if you are using an electronic version.

Feedback, Errors, and Copyright Protection

Feedback

Your feedback is always welcome. If you have any suggestions or comments about this training course, you can contact us via the publisher's website or email.

Your input helps improve the quality of this course and ensures a better learning experience for future readers.

Errata

Despite our best efforts, some errors may still occur. If you spot any mistakes or inaccuracies, please report them so we can correct them promptly.

You can view previously reported issues and submit your own via our GitHub Issues page.
Please:

- Choose the appropriate category (Errata, Feedback, etc.)
- Provide as much detail as you can
- Suggest a fix if you have one
- Attach files or screenshots if helpful

Your contributions help make this book more accurate and helpful for everyone.

Handling Feedback and Errors

- **Critical Errors**
  Will be addressed as soon as possible. Corrected files or updates will be posted on the GitHub repository or official website.
  Note: For books purchased via retailers (e.g. Amazon), updated versions may not be automatically delivered. Please check the GitHub repository for the most current files and resources.
- **Non-Critical Errors**
  Reviewed and corrected in the next scheduled update or release.
- **Feedback & Suggestions**

All feedback is reviewed. Suggestions aligned with the course goals may be added to future editions. If you're reporting something related to the difference between print and online features (e.g. popups, tooltips), rest assured the book is designed to ensure full usability in both formats.

> **Note:** This book is designed to support both printed and online use. While some interactive features may appear in digital formats, printed readers will find equivalent examples and explanations included to ensure a complete learning experience.

Piracy

It is illegal to share or distribute copyrighted material without permission.
If you discover unauthorized copies of this training course online, please report them:

To report piracy,

Scan or click the QR Code to send a report via email

Please include:

- The name of the website or platform
- A direct link to the pirated content

Only authorized personnel will review your report. Any personal information you provide will be used solely to investigate the issue.

Your help protects the integrity of this work and supports respectful, legal learning.

About This Book

Mastering Excel for Home Budgeting is designed to take you from beginner to confident Excel user by guiding you through the creation of a real-world home budgeting system.

Each chapter builds your skills step-by-step, using clear examples, practical exercises, and real-world scenarios. You'll not only learn how to use Microsoft Excel but also how to apply your knowledge to manage your personal finances more effectively.

Wherever possible, this book also provides guidance for LibreOffice Calc users, ensuring that both Excel and open-source spreadsheet users can benefit from the lessons and techniques taught throughout.

Whether you're completely new to spreadsheets or looking to sharpen your existing skills, this book provides an approachable, hands-on learning experience.

At the end of each chapter, you'll find a quiz, answer section, and a self-assessment to help reinforce your understanding and measure your progress.

Get ready to open Excel or LibreOffice, build your budget, and take control of your financial future!

A Personal Note

Thank you for picking up this book and taking the first steps toward mastering Excel and budgeting.
I hope you find this guide practical, supportive, and empowering as you build the tools you need for your financial journey.

Here's to your success!

— Thomas W. Pettit

Table of Contents

Important Information

Before diving into the content, please review the following disclaimers to understand the scope and limitations of the information provided.

Financial Advice and Liability Disclaimer

This book is not intended to provide financial, legal, or tax advice. The information presented is for educational purposes only. Readers should consult qualified professionals for specific advice tailored to their individual circumstances. The author and publisher shall not be liable for any damage or losses arising from the use of this book. This includes, but is not limited to, any direct, indirect, incidental, or consequential damages. Readers use the information in this book at their own risk.

Accuracy Disclaimer

While every effort has been made to ensure the accuracy of the information provided in this book, errors and omissions may occur. The author and publisher make no warranties, expressed or implied, about the completeness, reliability, or accuracy of the information. This book should be used as a guide, and users are encouraged to verify the information with other sources.

Software and Tools Disclaimer

This book references specific software (e.g., Microsoft Excel) and tools. The author and publisher are not responsible for any issues related to the use or performance of these software and tools. Readers should refer to the software's official documentation for the most accurate and up-to-date information.

Updates and Changes Disclaimer

Software updates and changes may affect the functionality and features described in this book. The author and publisher are not responsible for any discrepancies that arise due to software updates. Readers are encouraged to refer to the latest official documentation or resources for current information.

AI Usage Disclaimer

The primary expertise of the author lies in Excel, not in professional writing. While the initial content of this book was created by the author, it has been enhanced with the assistance of artificial intelligence (AI). This support was used to refine and improve the text for clarity and coherence. The integration of AI does not diminish the authenticity or originality of the work. The ideas, methodologies, and instructions throughout this book remain the author's own work — AI simply aided in expressing and organizing them.

Mastering Excel for Home Budgeting

Software Needed

To follow along with this book, you will need access to a spreadsheet program that supports macros.

- **Microsoft Excel** installed on your computer (preferably Excel 2016 or later. Excel 365 is ideal, but older versions should still work—though menus may differ slightly).

  ⚠ **Important**: The free **Excel Online** version does not support VBA macros. If you're using Excel through a web browser (e.g., Office.com), many of the features in this book, especially automation tasks, will not work.

- **OR** you can use **LibreOffice Calc** (latest version), which is free and open-source. While it uses a different macro language (LibreOffice Basic instead of VBA), most of the budgeting techniques covered in this book can still be followed manually, and we include fallback instructions where possible.

Download and installation instructions for LibreOffice appear in a later section.

> **Note for LibreOffice Calc Users**
> While this book primarily teaches Microsoft Excel, all major features and steps are also available in LibreOffice Calc, a free and powerful alternative to Excel.
>
> Where necessary, notes and guidance are provided to help LibreOffice users adapt the instructions smoothly.

Is this course for you?

The course is intended for individuals with no prior experience with Excel or other spreadsheet applications who want to learn how to create a useful tool for managing their personal finances.

The course will guide the reader through the process of creating the spreadsheet and provide the skills to modify and continue using it after completing the training course.

You'll be working hands-on from the very beginning, building your own personalized home budgeting workbook — one step at a time!

What You'll Learn

This training course covers the following, plus more.

- Creating, opening, and saving spreadsheets
- Formula
- Cell referencing on same worksheet and other worksheets.
- Named Ranges, Graphs and Charts
- Security, i.e., Protecting and locking cells, worksheets, workbook.

> ***Note:***
> Although this course uses Microsoft Excel, LibreOffice Calc users can follow along successfully with minor adjustments. Full details are provided where needed.

Course Structure

This training course is designed to provide targeted exercises and activities that will teach you the necessary skills for creating spreadsheet applications. The course is structured into several chapters, each focusing on different aspects of Excel and personal budgeting. Here's a detailed breakdown of what each chapter covers:

1. Introduction to Microsoft Excel

Overview of Excel and its interface, Basic navigation and functionalities

2. Creating Workbooks and Worksheets

Have you ever wondered how to keep your Excel workbooks organized right from the start?

3. Basic Formulas and Functions

Introduction to formulas, Basic arithmetic operations and common functions

4. Advanced Formulas and Data Analysis
Advanced functions like SUM, AVERAGE, VLOOKUP, Absolute and relative references and also Nested Formulas

5. Creating and Organizing the Home Budget Workbook
Setting up the income and expenses worksheets, Planning and organizing data

6. Worksheet Tutorials
Detailed tutorials on creating and formatting various budget-related worksheets (Income, Expenses, Loans, etc.)

7. VBA Macros
Introduction to VBA, Creating and using macros for automation

8. Modifying and Enhancing Worksheets
Dynamic worksheet modifications, Inserting, moving, copying, and deleting data

9. Security and Protection
Protecting workbooks and worksheets, Managing user input cells

By the end of the course, you will have gained the skills and confidence to create your own spreadsheet applications for personal and professional use. Each chapter includes practical exercises and real-life examples to help you apply what you've learned.

Maximize Your Learning

To fully benefit from this course, it is recommended that the learner has the following:

- Basic computer skills, including starting the computer, finding and starting applications, opening and saving files, and using a mouse or touchpad/touchscreen and keyboard.
- Microsoft Office with Microsoft Excel installed.
- The use of a second monitor is highly recommended, ideally a large format monitor, as it can enhance the learning experience. However, the

course can be completed using a laptop, tablet or single monitor desktop computer.

Get Your Sample Files Here

All sample files, sample code, exercises and future updates to the public files will be put in here.

Access Color Images

If you purchase a black and white printed version of this training course, all images in this book are also compiled in full color in a companion PDF, which can be downloaded from here.

The printed version is available in black and white only, to keep the cost as low as possible. The eBook version is in full color.

In particular, some worksheet images in this book use **yellow highlighting** to indicate input areas. Please note that this highlighting may not be clearly visible in the black and white print version. The full-color images in the companion PDF will display these highlights clearly.

How To Use This Book

Reader Note: Print vs. Online Features
This book is designed so you can work through it either from a printed copy or on screen — whichever you prefer. Everything you need is included in the book itself, but online readers may also see some extra features like pop-up tips or interactive examples. If you're reading the print version, don't worry — wherever an online feature is mentioned, I've made sure there's also a printed example or note you can follow. You won't miss out on any key information, whichever way you choose to learn.

There are several conventions used throughout this training course.

Tips, tricks, and important notes
Will appear in a box like this.

Italics

Indicates code words in text, database table names, folder names, filenames, file extensions, pathnames, URLs, user input, and Twitter handles.
Here is an example: "We used *WHERE* to filter out the rows we were interested in."

Bold

In a standard text block or paragraph Indicates something new, an important word, or words that you will see onscreen. For instance, words on menus or dialog boxes will appear in bold.
Here is an example: "**Dbl-Click** in cell I**8** and type **=G8*H8**"

Cell Range references

In Excel, the colon (:) in a cell range, such as A10:A25, signifies a continuous range of cells. This range can be within a single column, a single row, or span multiple columns and rows.

For example,

- **A1:A5** refers to cells in a single column

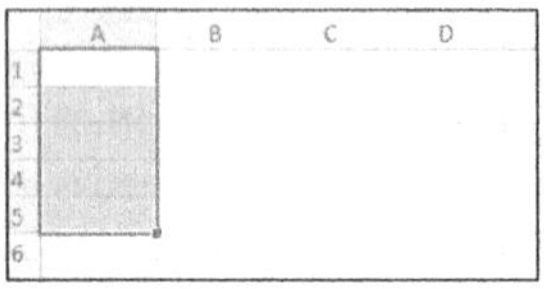

- **A1:D1** refers to cells in a single row

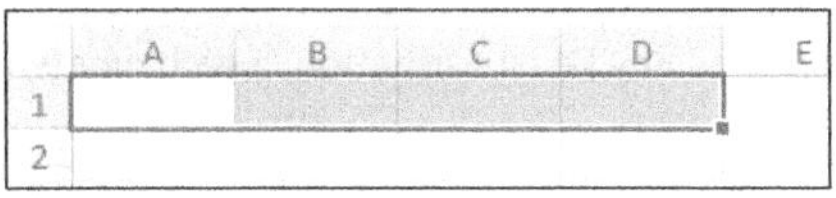

- **A1:D5** includes cells across multiple columns and rows.

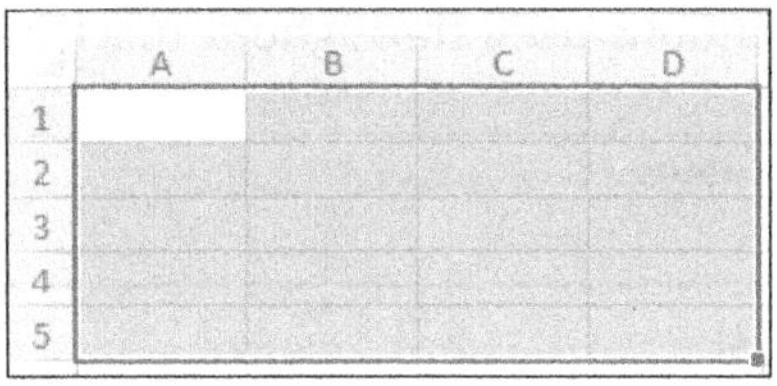

Using a colon helps define these blocks of cells for functions and formulas, making it easier to perform operations like summing, averaging, or applying formatting to multiple cells at once.

Throughout this course, when we refer to a range of cells, we will use this convention.

Code snippets

are displayed like this and to draw your attention to a particular part of the code, the relevant lines or items will be bolded:

```
Sub CalculateSum()
  Dim total As Integer
  total = WorksheetFunction.Sum(Range("A1:A10"))
  MsgBox "The sum of values in Range A1:A10 is " & total
End Sub
```

Images

Screen images can have large areas that are blank or not relevant to the current lesson. To reduce the size of the image, we use the following technique to remove unnecessary sections and focus only on the important parts for the current lesson. This ensures that the images are clear and easy to understand, highlighting the specific areas of interest without any distractions and do not take up excessive space on the pages.

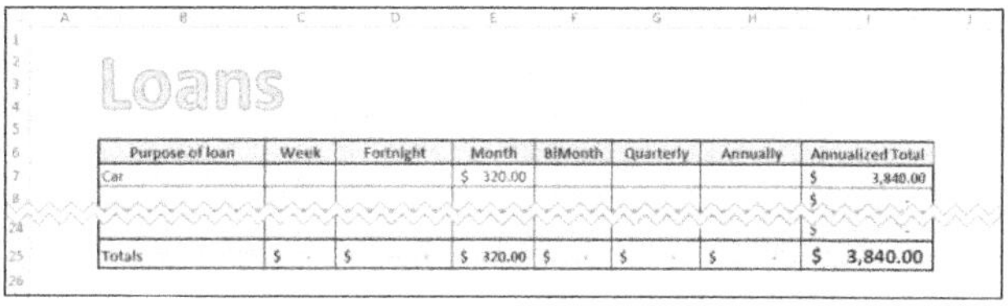

Loans

Purpose of loan	Week	Fortnight	Month	BiMonth	Quarterly	Annually	Annualized Total
Car			$ 320.00				$ 3,840.00
							$
							$ -
Totals	$ -	$ -	$ 320.00	$ -	$ -	$ -	$ 3,840.00

As we introduce new concepts, you will be guided in detail how to perform the tasks the first time, after the initial introduction, the instructions will become much less specific.

Handy Keyboard Shortcuts

Shortcut keys enhance productivity in Excel by allowing quick execution of tasks without navigating menus. They streamline workflow, save time, and improve accuracy, making it easier to handle large datasets and complex spreadsheets efficiently.

The next page has a list of shortcuts in common categories. You can also download the list to print and use as a handy Keyboard Shortcut Reference chart, scan or click the QR Code

Special mention: Ctrl-Z is a powerful undo command in Excel and almost all Windows applications that can reverse recent actions, helping to correct mistakes. You will use it a lot. However, it has limitations: it can only undo a finite number of steps (typically up to 100 depending on your version of Excel), cannot undo actions once the workbook is closed, and may not reverse some complex operations involving multiple steps or VBA code changes. Therefore, always use caution, ensure you have made a backup, and verify actions before executing major changes.

Useful Excel Keyboard Shortcuts

Blue text indicates the most commonly used

Basic Navigation

- **Arrow Keys**: Move one cell up, down, left, or right
- **Ctrl + Arrow Key**: Move to the edge of the data region
- **Home**: Move to the beginning of the row
- **Ctrl + Home**: Move to the beginning of the worksheet
- **Ctrl + End**: Move to the last cell with data

Selection

- **Shift + Arrow Key**: Extend selection by one cell
- **Ctrl + Shift + Arrow Key**: Extend selection to the last cell in the data region
- **Ctrl + Space**: Select the entire column
- **Shift + Space**: Select the entire row
- **Ctrl + A**: Select the entire worksheet

Editing

- **Ctrl + C** also **Ctrl + Insert**: Copy
- **Ctrl + X**: Cut
- **Ctrl + V** also **Shift + Insert**: Paste
- **Delete**: Clear the content of selected cells
- **F2**: Edit the active cell
- **Ctrl + Z**: Undo
- **Ctrl + Y**: Redo
- **Ctrl + D**: Fill down
- **Ctrl + R**: Fill right

Formatting

- **Ctrl + 1**: Open the Format Cells dialog box
- **Ctrl + B**: Bold
- **Ctrl + I**: Italic
- **Ctrl + U**: Underline
- **Ctrl + Shift + $**: Apply currency format
- **Ctrl + Shift + %**: Apply percentage format
- **Ctrl + Shift + #**: Apply date format

Formulas

- **= (Equals)**: Start a formula
- **Alt + =**: Insert the AutoSum formula
- **Ctrl + `**: Toggle between displaying cell values and formulas

Managing Worksheets

- **Ctrl + Page Up**: Move to the previous worksheet
- **Ctrl + Page Down**: Move to the next worksheet
- **Shift + F11**: Insert a new worksheet
- **Alt + H + O + R**: Rename the current worksheet

Miscellaneous

- **F4**: Repeat the last action
- **F9**: Calculate all worksheets in all open workbooks
- **Ctrl + F**: Find
- **Ctrl + H**: Replace
- **Ctrl + K**: Insert hyperlink

Data Management

- **Ctrl + T**: Create a table
- **Ctrl + Shift + L**: Toggle filters on/off
- **Alt + Down Arrow**: Open the filter drop-down menu
- **Ctrl + ;**: Enter the current date
- **Ctrl + Shift + :**: Enter the current time
- **Ctrl + Shift + "+"**: Insert a new row or column
- **Ctrl + "-"**: Delete the selected row or column
- **Ctrl + Shift + U**: Expand or collapse the formula bar
- **Alt + Enter**: Start a new line within a cell

For a comprehensive list of Excel keyboard shortcuts, you can refer to the official Microsoft support page: Excel keyboard shortcuts and function keys

Chapter 1: Introduction to Microsoft Excel

Overview of Excel and its interface, Basic navigation and functionalities

Background Concepts

Getting to know Microsoft Excel

Excel is a powerful tool for creating and managing spreadsheets. It offers a wide range of features, including the ability to perform calculations and data analysis, create charts and graphs, and automate tasks through the use of macros. Excel is widely used in businesses, finances, and other industries for tasks such as budgeting, data analysis, and record-keeping. This course will guide you in learning how to use Excel to create a Home Budget Spreadsheet and also help you to gain skills to create and modify other spreadsheets as well.

What is a spreadsheet?

Understanding the history of spreadsheets provides insight into their evolution and why Excel remains a powerful and versatile tool today.

A quick history of spreadsheets

The first electronic spreadsheet, **VisiCalc**, was released in 1979 for the Apple II computer.
It was developed by **Dan Bricklin and Bob Frankston**, and its popularity helped establish personal computers as essential business tools.

In the early 1980s, **Lotus 1-2-3** became the industry standard for spreadsheets, especially during the rise of IBM PCs.

Then in 1985, **Microsoft Excel** was launched for Macintosh, and later in 1987 for Windows — eventually becoming the most widely used spreadsheet software today.

Over time, spreadsheets evolved with new features like charting, data analysis, and macro programming, making them an essential tool in almost every industry today.

Unique Capabilities of Spreadsheets

Spreadsheets are unique among applications in that data can be placed in cells, and the application can use this data to perform calculations with formulas and place the results in other cells. More importantly, users can program these cells as they see fit and create bespoke applications. For example, businesses can create bespoke invoice systems or project trackers using spreadsheet functionalities.. These abilities have made spreadsheets a powerful tool for business and personal use alike. Having skills in programming spreadsheets can put you at the forefront for prospective employers.

Key Points:

1. **VisiCalc**: First electronic spreadsheet, released in 1979, developed by Dan Bricklin and Bob Frankston.
2. **Lotus 1-2-3**: Released in 1983, became the industry standard in the 1980s.
3. **Microsoft Excel**: Released in 1985 for Macintosh and in 1987 for Windows, eventually becoming the dominant spreadsheet application.
4. **Modern Features**: Sophistication increased in the 1990s and 2000s with graphing, data analysis, and macro programming.
5. **Versatility**: Unique capability to place data in cells, perform calculations, and create bespoke applications.

Layout of the spreadsheet page

The layout of a spreadsheet page consists of rows and columns.

- At the top of the Excel window, you will find the **menu bar** and the **ribbon**. The **menu bar** contains tabs like **File**, **Home**, **Insert**, and others. When you select one of these tabs, the ribbon below it displays a set of related buttons and commands. The **ribbon** is the primary interface for accessing the tools and features used to perform various tasks in Excel, such as formatting, data manipulation, inserting charts, and applying formulas.

> **Exercise**: Take a few minutes to explore each tab in the menu bar and identify the commands in each tab. Hovering your mouse pointer over the commands will display the help text identifying what each command does.

- In Excel, rows are represented by numbers, and columns are represented by letters. Column headings run horizontally across the top, while row headings run vertically on the left.
    - Regardless of whether you are using the **32-bit** or **64-bit** version of Excel, both versions allow access to the same maximum number of rows and columns.
        - **Rows**: 1,048,576 rows per worksheet.
        - **Columns**: 16,384 columns per worksheet, labeled from **A** to **XFD**.

  While the number of rows and columns is identical in both the 32-bit and 64-bit versions, the **64-bit version** is designed to handle larger datasets more efficiently. The 64-bit version can work with more memory (RAM) and is better suited for handling large, complex spreadsheets with heavy calculations, whereas the **32-bit version** has limitations in handling large files or memory-intensive operations.
- The cells are organized in a grid-like structure

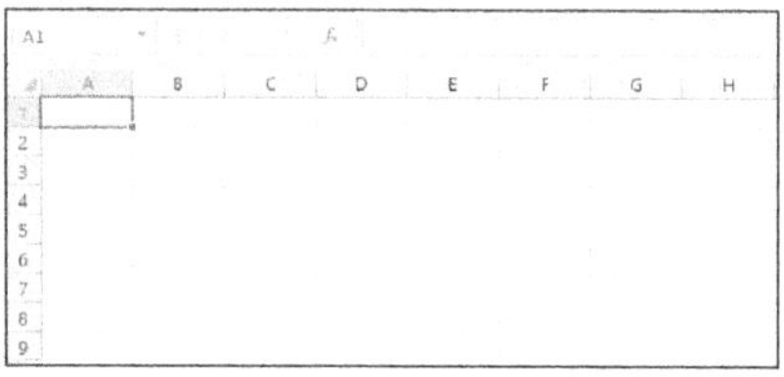

- Each intersection of a row and a column forms a cell where you can enter and edit data.
- Each cell can contain various types of data, including text, numbers, dates, and formulas. You can format the cells to change their appearance, such as the font style, size, color, and alignment.
- You can also use functions and formulas to perform calculations and analyze data in the spreadsheet.
- Additionally, you can insert charts, graphs, and other visual elements to help display and interpret the data in the spreadsheet.

Workbooks, worksheets, and spreadsheets

They sound similar, enough to be confused over what they are exactly, often people confuse these terms and use them interchangeably, let us clear this up.

- **Workbook**: A workbook in Excel is a file that contains one or more worksheets. It is the entire document that you save with the .xlsx extension (or another format compatible with Excel). Think of a workbook like a book containing multiple pages, where each page is a *worksheet*.
- **Worksheet**: A worksheet is a single "page" within a workbook. It consists of a grid of rows and columns where data is entered and manipulated. In Excel, worksheets are accessed via tabs at the bottom of the workbook window. Each tab represents one worksheet. A single workbook can contain multiple worksheets.
- **Spreadsheet**: This term is often used interchangeably with "worksheet," though it can also refer more broadly to the type of application (like Excel itself). A spreadsheet is any document created with a spreadsheet program that includes cells arranged in rows and columns. It can refer to a whole workbook or a single worksheet, depending on the context.

To avoid confusion:

- Use "workbook" when referring to the entire file containing all the data and sheets.
- Use "worksheet" when referring to a single tab within an Excel workbook.
- Use "spreadsheet" to refer to the general format or type of application, or when discussing the concept without specifying whether it is a single worksheet or an entire workbook.

Exercise: Open a new Excel file, and identify the workbook, worksheet tabs, and cells. Rename one of the worksheets to 'Practice Sheet'.

Spreadsheet programs

Microsoft Excel is by far the most popular spreadsheet application in use today, and this course will focus on using Microsoft Excel. However, there are several other spreadsheet applications available, many of which share similar layouts and functions. Most spreadsheet programs can open files from other applications, including MS Excel files.

Here are some notable spreadsheet programs:

- **Microsoft Excel**: A fully featured spreadsheet tool available as part of Microsoft Office 365.
- **Google Sheets**: A free, web-based spreadsheet program accessible via any browser. Google Sheets, unlike Excel, is cloud-based and allows real-time collaboration.
- **Apple Numbers**: Part of Apple's iWork suite, available for macOS and iOS.
- **LibreOffice Calc**: An open-source, free alternative to Excel. LibreOffice Calc, while free, might have some compatibility issues with Excel macros.
- **Lotus Symphony Spreadsheets**: A now-discontinued spreadsheet application.
- **Apache OpenOffice Calc**: Another free, open-source spreadsheet software.
- **VisiCalc**: Discontinued, but notable as the first spreadsheet program, credited with helping drive the success of personal computers for business use.

What are common uses of spreadsheets?

Spreadsheets have a wide range of applications in both business and personal contexts. Common uses include, but certainly not limited to:

- **Finance**: Spreadsheets are primarily used for financial management due to their ability to handle complex calculations.
  Examples include
  - personal and business budgets,
  - GST and taxes,
  - sales and transactions,
  - customer billing,
  - invoicing,
  - sales receipts,
  - stock control,
  - forecasting,
  - "what-if" financial scenarios,
  - and payment systems.
- **Forms**: Templates can be designed for easy data entry into databases, such as
  - inventory control,
  - time sheets,
  - client information,
  - and surveys.
- **Lists**: They can be used for maintaining
  - shopping lists,
  - to-do lists,
  - and contact information.
- **Sports**: Spreadsheets help in analyzing
  - player and team statistics,
  - tracking
    - high, low, and average scores,
    - win/lose ratios,
    - and other performance metrics.

This analysis supports data-driven decision-making.

Essentially, spreadsheets like Excel are invaluable wherever information needs to be calculated, analyzed, or organized in lists.

In this section, you learned:

1. An introduction to Microsoft Excel, including its user interface and layout.
2. How to create and name workbooks and worksheets, along with basic formulas and useful tips.
3. A breakdown of spreadsheet and worksheet creation, layout design, and the use of basic formulas.
4. An overview of other spreadsheet programs such as Google Sheets.
5. Explored different practical uses of spreadsheets, including finance, forms, lists, and sports.

Conclusion

In this chapter, you gained foundational knowledge about Microsoft Excel, including an overview of its interface, navigation, and essential functionalities. Understanding Excel's layout, including the difference between workbooks, worksheets, and spreadsheets, equips you with the vocabulary and skills to navigate this powerful tool confidently. You also explored practical applications of spreadsheets and were introduced to other spreadsheet programs, which helps position Excel within the broader landscape of spreadsheet applications. This foundational knowledge sets the stage for building and managing organized, efficient workbooks and workspaces as you move through this course.

Quiz

1. What is the primary function of a workbook in Excel?

2. Which of the following is a cell reference?

    - a) Row 10
    - b) Column D
    - c) B5
    - d) Worksheet

3. True or False: Excel files created in 32-bit and 64-bit versions have different maximum row and column counts.

4. Which term is often used interchangeably with "worksheet"?

5. Name three common uses of spreadsheets in business or personal tasks.

Quiz Answers

1. A workbook is the entire Excel file that contains one or more worksheets.
2. c) B5
3. False – Both versions have the same row and column limits.
4. Spreadsheet
5. Examples include budgeting, financial forecasting, data analysis, project tracking, or maintaining contact lists.

Self-Assessment

Key Takeaways

- **Workbooks and Worksheets:** Understanding the difference helps with organizing data efficiently.

- **Excel Interface and Layout:** Familiarity with Excel's user interface and navigation makes it easier to access the program's tools.

- **Spreadsheet Functions and Uses:** Knowledge of basic uses gives insight into how Excel can support personal and business tasks.

- **Different Spreadsheet Programs:** Being aware of alternative tools, like Google Sheets, broadens your options for collaboration and file compatibility.

Reflective Questions

1. How do workbooks, worksheets, and spreadsheets differ, and why is it important to distinguish between them?

2. Which features of the Excel interface do you find most intuitive? Which might require more practice?

3. How could learning about other spreadsheet applications benefit your work, especially if collaborating with others who may use different software?

With this foundation, you are now ready to dive deeper into creating workbooks and building basic formulas that bring your data to life in Excel.

Chapter 2: Creating Workbooks and Worksheets

Keeping your Excel workbooks organized right from the start?

Creating a workbook and worksheet

Here we will learn how to create and name a workbook and worksheet in Microsoft Excel.

You will.

- Start by opening Excel and creating a new workbook.
- Learn how to name the workbook and save it to our computer.
- Create new worksheets within the workbook and give them meaningful names.
- Learn how to navigate and switch between worksheets within a workbook.

By the end of this chapter, you will have the skills to create and organize your own Excel workbooks and worksheets.

Let's get started.

Microsoft Excel

Starting Excel

There are several ways to start Excel, depending on your specific setup. Throughout this course we will use the ***Windows Icon*** on the ***toolbar.***

1. Click the Windows Icon on the toolbar.

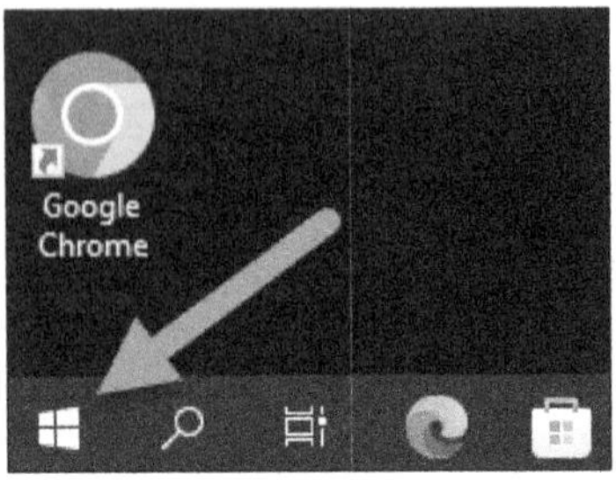

2. Start typing **Excel**, lowercase is fine. At some point the Excel Icon will be displayed at the top of the list

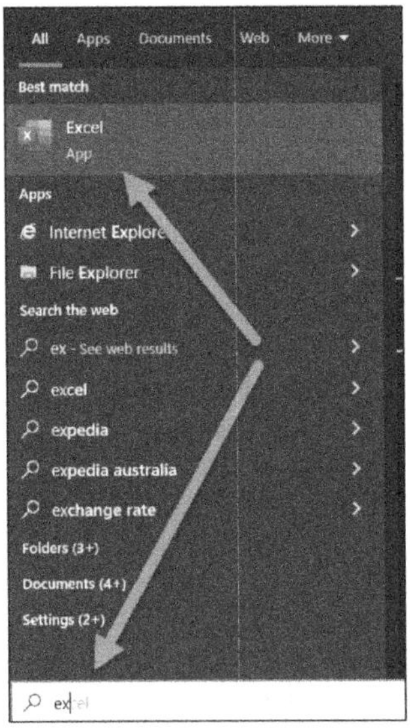

3. When the Excel Icon is displayed, click it, Excel will open.

A quick tour of the opening screen

The Excel opening screen typically displays a blank spreadsheet with a grid of rows and columns. There may also be a ribbon of tabs and buttons at the top of the screen for performing various tasks, such as formatting cells, creating charts, and running calculations.

Depending on your version, you might also see a 'Start' menu or button with options for creating new spreadsheets, opening existing ones, or choosing templates. The Screen layout may vary depending on the version of Excel you are using.

This course is based on **Excel for Microsoft 365**.

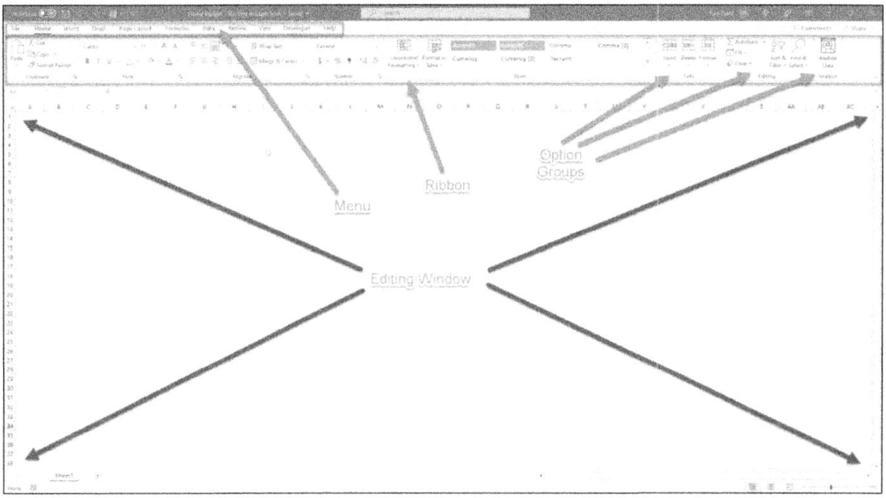

Exercise: Take a few minutes to explore the tabs and buttons at the top of the Excel window. Try hovering over each tab to see the tooltips, which describe what each option does.

1. Click **File** in menu

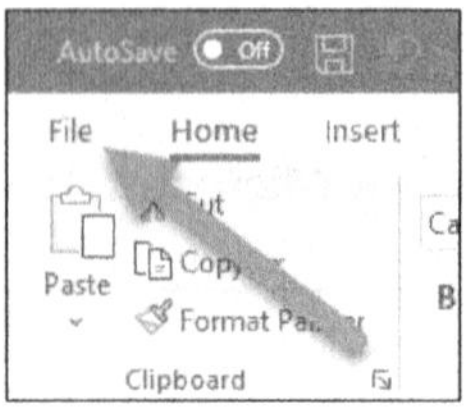

and the **file options** screen will open

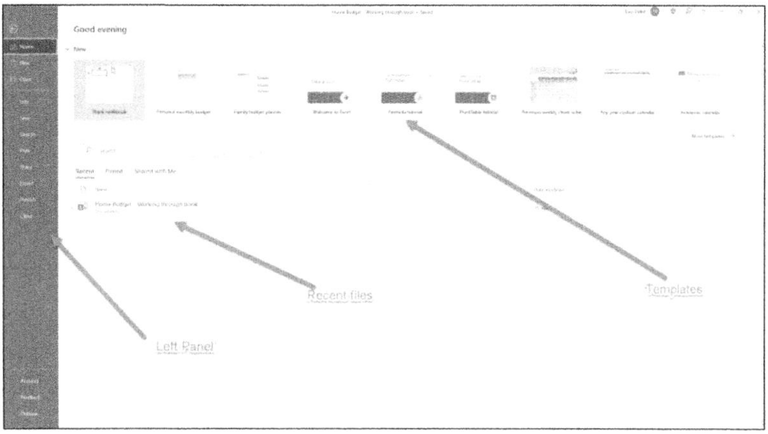

Exercise: Click on each option and take note of what they provide. This exploration will help you become more familiar with the tools available.

2. Left vertical panel

   Options in here are.

   a. ***Home***, this screen.
   b. ***New***, create a new workbook or open a template.
   c. ***Open***, open an existing workbook.
   d. ***Account***, lets you work with your Microsoft Account, do updates, etc.
   e. ***Feedback***, Send feedback or suggestions to Microsoft about Excel
   f. ***Options***, set the Excel options, be careful here as settings can affect the way Excel works. In good time we will be making some changes here when required, but not now.

3. Template panel
   Presents a list of templates you can use. There are many templates here plus others available online. They cover a wide variety of applications and demonstrate some of the many uses of Excel. These are workable and are often basic in nature, however they are a good starting point for many projects. You can use these templates, along with the skills you learn on this training course to modify them to better fit your needs.

4. Recent files panel
   Displays the recent files you have worked on, if the file you wish to work on is here, clicking on it will open it for you.

The Workbook

The workbook will contain all the worksheets, code and macros used in your application; let us have a quick look at it.

Creating a new workbook

- The template panel if shown will have a ***Blank workbook*** template as the first template, click it and a new, blank workbook is created.
- Alternatively, you can click ***New*** in left panel, this will change the main panel to available templates with the ***Blank workbook*** template at the top, click it to create the new workbook.

Exercise: Create a new workbook and give it a meaningful name, like 'Practice Workbook'. Experiment with switching between different templates to see what's available.

Saving Your Workbook

Once you have created your blank workbook:

- **Click File > Save As.**
  Choose the folder where you want to save your budget project.
  (If you haven't created a folder yet, now is a great time to do so — perhaps call it "Home Budget Project.")
  3. Name the file "Home Budget.xlsx".

Tip: It's a good habit to save your workbook regularly as you work, especially after entering new information.

A quick tour of the new workbook

The new workbook has the following.

- Ribbon, all the basic tools you need all grouped with similar tools and each menu item (Home, Insert, etc.) will give you another set of tools to work with. As you work through the training course, you will be introduced to several of the tools.

- One blank worksheet named Sheet1 to get you started.

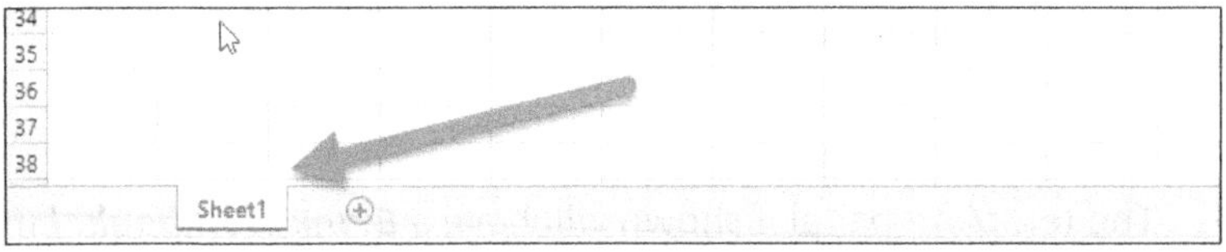

(Don't worry — we'll be creating the actual worksheets later step-by-step. For now, we're just planning.)

The blank worksheet

Information about worksheets

About the worksheet

1. The worksheet is made up of rows and columns; rows are numbered 1, 2, 3, etc. and columns have alphabet letters allocated to them, A, B, C, etc.
2. The intersection of the rows and columns are the ***cells,*** and each cell is uniquely identified by its Column/Row coordinate, A1, D3, F5, etc. Click on any random cell and you will see its coordinate shown in the **Name Box** just above the A column. The row and column heading will also be highlighted for the current cell or range selection, try it, drag your mouse on the worksheet.

3. Excel versions 2003 and earlier have a maximum of 65,000 rows and 255 columns.
4. Excel versions 2007 and above have a row count of 1,048,576 rows and 16,384 columns.
5. Column lettering adds another letter when it reaches Z.
    a. 27 columns range from A to AA
    b. 16,384 columns will range from A to XFD
6. Excel does not limit the number of worksheets in a workbook, but the amount of memory on your computer may limit the number of worksheets you can have. If you have too many worksheets and your computer is running out of memory, close unnecessary programs or add more memory to your computer, or create a new workbook for the other sheets, data. You can link workbooks together.
7. It is also worth noting that as the number of worksheets and the amount of data in a workbook increases, it can start to slow down the performance of Excel, especially if you are using complex formulas and calculations. It is a good idea to keep your workbook organized and only include the worksheets and data that you need for your specific task or project. Additionally, you can use Excel's built-in tools such as data validation, conditional formatting, and filters to help you manage and analyze your data more efficiently.

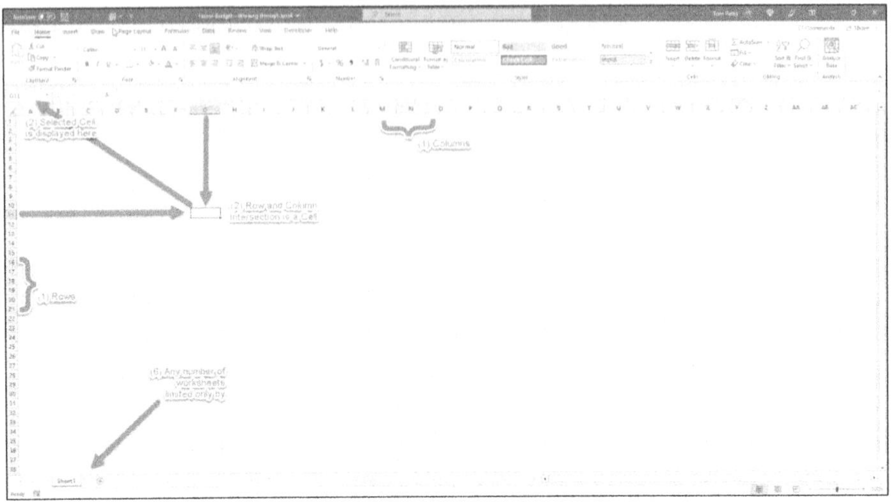

Exercise: Click on a few random cells and note their addresses in the Name Box. Try navigating to cell 'F5' by typing 'F5' into the Name Box and pressing Enter.

Naming the worksheet

Renaming your worksheets appropriately is important for the following reasons.

- Appropriate naming makes it easier to locate specific sheets and data, Sheet1, Sheet2, Sheet3, and so on is too generic and not useful.
- It is easier to refer to worksheets by name in VBA code, we will be doing a little bit of that later.
- Once named, do not change the name of a worksheet when it has been used in a formula or in VBA code, renaming the worksheet could break the formula and/or code and render the worksheet, other worksheets if they reference it or parts of them inoperable.
- Try to use descriptive names for the worksheets so you can tell at a glance what the sheets function is, this is useful when you have several worksheets.

The sheet's name is in the tab at the bottom of the sheet, to change the name of the sheet do the following.

- **Right-Click** the sheets name tab

- Select **Rename,** the name in the tab will be highlighted and you will see the cursor flashing.
- Type the new name, name it as **Dashboard** and press **Enter**, you have now renamed the sheet.

Alternatively

- Just **Dbl-Click** the tab and enter the new name then press **Enter**.

Creating a new worksheet

A workbook can consist of 1 or even thousands of worksheets,

- **Click** on the plus symbol 
- to the right of the tab to add a new worksheet to the right of the current active tab, it will be named Sheet2, Sheet3, Sheet4, and so on by default.
- As soon as you add a new worksheet, it is a good habit to immediately rename it before you start to use or refer to it, rename this one to **Income**, this will be the start of our Home Budget.

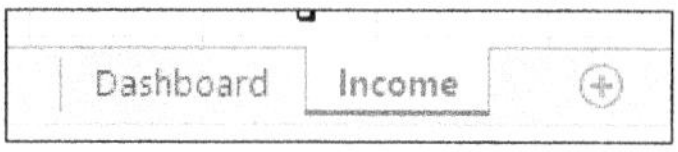

Naming and saving the workbook.

Of course, you need to constantly save your workbook as you are developing or using it to ensure you do not lose work if there is a crash. The first time you save it you will need to name it, after that just save it as you go. You may have already done this earlier, just a quick reminder here.

To name and save your workbook.

- Click **File** on the top menu

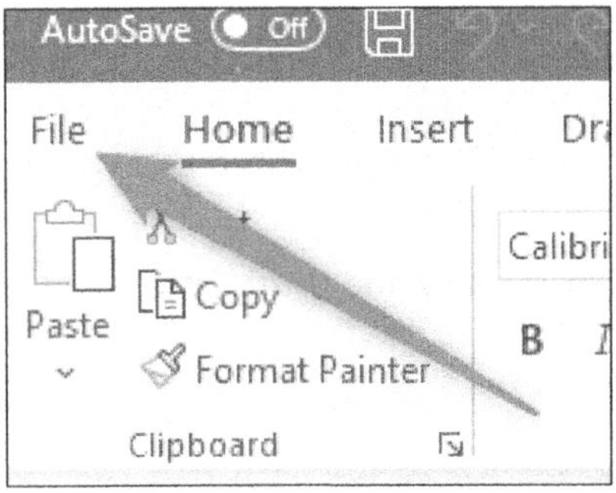

- Select **Save As,** if the file has not previously saved
- Select **Save** to save the file keeping the current filename.

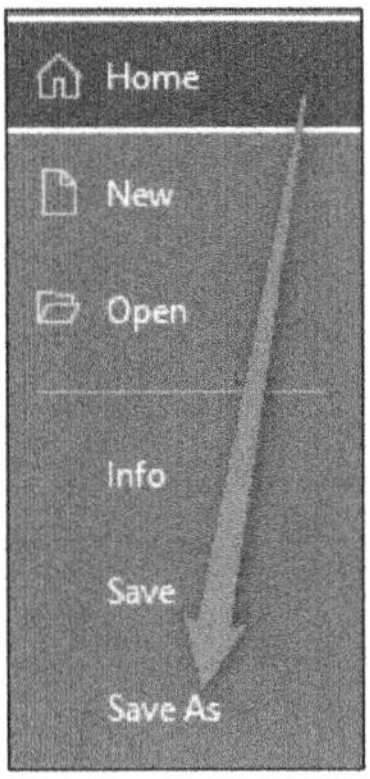

- Click where you want to save the file, this will be **This PC** but can be any of the options, we will go with This PC for now.

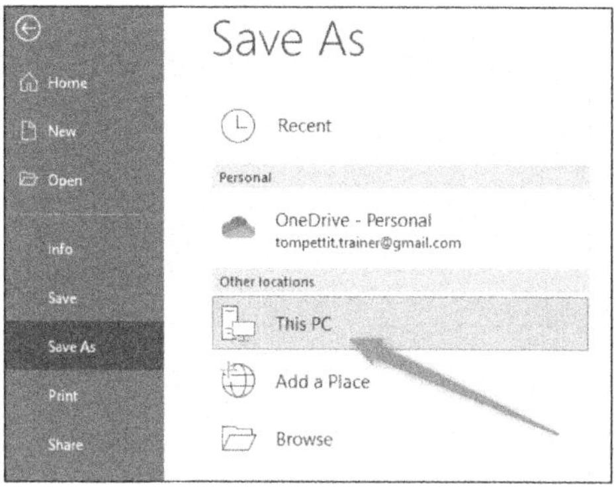

- Add the name you want to call the file, we have named it **HouseHold Budget**, it is recommended you use this name whilst doing this course, you can rename it later if you like.
  Default path/folder will be your Documents folder, click on Documents to use a File Explorer to locate the folder and name the file or you can use New Folder to add a new folder.

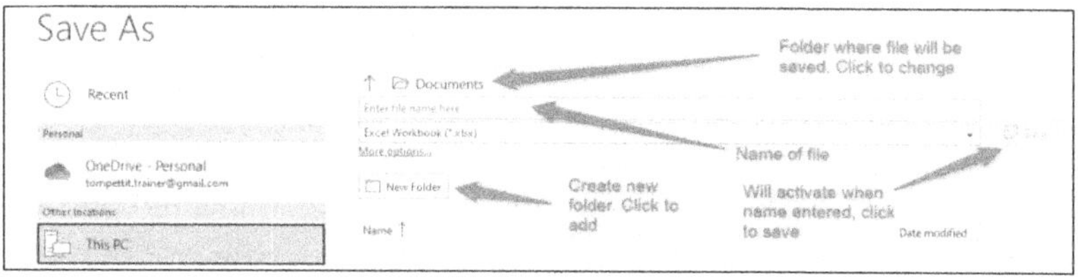

- Note, the image above shows the default Excel filename of **.xlsx**, this will be fine for most workbooks however at the end of the course we will be adding Macro's and VBA code, and these will not run in an xlsx file.
  Excel will only run Macro's in a Macro Enabled workbook with a file extension of **.xlsm**
  Use the dropdown to locate the Macro Enabled Workbook option and select that.

- Click the **Save** button, see the above image.

Congratulations, you have now named and saved the workbook. From now on, you only need to click the disk icon or select File/Save to save the file.

Note for Excel and LibreOffice Users
If you are using Microsoft Excel, it is recommended to save your workbook as a .xlsm (Macro-Enabled Workbook) to ensure all macros continue to function correctly.

LibreOffice Calc users should save their files as .ods (Open Document Spreadsheet) for best compatibility.

While Microsoft Excel can open .ods files, any macros created in LibreOffice may not work inside Excel. Only the worksheet data and basic formulas will be preserved.

AutoSave

Imagine you are working away in Excel, and you have just finished putting in a large number of changes, you have not been saving regularly and the power goes out. When you restart your computer and Excel, all that work is gone. To avoid losing unsaved work, it is recommended that you save your work frequently while working in Excel. This can be done by clicking the "Save" button in the Quick Access Toolbar or by using the keyboard shortcut "Ctrl + S".

Excel now offers an AutoSave function which will save your work automatically if you suffer a power outage or computer crash, you will only lose your work after the last save point.

The Excel Autosave feature saves changes frequently, typically every few seconds. This setting is designed to automatically save the latest version of your workbooks to prevent data loss. You can adjust the frequency of autosaves or turn the feature on or off by accessing the Autosave settings in the File tab under Options. For Office 365 subscribers using Excel, Autosave is often enabled by default and saves every few seconds when the file is stored on OneDrive or SharePoint.

To turn it on or off

- Click the AutoSave icon, if it says **Off**

- A window will popup explaining the file needs to be uploaded to OneDrive to allow AutoSave, there will be one icon for OneDrive, click it and the file will be uploaded, and AutoSave will be activated.

The Autosave feature in Excel specifically for Office 365 subscribers works only when the file is stored on OneDrive, SharePoint, or similar cloud services supported by Microsoft.

Congratulations, if you are using a cloud service, AutoSave is now turned ON and your work will be saved regularly. Other MS Office and Office 365 applications also have this feature, be sure to turn it on there as well.

If your file is not stored on one of these cloud services, the Autosave feature will not be active. However, Excel does have an "**AutoRecover**" feature that can help recover unsaved work in case of a crash.

AutoRecover

This feature is different from Autosave and can be configured to save a recovery version of your file locally at specified intervals. You can adjust AutoRecover settings via the File tab under Options, where you can set how often you want the program to save a recovery file, see image below.

Once the AutoRecover feature in Excel is turned on, it operates by periodically saving a copy of open workbooks in a temporary file at a specified interval. Here is how it works:

- **Configuration**: You can enable and configure AutoRecover in the Excel Options menu. This involves selecting the frequency of autosaves (e.g., every 10 minutes) and specifying the location where the recovery files should be saved.
- **Saving Temporary Files**: At the chosen interval, Excel will save a temporary recovery file automatically. This does not affect the actual file you are working on but acts as a backup that Excel can revert to if the program closes unexpectedly.
- **Recovering Files**: If Excel closes due to a power failure, crash, or system error, upon restarting Excel, it will detect the presence of AutoRecover files and prompt you to open them. This allows you to recover unsaved changes up to the last AutoRecover save point.

- **File Deletion**: After you successfully save your work manually, Excel deletes the temporary AutoRecover files associated with that session, as they are no longer necessary. If you continue making changes, a new AutoRecover file will be created when the next save point is reached.

AutoRecover is a safeguard for unexpected shutdowns but is not a substitute for regularly saving your work, especially as it only captures the state of the document at the last autosave interval, not every change up to the moment of a crash.

Conclusion

In this chapter, you have established the foundational skills for creating and organizing Excel workbooks and worksheets. From opening Excel and naming your workbook to creating worksheets and navigating through the workbook, these fundamental tasks are essential for structuring and managing your data effectively. You have also learned about AutoSave and AutoRecover features, ensuring that your work is protected even in the event of unexpected disruptions. By mastering these initial steps, you are well-prepared to build organized, reliable workbooks as you progress in Excel.

Note for LibreOffice Users

LibreOffice Calc does not have real-time AutoSave linked to the cloud, like Microsoft Excel does with OneDrive or SharePoint

However, it can automatically create backup copies at regular intervals.

To enable this feature, go to Tools → Options → Load/Save → General and turn on "Save AutoRecovery information every X minutes."

This saves a recovery copy. If LibreOffice crashes, you will be offered the chance to restore your last auto-saved file when reopening. Be sure to turn this on at 5 or 10 minute intervals, should your computer crash, you will only lose work since last backup.

Quiz

1. Which tab do you select to create a new workbook?
    - a) Insert
    - b) File
    - c) Home
    - d) Data
2. What is the shortcut for saving your workbook in Excel?
    - a) Ctrl + A
    - b) Ctrl + N
    - c) Ctrl + S
    - d) Ctrl + Z
3. Why is it important to name your worksheets in Excel?
    - a) To help locate specific sheets quickly
    - b) To make the workbook look professional
    - c) To prevent breaking references in formulas or VBA code
    - d) All of the above
4. Which feature saves your workbook automatically if stored on a cloud service like OneDrive?
    - a) AutoRecover
    - b) AutoSave
    - c) Quick Access Save
    - d) Instant Save

Quiz Answers

1. b) File
2. c) Ctrl + S
3. d) All of the above
4. b) AutoSave

Self-Assessment

Key Takeaways

- Creating and naming workbooks and worksheets lays the groundwork for organized data management in Excel.
- Naming your sheets meaningfully improves navigation and prevents formula errors when they are referenced in other parts of the workbook.
- AutoSave and AutoRecover are essential features for protecting your data, especially when working on cloud-based platforms.

Reflective Questions

- How can I use organized naming conventions to make my workbooks more intuitive and easier to navigate?
- In what situations would AutoRecover be more beneficial than AutoSave, and how can I ensure that my data is always backed up?

By considering these questions, you can refine your approach to structuring Excel workbooks, ensuring that they remain both user-friendly and resilient to unexpected interruptions.

Chapter 3: Basic Formulas and Functions

Introduction to formulas, Basic arithmetic operations and common functions

Before diving into creating our workbooks, we will first explore both basic and advanced formulas. This foundational knowledge will ensure you understand how formulas work and can confidently use them when needed. We will cover simple arithmetic operations to more complex functions like VLOOKUP, nested formulas and IF statements. This will prepare you to handle the calculation requirements as you build your budgeting application.

What is a formula?

A formula in Excel is an expression used to perform calculations, manipulate data, and return values. It typically starts with an equal sign (=) which tells Excel this is a formula and can include numbers, cell references, arithmetic operators, and functions to compute results dynamically within a worksheet. A formula is placed in a cell and the results are displayed in the same cell. If a cell has a formula, it will be displayed in the formula bar when the cell is selected. Below are some samples.

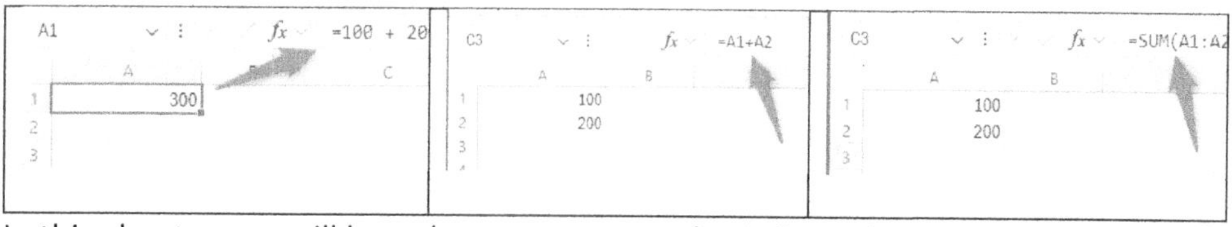

In this chapter, we will learn how to use some basic formulas and functions to perform calculations in Excel.

> **Tip for LibreOffice Users**
> Most formulas and function names work the same way in LibreOffice Calc as they do in Excel.
> If you encounter small differences, check Appendix A for tips on adjusting formulas if needed.

Understanding formula in Excel

Formulas are the backbone of Excel's functionality, enabling it to perform a wide range of calculations. These calculations are essential for analyzing data, making projections, and automating tasks within your spreadsheet.

Basic Formula Components

- **Operators**: Most basic formulas use arithmetic operators such as addition (+), subtraction (-), multiplication (*), and division (/). These operators help perform calculations on data values retrieved from other cells.
- **Cell References**: Formulas typically operate on data contained in other cells. For example, if you want to sum the values in cells A1 and A2, your formula in cell A3 would be =A1 + A2.
- **Result Display**: The outcome of a formula is displayed in the cell where the formula is entered

Entering formula

Before we start practicing entering formulas, here is a quick overview of what you need to know about them.

Some basic formula information

- Formula in Excel always begins with an equal sign (=), this tells Excel that what follows is a formula. If you actually need the equal sign as the first character in a text value, precede it with a space (=) and Excel will treat it as text.
- Excel, like most computer programs, uses specific characters to represent mathematical operators. Throughout this course, we will only use the symbols recognized by Excel, as shown in the table on the next page:

Character	Use	Sample
+	Addition	2 + 2 = 4
-	Subtraction	5 – 2 = 3
/	Division	6 / 3 = 2
*	Multiplication	6 * 3 = 18
^	Exponentiation	2 ^ 3 = 8
( )	Calculate first	2 + (3 * 2) = 8

These symbols are essential for performing calculations in Excel and understanding them will help you create and use formulas effectively.

- The order of operations used by Excel is **PEMDAS**
  If your calculations do not come out right, check the order of operations. The formula we use throughout this training course will be simple and not rely too much on PEMDAS, but it is important you know about it, a very brief explanation is below

  - **P**arentheses, (1+2), are done first. If there are parentheses within parentheses
    (2 * (1+2)), the inner most parentheses are always the first calculated.
  - **E**xponents, ^
  - **M**ultiplication and **D**ivision, * and /, in order left to right.
  - **A**ddition and **S**ubtraction, + and -, in order left to right.
  - Here are some samples of PEMDAS operations.
    - *5 + 3 * 4 = 17*

    - According to PEMDAS, we first perform multiplication, then addition. So, we multiply 3 and 4 to get 12, and then add 5 to get the final answer of 17.
  - *(10 + 5) * 2 / 3 = 10*
    - We first perform the parentheses, which gives us 15. Then we multiply by 2 to get 30. Finally, we divide it by 3 to get the final answer of 10.
  - *6 * 2 + 4 / 2 - 1 = 13*
    - We first perform multiplication and division, then addition and subtraction. So, we start by multiplying 6 and 2 to get 12 then dividing 4 by 2 to get 2. We then add 12 and 2 to get 14. Next, we subtract 1 from 14 resulting in 13.
  - *2^3 * (4 + 1) / 5 - 1 = 7*
    - Start by performing parentheses, which gives us 5. Then we raise 2 to the power of 3 to get 8. Next, we multiply 8 by 5 to get 40. Finally, we divide 40 by 5 to get 8, and then subtract 1 to get the final answer of 7.
  - *20 / 5 * (3 + 2) - 1 = 19*
    - We first perform the parentheses, which gives us 5. Then we divide 20 by 5 to get 4. Next, we multiply 4 by 5 to get 20. Finally, we subtract 1 from 20 to get the final answer of 19.

We will now do a little practice on entering formula, as we progress through the following formulae, you will be introduced to several tips and tricks, for entering formula easily and quickly, let us begin.

Creating a Basic Formula

- **Enter values** in cell **A1** and **A2**, we need something to calculate with.
  A1 = 101
  A2 = 202

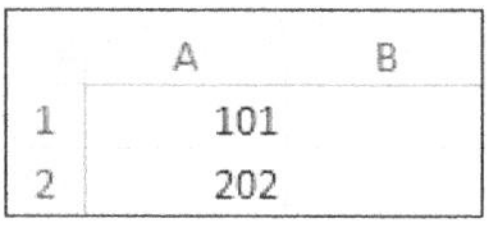

- **Select a Cell**: Click on the cell where you want the result of the calculation to appear, select **C1**.

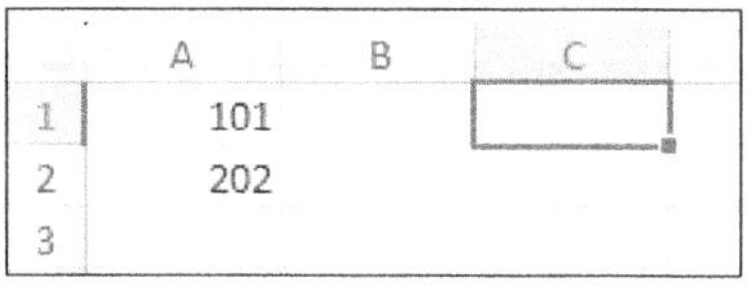

- **Enter Formula Mode**: Type the equal sign (=) to tell Excel that you are about to enter a formula.

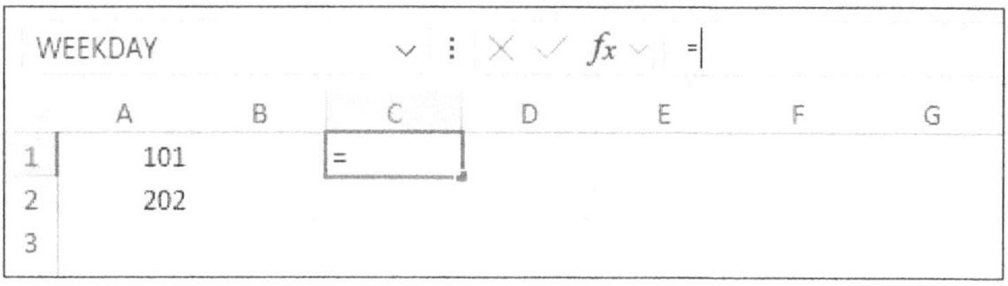

- **Insert Cell References and Operators**: Type in the cell references along with the necessary operators to define your calculation.

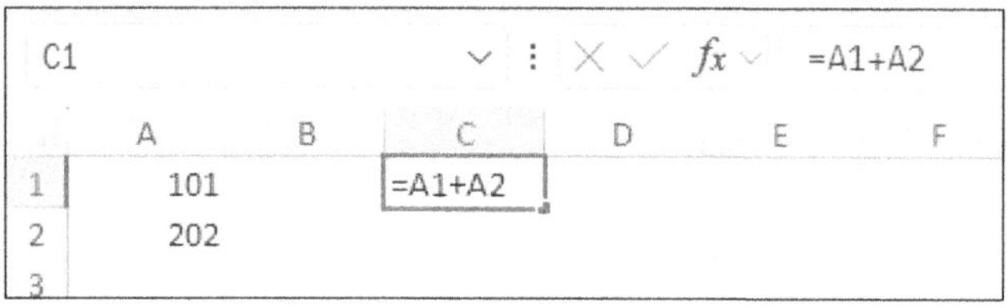

- **Press Enter**: Once you complete the formula, press Enter. Excel will calculate and display the result in the selected cell.

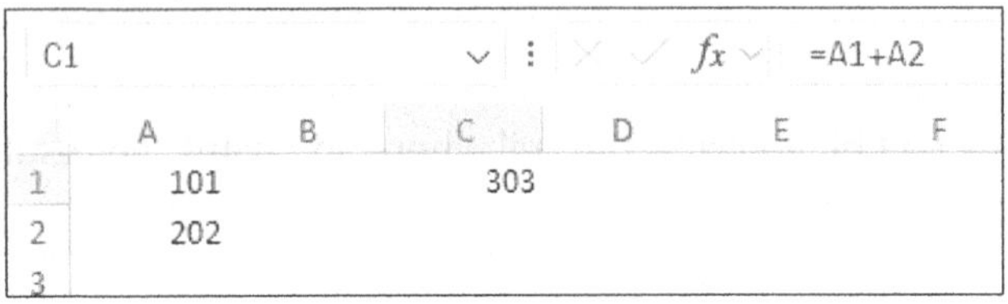

- **Finally,** change the values in A1 and A2 and see the calculation change accordingly

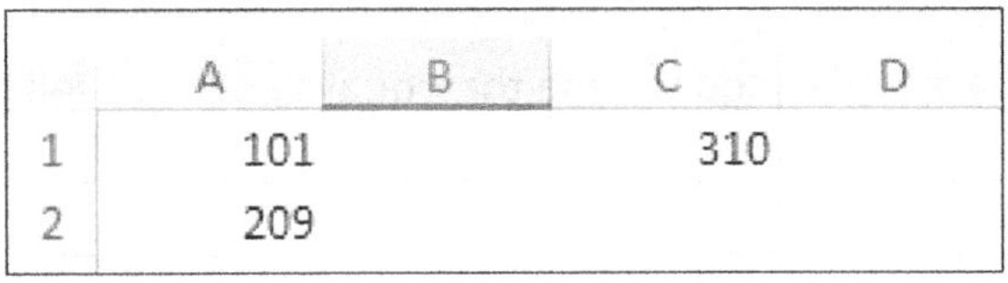

Significance of Using $ in Cell Formulas

During the course of this book, you will be creating formulas in a cell and copying them to other cells in the column or row. Excel will adjust the formula as required to ensure everything works, this saves much time entering many similar formulas. However, some formula you may not want to change a specific cells reference, there is a way to lock it in.

In Excel, the dollar sign ($) is used to create absolute references, which do not change when you copy the formula to another cell. You can use the $ for one or both coordinates (column or row).

Example Formula: D7*(52 * $J$4)

- **D7**: A relative reference to a workday expense (like coffee). This will change if the formula is copied to another cell.
- **$J$4**: An absolute reference to the number of days worked per week. The dollar signs keep this reference fixed, no matter where the formula is copied.

Types of References:

- **Relative (e.g., D7)**: Changes when copied to another cell.
- **Absolute (e.g., $J$4)**: Both coordinates are fixed and will not change when copied.
- **Mixed (e.g., $J4 or J$4)**: One coordinate is fixed, the other can change.

Why It Matters:

Using **$J$4** ensures that the reference to days worked per week stays the same, providing consistent and accurate calculations even when the formula is copied to other cells. This helps avoid errors and makes your formulas more dependable. We will be working on this later, for now, you just need to know that you can lock in a cell reference in formula.

Recap of Key Topics Covered

In this section you have learned.

- **Starting Excel**:
  - Opening Excel using the Windows Icon.
  - Navigating the Excel startup screen and understanding its various components.
- **Creating and Naming Workbooks**:
  - Creating new workbooks from scratch or templates.
  - Saving and naming workbooks appropriately to maintain organization.
- **Managing Worksheets**:
  - Adding new worksheets and giving them meaningful names.
  - Navigating between different worksheets within a workbook.
- **Basic Navigation**:
  - Understanding the layout of the Excel interface, including ribbon tabs and tool groups.
- **Basic Formula Creation**:
  - Using basic arithmetic operators to perform calculations.
  - Understanding cell references and the result display in formulas.

- **AutoSave and AutoRecover Features**:
    - Setting up AutoSave to automatically save work to cloud storage.
    - Configuring AutoRecover to save local backup copies at set intervals.
    - LibreOffice Calc AutoSave.
- **Excel Version Differences**:
    - Discussing the variations in capabilities and layout between different Excel versions.

Each of these areas builds your competence in using Excel, preparing you for more advanced operations and functions in subsequent sections of the course.

Conclusion

In this chapter, we covered essential concepts of creating and using basic formulas and functions in Excel. We discussed the structure of formulas, explored basic arithmetic operations, and understood how to utilize cell references to create dynamic calculations. Understanding formula basics provides the foundation needed to build effective, accurate spreadsheets, which is crucial as you develop your budgeting application. We also explored the significance of Excel's order of operations (PEMDAS) and learned about relative, absolute, and mixed references, which allow for flexibility in calculations. With these skills, you are now well-equipped to handle the core mathematical and logical requirements of your budgeting application confidently.

Quiz

1. **What symbol must a formula start with in Excel?**
   a. *
   b. =
   c. $
   d. /

2. **What is the result of the formula =(10 + 5) * 2 / 3 following the order of operations?**
   a. 30
   b. 7.5
   c. 10
   d. 5

3. **In formula =A1 + $B$2, what does $B$2 represent?**
   a. A relative reference
   b. A mixed reference
   c. An absolute reference
   d. A calculated reference

4. **What is the primary advantage of using cell references in Excel formulas?**
   a. It displays cell formatting
   b. It allows easy updates when data changes
   c. It hides formulas from view
   d. It automatically applies bold text

5. **How does Excel handle the order of operations in formulas?**
   a. By performing addition and subtraction first
   b. By ignoring parentheses
   c. By following the PEMDAS rule
   d. By calculating from right to left

Quiz Answers

1. b) =
2. c) 10
3. c) An absolute reference
4. b) It allows easy updates when data changes
5. c) By following the PEMDAS rule

Self-Assessment

Key Takeaways

- **Formula Structure**: Always start a formula with an equal sign, which tells Excel to treat it as a calculation rather than a regular entry.
- **Order of Operations (PEMDAS)**: Familiarity with the PEMDAS rule ensures that complex calculations are executed correctly.
- **Cell References**: Understanding relative, absolute, and mixed references makes formulas adaptable and dynamic, reducing manual data entry.
- **Arithmetic Operators**: Mastering operators (+, -, *, /, ^) allows you to perform essential calculations in Excel with confidence.

Reflective Questions

- How does understanding absolute and relative references enhance the flexibility of your formulas?
- When might using parentheses be essential in a formula, and how does it impact your calculations?
- How can building a strong foundation in basic formulas and arithmetic operations benefit your overall Excel skills in budgeting applications?

Reflecting on these points will solidify your grasp of fundamental Excel formulas and functions, preparing you for more advanced topics in future chapters.

Chapter 4: Advanced Formulas and Data Analysis

Advanced functions like SUM, AVERAGE, VLOOKUP, Absolute and relative references and also Nested Formulas

Advanced Formulas

As we progress through the training, we will explore more complex formulas that involve additional functionalities like:

- **Functions**: Built-in functions like SUM(), AVERAGE(), and VLOOKUP(), which provide more advanced calculation capabilities.
- **Conditional Logic**: Formulas that use conditions, such as IF statements, to perform different calculations based on certain criteria.

Each of these basic and advanced formulas will be explained in detail as they are introduced in the course. Understanding and utilizing both basic and complex formulas will enhance your ability to manage and analyze data effectively in Excel. For now, this is a brief introduction.

SUM Function

Formula: =SUM(A1:A10)

Explanation: The SUM function adds all the numbers in a specified range. In this case, it sums all the values from cell A1 to A10.

AVERAGE Function

Formula: =AVERAGE(B1:B10)

Explanation: The AVERAGE function calculates the average of a range of numbers. Here, it computes the average values from cell B1 to B10.

VLOOKUP Function (Vertical Lookup)

- V stands for Vertical.
- Searches for a value in the first column of a range (top to bottom).
- Returns a value from a specified column in the same row.

Example:

A6 fx =VLOOKUP("Rent", A1:B4, 2, FALSE)

	A	B	C	D
1	**Category**	**Limit**		
2	Rent	18000		
3	Utilities	2400		
4	Food	20000		
5				
6	18000			
7				

=VLOOKUP("Rent", A1:B4, 2, FALSE)

Returns 18000

- "Rent" – The value to search for in the first column of the range.
- A1:B4 – The range of cells containing the lookup table.
- 2 – The column number in the range from which to return the value (in this case, column B).
- FALSE – Tells Excel to find an exact match for "Rent".

Explanation: The VLOOKUP function searches for a value in the first column of a range and returns a value from the same row in a specified column. In this example, it searches for the word "Rent" in the range A1:A4 and returns the corresponding value from the 2nd column in the range (B) in the same row.

> **Tip:**
> VLOOKUP is commonly used more than HLOOKUP because most data is organized in vertical columns. The one you use will be determined by the layout of the data being accessed.

HLOOKUP Function (Horizontal Lookup)

- H stands for Horizontal.
- Searches for a value in the first row of a range (left to right).
- Returns a value from a specified row in the same column.

Example:

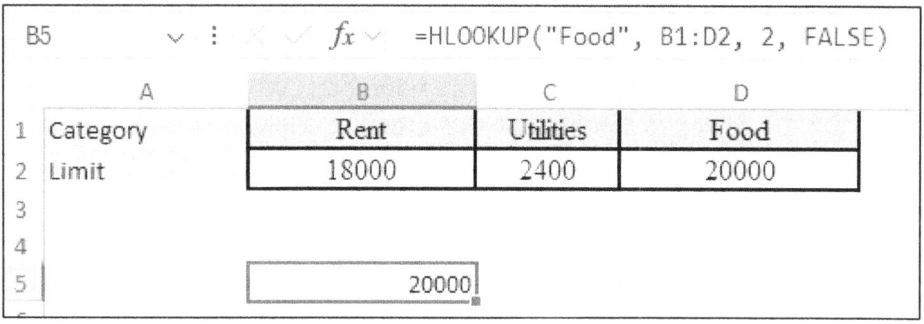
B5 fx =HLOOKUP("Food", B1:D2, 2, FALSE)

	A	B	C	D
1	Category	Rent	Utilities	Food
2	Limit	18000	2400	20000
3				
4				
5		20000		

=HLOOKUP("Food", B1:D2, 2, FALSE)

Returns 20000

- "Food" – The value to search for in the first row of the range.
- B1:D2 – The range of cells containing the lookup table.
- 2 – The row number in the range from which to return the value (in this case, row 2).
- FALSE – Tells Excel to find an exact match for "Food".

Explanation: The HLOOKUP function searches for a value in the first row of a range and returns a value from the same column in a specified row. In this example, it searches for the word "Food" in row 1 of the range B1:D2 and returns the corresponding value from the second row.

Absolute and Relative References

In Excel, cell references are classified into three types: relative, absolute, and mixed. The `**$**` sign is used to indicate absolute references. Each type behaves differently when formulas are copied to new locations.
Here's an overview with examples:

- **Relative Reference**
  - **Example:** =A1+B1
    Both A1 and B1 are relative references. When this formula is copied to another cell, the references will adjust relative to the coordinates where the formula is placed.
- **Absolute Reference**
  - **Example:** =$A$1+$B$1
    Both $A$1 and $B$1 are absolute references. When this formula is copied to another cell, the references will not change.
- **Mixed Reference**
  - **Example:** =A$1+$B1
    In this formula, A$1 is a mixed reference with an absolute row and relative column, while $B1 has an absolute column and relative row.
    When copied, only the relative parts will adjust.

Nested Formula

An Excel formula with more than one formula within it is called a **nested formula**. This means it contains multiple functions or operations that are combined to produce a single result. Below are samples of two nested formulas, similar to what we will be using later.

Arithmetic Nested Formula

Arithmetic Nested Formula will use two or more distinct formulas to calculate a single value. The formula below involves nested arithmetic operations and functions within the parenthesis. It uses the SUM function nested within a multiplication operation

=D5*(SUM(B2:B6) + (D2*D3)), the SUM function and the multiplication operation within parentheses are nested within the overall formula. Excel will use the PEMDAS order of operations when calculating the formulas

=D5*(SUM(B2:B6) + (D2*D3)) step by step to understand how it works:

1. **Inner Calculations:**
    - **SUM(B2:B6):** This part of the formula calculates the sum of the values in cells B2 to B6.
    - **(D2*D3):** This part multiplies the value in cell D3 by D2 (total kids pocket money).
2. **Combining the Inner Results:** (for the outer brackets)
    - The results of SUM(B2:B6) and (D3*D2) are then added together. So,
if SUM(B2:B6) returns 15
and (D3*D2) returns 10,
the combined result will be 25.
3. **Multiplication with D2:**
    - Finally, the combined result from the addition (in our example, 25) is multiplied by the value in cell D5. So, if D5 contains the value 4 (quarterly), the final calculation will be 4 * 25, which equals 100.

Summary: The formula =D5*(SUM(B2:B6) + (D2*D3)) performs the following steps:

1. **Inner Parenthesis:** Sums the monthly expenses values in the range B2:B6 using the SUM(B2:B6) function.
2. **Inner Parenthesis:** Multiplies the value in cell D3 by D2 to calculate the total kids pocket money for the month.

3. **Outer Parenthesis:** Adds the result of the sum to the result of the multiplication to get the total expenses and pocket money amount for month.
4. Multiplies this combined result by the value in cell D2 to get the quarterly value (in this case, it could be 6 for bi-annual or 12 for annual).

This nested formula allows you to perform multiple operations within a single formula, making your calculations more efficient and dynamic.

Exercise: Test this by creating the following mini spreadsheet, enter the numbers in yellow in the same places as shown and the formula should go into cell D6.

=D5*(SUM(B2:B6) + (D2*D3))

I use simple numbers to make it easier to test the formula. When you get the same result with these numbers, add some more realistic numbers in the yellow cells.

Note: This is only to test the nested formula concept, don't get too concerned about formatting, we will have plenty of that later.

	A	B	C	D
1	**Expenses**	**Month Value**		
2	*Rent*	1	**Kids Pocket Money**	5
3	*Electricity*	2	**Kid Count**	2
4	*Groceries*	3		
5	*Petrol*	4	**Quarterly Multiplier**	4
6	*Loan Repayment*	5	**Total**	100
7				

Logical Nested Formula

Logical functions in Excel perform some form of comparison and depending on the result can then perform other tasks or functions, in the following samples we will use the IF function, this is the most common logical function you will use.

Syntax: IF(logical_test, value_if_true, value_if_false)

logical_test: The condition you want to check, result MUST be TRUE or FALSE

value_if_true: The result if the condition is TRUE.

value_if_false: The result if the condition is FALSE.

The **IF function** in Excel checks a condition and returns one value if the condition is TRUE and another value if it is FALSE.

The formula below is a nested logical formula; it uses the IF function with the SUM function nested inside it to perform a logical test and based on the result will display one of two messages.

Formula: =IF(SUM(A1:A10) > 100, "Above 100", "Below 100")
This nested formula uses the IF function with the SUM function inside it. It first sums the values in the range A1:A10. If the result is greater than 100, it returns "Above 100"; otherwise, it returns "Below 100".

Combining the Concepts: Advanced Nested Formula Example

Formula: =IF(D2 > 50, SUM(A1:A10), AVERAGE(B1:B10))
This formula combines several advanced concepts:

- **Conditional Check:** The IF function checks if this value in D2 is greater than 50.
- **Nested Functions:** If the condition is
  - true
    - returns the sum of the range A1:A10
      - (SUM(A1:A10)).

- False
  - returns the average of the range B1:B10
    - (AVERAGE(B1:B10)).

To test the formulas using the IF function, recreate the following by

	A	B	C	D	E
1	1	2			
2	2	4		Sum of B1:B10	**110**
3	3	6			
4	4	8			
5	5	10		Test Column A1:A10	**Below 100**
6	6	12		Test Cell E2	**55 (SUM)**
7	7	14			
8	8	16			
9	9	18			
10	10	20			
11					

- Enter the numbers in column **A1-A10**, **B1-B10** as shown
- Enter the labels in cells **D2, D5** and **D6** as shown
- Enter the following formula in cell **E2**
  - **=SUM(B1:B10)**
- Enter the following formula in cell **E5**
  - **=IF(SUM(A1:A10) >= 100, "100 or Above", "Below 100")**
- Enter the following formula in cell **E6**
  - **=IF(E2 >= 100, SUM(A1:A10) & " (SUM)", AVERAGE(B1:B10) & " (Average)")**

To test the formulas work

- **E2,** the value of the sum of **B1:B10**
  - the **SUM** with the sample numbers is *110*, you should see *110*
  - This is used in the formula in E6 to indirectly test the sum of B1:B10
- **E5**, testing the sum of **A1:A10**
  - The sum with the sample numbers is *55*, you should see **Below 100**
  - Change **A5** to *100*, the result should change to **100 or Above**

- **E6,** The value of **D2**
  - in the sample data, **D2** is *110*, the test is checking to see if it is greater than or equal to 100 so the value shown will be the **SUM** of cells **A1:A10** which is **55** with the word **(Sum)** appended
  - Change the value in column **B10** to *1*, **D2** will change to *91*, below 100 so the value shown in **E6** will be the **AVERAGE** of **B1:B10** which is *9.1*

By combining conditional logic with nested functions, Excel allows for powerful and flexible calculations. The formulas we explored illustrate how complex decision-making and multiple operations can be condensed into a single expression. Practicing these examples will help you understand how to apply similar logic to a wide range of data analysis tasks, enhancing your ability to solve problems dynamically and efficiently. We will be doing more of this as we start building our budget application.

Conclusion

In this chapter, you have expanded your knowledge of Excel formulas to include advanced functions and data analysis tools. By working with SUM, AVERAGE, and VLOOKUP, as well as mastering absolute and relative references, you've learned the tools to tackle more complex data scenarios. These advanced formulas, combined with conditional logic and nested structures, empower you to create dynamic, responsive calculations within your workbook. With these skills, you're now prepared to analyze data in depth and create formulas that adapt seamlessly to changes, a crucial step in building a powerful and functional budgeting application.

Quiz

1. What does the SUM function do in Excel?

2. Which of the following will maintain a fixed reference when copied to another cell?

   - a) A1
   - b) $A$1
   - c) A$1
   - d) $A1

3. What is the purpose of the VLOOKUP function?

4. What will the following formula return if the sum of A1:A10 is 75?
   =IF(SUM(A1:A10) > 100, "Above 100", "Below 100")

5. In the following formula what result will be displayed if D2 is 30?
   =IF(D2 > 50, SUM(A1:A10), AVERAGE(B1:B10))

Quiz Answers

1. It adds all the numbers in a specified range.
2. b) $A$1
3. VLOOKUP searches for a value in the first column of a range and returns a corresponding value from a specified column in the same row.
4. "Below 100"
5. The average of the values in the range B1

Self-Assessment

Key Takeaways

- **Advanced Functions:** Functions like SUM, AVERAGE, and VLOOKUP enable you to perform a wide range of data calculations quickly.
- **Absolute and Relative References:** Use $ signs to lock cell references in formulas, maintaining accurate calculations when formulas are copied.
- **Nested Formulas:** Embedding multiple functions within a single formula enables complex calculations in one cell.
- **Conditional Logic with IF Statements:** Allows you to set conditions for calculations, making formulas responsive to different data scenarios.

Reflective Questions

1. How could using absolute references improve the accuracy of your formulas in large datasets?
2. Why might you nest multiple functions within a single formula? How does this benefit your workflow?
3. In what situations would the VLOOKUP function streamline data retrieval in your workbook?

By practicing these advanced functions and formula structures, you're now equipped to take on sophisticated calculations and data analysis tasks in Excel.

Chapter 5: Creating and Organizing the Home Budget Workbook

Setting up the income and expenses worksheets, Planning and organizing data

Start the Home Budget

Why do we need a Home Budget?

A home budget is a financial plan that outlines how much money is coming in and how it is going out of the household each month. A budget can help individuals and families keep track of their expenses, set financial goals, and make sure they are living within their means and also to assist in saving for that holiday or special item you want to purchase.

Having a budget in place can also help identify areas where money is being wasted, so adjustments can be made to save more money or redirect money to pay down your loans. Additionally, creating a budget can help individuals and families prepare for unexpected expenses and plan for future financial milestones, such as buying a home, saving for a holiday or saving for retirement.

Overall, a home budget is an important tool for managing personal finances, paying loans, saving, and achieving financial stability and security. Without a complete financial picture of the household, it is difficult to make informed decisions, plan for future expenses, or identify areas where adjustments are needed to stay on track financially.

Creating the Home Budget workbook

When planning an Excel workbook for budgeting, there are several key steps to take to ensure that the workbook is effective and easy to use:

1. **Define your budgeting goals**: Determine what you want to accomplish with your budget, such as reducing debt, increasing savings or getting an overview of your financial situation.
2. **Gather all necessary financial information**: Collect all of the financial data that will be used in the budget, including income from all sources, expenses, and loans.

3. **Create a template or use a pre-made budget template**: Create a template or use a pre-made budget template that includes all of the necessary categories and columns for organizing and tracking your financial information. In this course, you are going to create the Home Budget Workbook.
4. **Design and format the workbook**: Make the workbook visually appealing, easy to read and understand, and easy to use.
5. **Set up formulas and calculations**: To automatically calculate and present totals, averages, and other important financial metrics.
6. **Create charts and graphs**: To help you visualize the data in your budget, you can create charts and graphs to show the distribution of your income, expenses, and net worth over time.
7. **Input data**: Input all of the financial data into the template, being sure to keep the data organized, up to date and accurate.
8. **Review and update your budget regularly**: Review the budget regularly and adjust as necessary to ensure that it remains accurate and effective.

By following these steps, you can create an effective and easy-to-use Excel workbook for budgeting that will help you manage your finances better.

Planning your worksheets

When creating a new workbook in Excel, it is important to have a clear understanding of the goals and objectives of the application. This will help guide the planning and development process, including identifying the necessary worksheets to include in the workbook. As the development process progresses, additional worksheets may be added, combined, or removed as needed to achieve the desired outcome. It is important to regularly review and assess the worksheets in the workbook to ensure they are effectively supporting the goals of the application.

Having thought about what the goal is in the application, it has been determined, for this course, that initially, the following features are required in the budget spreadsheet, *Home, Income, Expenditure - Budget – Actuals, Loans, Holiday Planning, Misc. Costs*. Each of these will be a worksheet. So now we start by creating the worksheets and naming them.

Add the worksheets

Here we will begin by inserting and naming the basic worksheets we need all at once and we will start working by fleshing them out.

At this stage, we know we want several worksheets, let us begin by adding them.

1. Start by clicking the **New Sheet** icon nine (9) times (because you already have two worksheets, Home and Income. You will now have 11 worksheets named Home, Income, and 9 more named Sheet ##. If during your trying things out earlier the sheet names are different to the below, it does not matter, as long as you have 11 worksheets to rename in the next exercise.

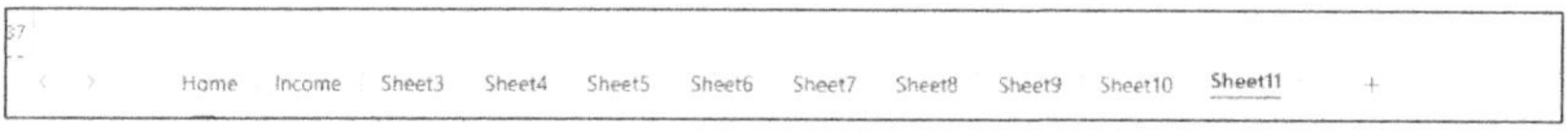

2. The names Excel provides are not informative of what the contents of the worksheets will, we need to rename them all, doing this now will.

3. For each of the worksheets, Dbl-Click on the worksheets tab, the name will be highlighted, change the names to

    1. *Home*
    2. *Income*
    3. *Expenses – Budget*
    4. *Expenses - Actuals*
    5. *Loans*
    6. *Mortgage*
    7. *Holiday Planning*
    8. *Misc. Costs*
    9. *New Job Pay Comparison*
    10. *Lookup Tables*
    11. *Work Sheet (this is a work space for you to test formula, etc.)*

> **Tip:** Be sure to use the names exactly as shown above whilst working through this course to ensure refences to the tabs work.

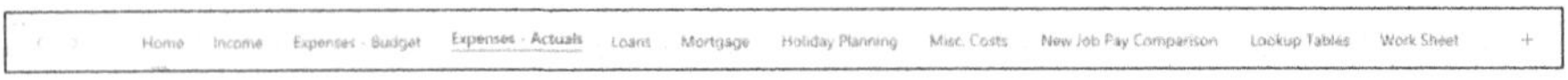

A brief rundown on the purpose of each of the sheets.

Home

The first worksheet, also known as the "Home" worksheet, is an important tool for providing a clear and concise summary of the key information contained in the other worksheets of the workbook. This worksheet will display totals for income, expenditure, and remaining income, broken down by different time periods such as yearly, weekly, and monthly. Information for this worksheet is derived from information held in the other worksheets, tying it all together. Additionally, the worksheet will include a pie chart that visually represents your financial expenditure, making it easy to understand your overall financial picture at a glance. This worksheet is designed to be the first visible worksheet when the workbook is opened, providing you with easy access to the most important information. It requires no user input once created.

Income

This worksheet is used to record and forecast annual income and serves as the foundation for other financial calculations in the workbook. It includes multiple sources of income.

The total income from this worksheet will be used in other worksheets, such as the Home worksheet, to calculate overall financial, expenditure and remaining income. This worksheet is designed to be easy to update and maintain, with clear instructions on how to input and format data correctly.

It is designed to be able to manage different types of income and their frequency. This will help to ensure that the financial calculations in the workbook are accurate and dependable.

Expenses – Budget

This worksheet is where all of your living and entertainment expenses will be recorded, including the amount and frequency of each expense.

The *Expenses – Budget* worksheet is designed to provide a detailed breakdown of expenses, including annual totals, the percentage of total expenses each expense represents, the percentage of total annual income each expense represents, and the budgeted amount required to service the expense based on your selected pay frequency. To facilitate this, the worksheet includes columns for inputting the frequency of pay days, which are used to calculate the budget amount. This worksheet is a valuable tool for understanding expenditure patterns and finding areas where expenses can be reduced.

Expenses – Actuals

This worksheet is where you enter the actual spending for each budget item, and comments. At the end of the spending for the pay period, you will see how you performed with your budget and be able to see where you might need to adjust for the next budget period.

You can archive the worksheet and its data at the end of the budget period and retain this information for future reference

Loans

This worksheet, known as the "Loans" worksheet, is where Loans are recorded, including the repayment amount and frequency of payment. The information entered into this worksheet is automatically transferred to the Expenses - Budget worksheet, loan repayments are considered an expense.

This worksheet is designed to provide a detailed breakdown of loans, including the total outstanding balance, the interest rate, and the monthly or annual repayment amount. Additionally, the worksheet has columns for inputting the frequency of Loan payments, so you can see the total amount of loan repayments made in a year.

It also includes columns for recording the remaining balance, interest and the total amount paid. This worksheet can be a valuable tool for managing and tracking loans and creating a plan to pay off debt.

Mortgage

This worksheet will assist you in keeping track of the mortgages you currently service and link the total cost back to the budget.

There is a mortgage calculator to help you evaluate the impact of changes to your mortgage, such as how a change in the interest rate might affect your finances. You can copy the calculator and use several of them side by side to make comparisons.

Note: Rent should be entered in the *Expenses – Budget* worksheet as a budget item.

Holiday Planning

This worksheet is designed for planning holidays by recording planned expenses and calculating the savings goal and the weekly payments required to reach that goal.

It includes columns for inputting information such as the destination, travel dates, estimated costs, and any other expenses related to the holiday.

The worksheet also has a feature that calculates the total cost of the holiday, and the savings goal required, based on the input information. Additionally, it includes a column that calculates the weekly payments needed to reach the savings goal. These values are entered into the budget worksheet, so you can track their progress and adjust as needed to ensure you reach your holiday savings goal. This worksheet can be a valuable tool for planning and saving for future holidays and staying on budget.

Misc Costs

This worksheet, known as the "Misc. Costs" worksheet, is designed to record miscellaneous costs and have the values included in your budget.

It includes columns for inputting information such as the name of the expense, the cost, and the frequency of the expense.

The worksheet also has a feature that calculates the total cost of all miscellaneous expenses, and the budgeted amount required to service the expense.
These values are entered into the budget worksheet, so you can track their progress and adjust as needed to ensure you stay on budget. This worksheet is a valuable tool for tracking and managing miscellaneous expenses, which can often be overlooked or forgotten in a budget such as new tyres, car registration, etc.

New Job Pay Comparison
Throughout your career, you are likely to change jobs several times, sometime voluntarily, sometimes not. The Job Pay Comparison worksheet allows you to compare the financial details of two jobs, your current and the prospective job, so you can make an informed decision on how the change will affect your financial situation.
There is also a section on how it will affect your payments if you are on Job Support income. This part is mainly for Australia but can be modified for other countries, now there's a task for you, if required.

Lookup Tables
The *Lookup Tables* worksheet is a storage space for information you will need in the budget to keep it organized, provide a single point of reference for the information and allow it to be adjusted when required, like when the tax rates change so these changes will automatically reflect throughout your budget.

Work Sheet
The *Work Sheet* is your scratchpad, somewhere where you can test formulas, formatting or anything you want so you do not risk messing up your working worksheets. Create and delete these at will.

Exercise 2.0 – Create a test worksheet

- Create another worksheet.
- rename it to **Test Worksheet**.

- Move it to the last tab
  The right most position, by clicking and holding on the tab and dragging it to the right, let go when it is last.

This sheet will be your test sheet to practice before applying changes to the other sheets. You can remove this worksheet when you have completed the course.

Conclusion

In this chapter, you've set up the foundational structure of your home budget workbook, creating worksheets that categorize income, expenses, loans, and other financial elements essential for personal financial management. A well-organized workbook is key to effectively managing your budget, offering clarity on where your money is going, helping you set realistic financial goals, and allowing you to adjust as needed. This setup also introduces various planning techniques and considerations for structuring financial data in a way that is practical, functional, and easy to update over time.

Quiz

1. Why is it important to create a budget in Excel?

2. Which of the following is NOT typically included in a personal budget workbook?

    - a) Income
    - b) Expenses
    - c) Loan Repayments
    - d) Social Media Profiles

3. True or False: A new worksheet can be added to an Excel workbook by clicking the New Sheet icon.

4. Name two specific uses for the Misc. Costs and Holiday Planning worksheets in your budget workbook.

5. Why is it useful to have a worksheet specifically for testing or scratch work?

Quiz Answers

1. To track income and expenses, set financial goals, prepare for unexpected costs, and achieve financial stability.
2. d) Social Media Profiles
3. True
4. Misc. Costs helps track miscellaneous expenses, while Holiday Planning is used to save for and organize holiday expenses.
5. A test worksheet provides a safe space to experiment with formulas and layout without impacting the main budget workbook.

Self-Assessment

Key Takeaways

- **Budget Structure:** Setting up distinct worksheets for income, expenses, loans, and savings goals allows for an organized and comprehensive view of your finances.

- **Worksheet Purpose:** Each worksheet serves a unique role in categorizing and tracking specific financial data, enhancing clarity and usability.

- **Planning and Goal Setting:** A well-planned budget workbook helps you visualize financial goals and track progress toward achieving them.

- **Future-Proofing Your Budget:** Organizing your workbook early on makes it easier to adjust in the future as your financial situation or goals change.

Reflective Questions

1. How does creating separate worksheets for each aspect of your budget improve clarity and usability?

2. Which worksheets do you expect to update most frequently? Why?

3. How could planning your workbook structure in advance help you as your financial needs or goals evolve over time?

With the foundational structure in place, you are now well-equipped to begin populating your worksheets with financial data, enabling accurate tracking and analysis of your finances.

We are off to a good start; we have had a lot to cover up to this point to prepare for the upcoming worksheet development.

Now we can start creating the worksheets, the first task is to get the headings on each of the main tabs.

Let's get started.

Chapter 6: Worksheet Tutorials

Detailed tutorials on creating and formatting various budget-related worksheets (Income, Expenses, Loans, etc.)

> **Tip for LibreOffice Users**
> You can format cells in LibreOffice Calc by right-clicking a cell and selecting Format Cells, or by using the *Format → Cells* option from the top menu.
> The available formatting options (like Number, Currency, Bold, Fill Color, Borders) work similarly to Excel, although the dialog layout will look different.

Work Sheet Headings

The main purpose of a heading is to clearly identify the purpose or function of the worksheet. It should be prominent and easily readable, often located at the top of the worksheet. While headings don't need to be fancy, we will be using WordArt in Excel and FontWork in LibreOffice Calc to introduce you to them, you can get as fancy as you like.

> **LibreOffice Users**
> To get access to FontWork, activate the Draw Toolbar by selecting *View → Toolbars → Drawing*
> The toolbar will appear on screen, most likely at the bottom screen. Fontwork can be activated with the outlined "F" icon

You can create a heading in one worksheet, and then copy and paste it to other worksheets, which can save time and ensure consistency across multiple worksheets. You can then simply change the text as needed to reflect the specific function of each worksheet.

It is also good practice to format the heading text to make it stand out, for example using different fonts, bold, larger or different color to make it easily visible and distinguishable from the other contents.

Create the heading by

1. Activate the **Income** Worksheet by Clicking on the **Income** worksheet tab.
2. Place your cursor in cell **A1**, top left of the screen.

3. Select **Insert** from the top menu and select **WordArt** from the ribbon – way over to the right

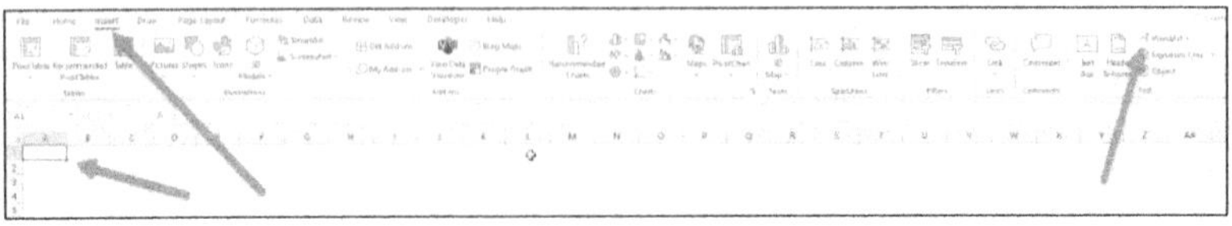

LibreOffice users

4. Select one of the styles presented by clicking on it.
   A text box will open with the words ***"Your Text Here"***, LibreOffice Calc will open with the name of the style

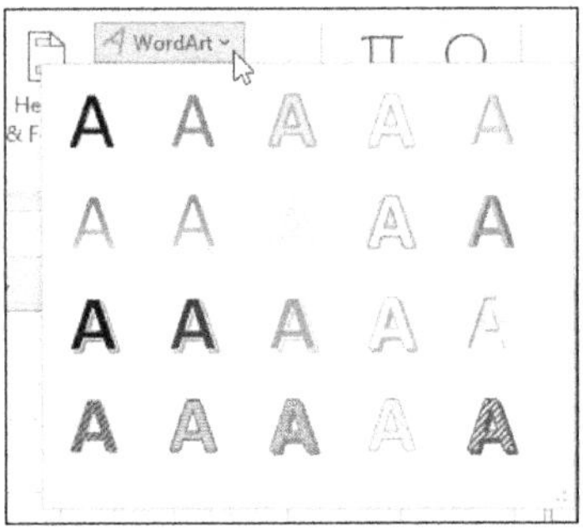

5. Type the heading, for now, type **My Heading**
   Note: If you lose focus on the text box, just double click on one of the letters to regain focus.

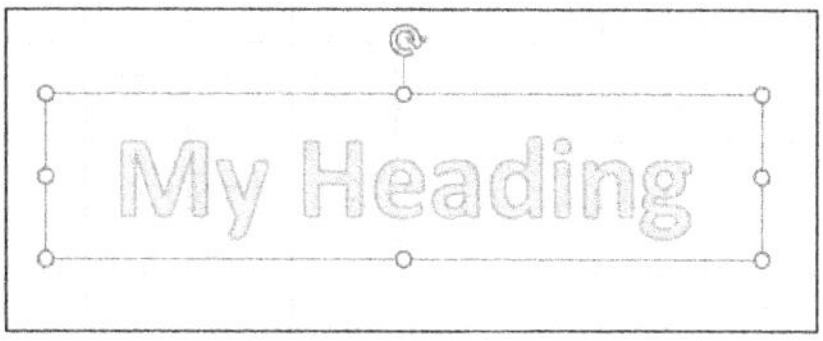

6. Select all characters in the text box by left clicking in front of the first letter and dragging the pointer to the right, all selected text will be greyed, and a small dialog option box will appear

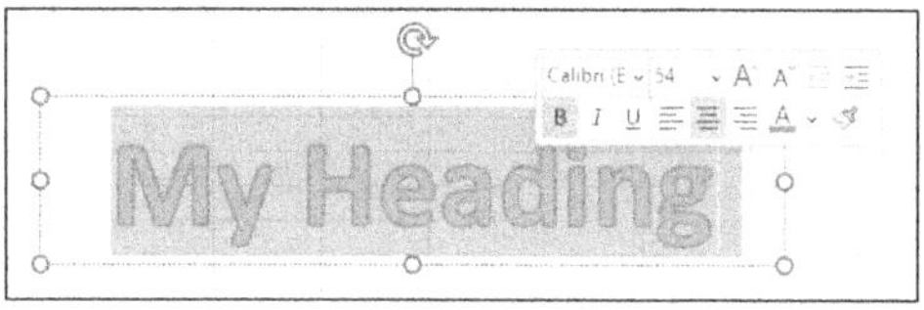

7. Set the font size to **54**, or other size to fit neatly in 3 rows
   You can also set any other formatting you wish.

   LibreOffice Calc, you do not need to set the font, resize the text box with your mouse.

Now let us practice the Copy/Paste so you can easily do the headings for the other worksheets.

8. There are two ways to copy the WordArt box into the clipboard
    a. Click on the new heading and then **right-click** the frame around it so it becomes solid, select **Copy** from the right-click menu. This can be a little tricky because you may get the short menu with *Copy Here* or the longer menu with *Copy*. You want the longer menu, the movement is so fine it takes some practice, but there is an easier way.
    b. Click in the new heading and then **right-click** the frame around it so it becomes solid, select **Copy** from the *Home*, *Clipboard* group. This will put the WordArt into the clipboard.

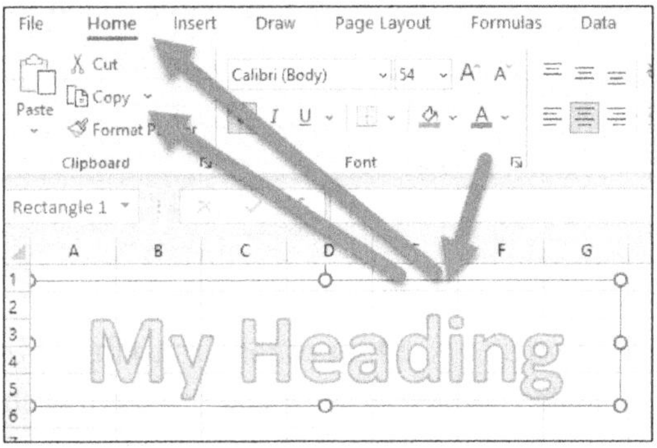

9. Select C**ell A1**
10. **Right-Click** and click **Paste** – To duplicate the heading.
11. Click or Dbl-Click the new heading, replace the text with the new heading name **Income** and reposition it properly in the top/left corner of the

worksheet. **LibreOffice Calcusers**, when text is changed, click on the worksheet outside of the box to set it.

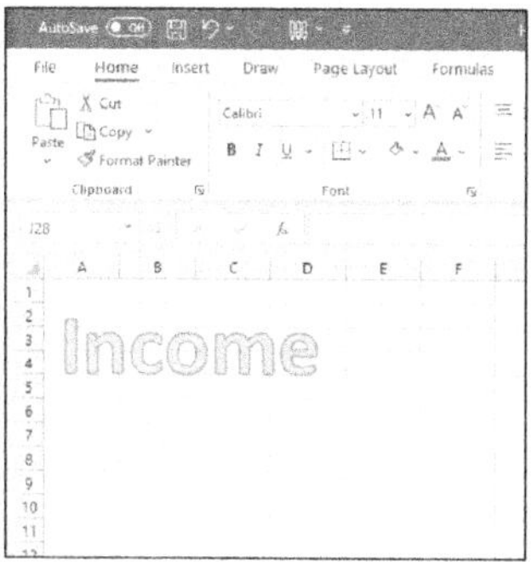

12. Remove the old heading by clicking in it, clicking on the line and press **Delete key on keyboard**

Now you know how to

- Add a heading.
- Copy/Paste and existing heading to a new worksheet to save time.

> **NOTE:**
> **Ensure to place the heading at cell A1 and limit the height to five (5) standard rows or less, all worksheets in this training course start on row 6.**

Exercise 6.1 – Setting up headings on other worksheets.

You can go ahead and set up the headings for the other worksheets you created earlier. Give them the following names to avoid confusion when we refer to them later, you can always change them after you have completed the course.

Tab Name	**Heading Text**
Home	My Budget
Income	Income
Expenses - Budget	Expenses – Budget
Expenses - Actuals	Expenses – Actuals
Loans	Loans
Mortgage	Mortgage
Holiday Planning	Holiday Planning
Misc. Costs	Misc. Costs
New Job Pay Comparison	Comparison - Current income with new job
Lookup Tables	Lookup Tables
Work Sheet	*No heading required*

Be sure to save the workbook after you have added the headings.

WS 1 – Lookup Tables

Introduction

Welcome to WS1 – Lookup Tables! Before we dive into creating specific worksheets for your budgeting application, we need to set up a foundational component that will make the entire process smoother and more efficient. The Lookups worksheet will house essential data tables and named ranges that we will use throughout the workbook. These lookup tables will enable us to automate data retrieval, ensure consistency, and reduce manual entry errors as we build and work with various worksheets.

> **Tip:** While you can't see Named Ranges on paper, they're an important part of many formulas — they make your spreadsheets easier to build and read. You'll see them used throughout this example.

In this section, you will learn how to:

- Create a dedicated Lookup Tables worksheet.
- Set up various lookup tables that will be referenced in subsequent worksheets.
- Define named ranges for easy and efficient data management.

By setting up the Lookups worksheet first, you will establish a robust framework that supports all other aspects of your budgeting application. This preparation will streamline the process of creating and using formulas, making your workbook more dynamic and user-friendly.

> **Tip for LibreOffice Users**
> Setting up lookup tables works the same way in LibreOffice Calc.
> To define a data range for lookup purposes, use Data → Define Range.
> This allows you to manage named data blocks similar to how Excel manages table areas.

Key Benefits

1. **Automation**: Lookups enable Excel to automatically retrieve relevant data, minimizing the need for repetitive manual inputs or locking values into formula.

2. **Consistency**: Using named ranges and lookup tables ensures that data used across multiple worksheets is consistent and up to date.
3. **Efficiency**: With lookups in place, you can quickly and easily reference important data, saving time and reducing errors.
4. **Ease of Changing and Personalizing Data**: When you need to update or personalize data, you can simply modify the lookup tables in one place. This change will automatically reflect across all related worksheets, making the process seamless and efficient.

This is what the Lookups Table worksheet will look like when completed. Please note that the details in these lookups are for Australia, we will discuss later how to change this for your location at the end of the course. Stay with these values until then so you check the results when using them as we work through the course.

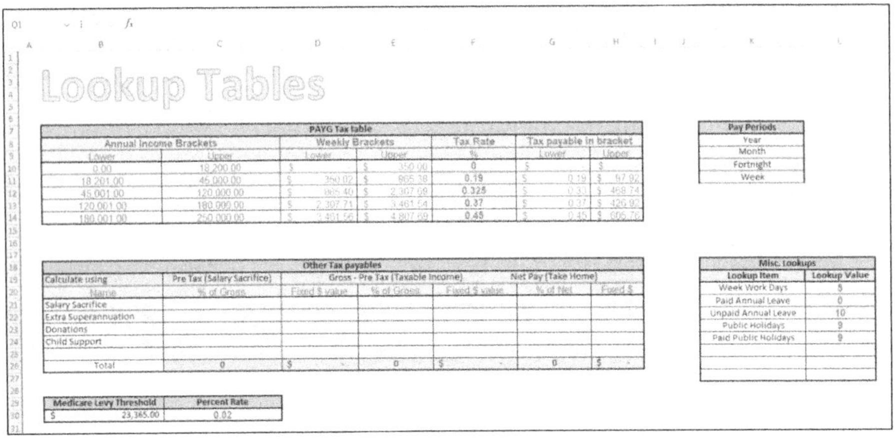

> **NOTE:** Throughout this course, you will see cell ranges referred to like this "A1:B5", for two or more adjacent cells, "A1:A2" or span rows and columns. In Excel, "A1:B5" refers to a range of cells that starts from cell A1 and extends to cell B5. This range includes all the cells in the rectangular area bounded by these two cells, specifically cells A1, A2, A3, A4, A5, B1, B2, B3, B4, and B5. The notation "A1:B5" is used to reference this group of cells in formulas, functions, and other Excel operations, allowing users to perform calculations or apply formatting to multiple cells simultaneously.

Let us get started by creating the Lookups worksheet and setting up the necessary tables and named ranges that will be essential for the rest of our workbook.

Creating the Lookups Worksheet

Follow these step-by-step instructions to build the Lookups worksheet and its tables/data. We will be more concerned about getting the details in correctly, not so much with formatting at this stage. We will work on formatting after the tables are created.

> **Hint:** Formatting is a trap, it pulls you in and before you know it, you have spent way too much time making it look perfect and will actually slow your development. When developing and creating, concentrate on getting the data and formula right, then and only then work on the formatting.

If you have not already added the Lookup Tables worksheet in the previous exercise, please do so now.

- **Open Excel** and add a new worksheet.
- **Rename the worksheet** to "Lookup Tables"
- **Add the heading**

Create the PAYG Tax Table

Tax brackets are ranges of income that are taxed at specific rates, forming a progressive tax system where higher income levels are taxed at higher rates. Each bracket applies to a portion of an individual's taxable income, meaning the first segment of income is taxed at the lowest rate, and as income increases, it enters higher brackets with correspondingly higher rates. This system ensures that those with higher earnings contribute a larger share of their income in taxes, while lower-income earners benefit from lower tax rates on their initial earnings.

This table provides a reference point to calculate the tax payable on your income.

Enter the Table Heading:

- In cell B7, type "PAYG Tax table"
  - Merge and center cells **B7:H7** by
    - Click in cell **B7**

- While holding down the **Shift** key, click in cell **H7**
  The range from B7:H7 will be selected
- Excel - **Alignment** menu in the **Ribbon**, click **Merge and Centre**
- Libre- **Home** menu in the **Ribbon**, click **Merge and Centre Cells**

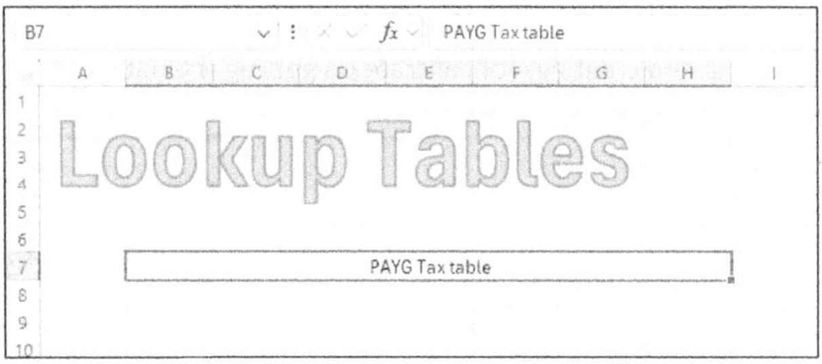

Enter Column Headings:

Adjust the column widths if required to see the headings properly as you add them

- In cell B8, type "Annual Income Brackets"
  - Merge and center cells B8:C8
- In cell D8, type "Weekly Brackets"
  - Merge and center cells D8:E8
- In cell F8, type "Tax Rate"
- In cell G8, type "Tax payable in bracket"
  - Merge and center cells G8:H8
- In cell B9, type "Lower"
- In cell C9, type "Upper"
- In cell D9, type "Lower"
- In cell E9, type "Upper"
- In cell F9, type "%"
- In cell G9, type "Lower"
- In cell H9, type "Upper"

Enter the Data:

- Enter the data as shown in the provided image
    - Columns B, C and F
- Example:
    - In cell B10, type "0.00"
    - In cell C10, type "18,200.00"
    - In cell F10, type "0"

> **Note**: We will be using formula to calculate the remaining values in this table. We will cover the topic of formula, formatting and security in detail in the next chapter, WS1-Income. We will then come back to them here.

Your unformatted table should look like this.

	A	B	C	D	E	F	G	H
6								
7					PAYG Tax table			
8		Annual Income Brackets		Weekly Brackets		Tax Rate	Tax payable in bracket	
9		Lower	Upper	Lower	Upper	%	Lower	Upper
10		0	18200			0		
11		18201	45000			0.19		
12		45001	120000			0.325		
13		120001	180000			0.37		
14		180001	250000			0.45		
15								

> **Note**: The tax brackets and tax rates in the above table were correct at the time of writing this training course, they may have changed. You can find the latest bracket and rates at the Tax Office website for your country.

Adapting to Your Country's Tax System

Although this workbook is based on Australian tax rules, you can easily customize it for any country!

- Simply update the Lookup Tables with your local tax brackets and rates.
- No changes to the macro code are needed.
- To verify, compare the results against a recent payslip or use your government's online tax calculator.

With a few simple edits, you can tailor the system to fit your local rules!

Create the Other Tax Payables Table

Tax deductions can occur at three stages:

1. Pre-Tax (Salary Sacrifice)
   Pre-tax deductions, such as additional superannuation contributions and health insurance premiums, reduce taxable income and thus lower overall tax liability. These reduce your taxable income, and you pay less tax.
2. Gross Pay (Taxable Income)
   Gross pay includes all earnings before taxes. Some deductions such as Child Support may be calculated using your Gross income. You will pay normal tax on these, but the calculated amount will be deducted from your Net pay.
3. Net Pay (Take Home).
   Net pay, the amount received after all deductions, reflects the employee's actual take-home income. You may have some deductions you want taken from your Net pay such as donations, etc.

Understanding these stages helps you manage your finances by knowing your true earnings and tax obligations. This table provides a method of entering these details so you can get a true indication of your income.

Enter the Table Heading:

- In cell B18, type "Other Tax payables"
- Merge and center cells B18:H18

Enter Column Headings:

- In cell B19, type "Calculate using"
- In cell C19, type "Pre Tax (Salary Sacrifice)"
  - Merge and center cells C18:D18
- In cell E19, type "Gross - Pre Tax (Taxable Income)"
  - Merge and center cells E19:F19
- In cell G19, type "Net Pay (Take Home)"
  - Merge and center cells G19:H19

- In cell B20, type "Name"
- In cell C20, type "% of Gross"
- In cell D20, type "Fixed $ value"
- In cell E20, type "% of Gross"
- In cell F20, type "Fixed $ value"
- In cell G20, type "% of Net"
- In cell H20, type "Fixed $ value"

Totals row

This table has a totals row, for now we only need to put the row heading in

- In cell B26, type "Total"

Enter the Data:

Enter the data as shown in the provided image, these are examples of what you can put in.

	B	C	D	E	F	G	H
16							
17							
18			Other Tax payables				
19	Calculate using	Pre Tax (Salary Sacrifice)		Gross - Pre Tax (Taxable Income)		Net Pay (Take Home)	
20	Name	% of Gross	Fixed $ value	% of Gross	Fixed $ value	% of Net	Fixed $ value
21	Salary Sacrifice						
22	Extra Superannuation						
23	Donations						
24	Child Support						
25							
26	Total						

Create the Medicare Levy Threshold Table

Enter the Table Heading:

- In cell B29, type "Medicare Levy Threshold"
- In cell C29, type " Percent Rate "

Enter the Column Headings and Data:

- In cell B30, type "$23,365.00"
- In cell C30, type "0.02"

	B	C
28		
29	Medicare Levy Threshold	Percent Rate
30	$23,365.00	0.02

Create the Pay Periods Table

This table is to store the possible pay periods for use in calculations, this will become important later.

Enter the Table Heading:

- In cell K7, type "Pay Periods".

Enter the Data:

- In cell K8, type "Year"
- In cell K9, type "Month"
- In cell K10, type "Fortnight"
- In cell K11, type "Week"

	J	K
7		Pay Periods
8		Year
9		Month
10		Fortnight
11		Week
12		

Create the Misc. Lookups Table

This table holds information we want to use throughout the workbook in calculations, but it is too few to require their own tables. In this course we will only be using "Week Workdays". The rest to give you a sample of what can go in here.

Enter the Table Heading:

- In cell K18, type "Lookup Item"
    - Merge and center cells K18:L18
- In cell K19, type "Lookup Item"
- In cell L19, type "Lookup Value"

Enter the Data:

- In cell K20, type "Week Workdays"
    - L20, type "5"
      If you work less days per week, you can enter that later, for now stay with 5
- In cell K21, type "Paid Annual Leave"
    - L20, type "20"
- In cell K22, type "Unpaid Annual Leave"
    - L20, type "0"
- In cell
    - K23, type "Public Holidays"
    - L20, type "9"
- In cell
    - K24, type "Paid Public Holidays"
    - L20, type "8"
    - Note: Some public holidays are only paid if they fall on a workday, i.e., Anzac Day

	J	K	L
17			
18		Lookup Item	
19		Lookup Item	Lookup Value
20		Week Workdays	5
21		Paid Annual Leave	20
22		Unpaid Annual Leave	0
23		Public Holidays	9
24		Paid Public Holidays	8

Note: Change these values as required.

Define Named Ranges

Named ranges in Excel are a feature that allows users to assign a meaningful name to a specific range of cells, making it easier to reference these cells in formulas and functions. Instead of using cell coordinates like A1:B10, you can use descriptive names such as "SalesData" or "TaxRates." The advantages of named ranges include improved readability and clarity of formulas, easier management of complex spreadsheets, and reduced errors since users can refer to data ranges by names that clearly describe their content or purpose.

> **NOTE**: Named ranges cannot contain spaces in their name, you can omit the spaces such as in PAYGTaxTable or replace them with underscores such as PAYG_Tax_Table. The choice is yours, use the name convention you find more readable, for this course we will be using underscores, you can change them later.

The named range should only include the data, not the headings, below we will step through the first table to name, the PAYG Tax Table

> **Tip for LibreOffice Users**
> Named Ranges work the same way in LibreOffice Calc.
> To create or manage named ranges, go to **Sheet → Named Ranges and Expressions → Define... or Manage....**
>
> *The dialog box may look slightly different from Excel's Name Manager, but the functionality is the same.*

Select the range for each table.

- The first range is from B10:H14, Select the range by
  - Click in cell B10
  - While holding down the shift key, click in cell H14

> **Note**: You will see the whole range go darker to indicate what is selected, except the cell B10, this is the selected cell in the range, the first you clicked on.

- **Go to the Formulas tab** and click "Define Name", the **New Name** window will open with the cell coordinates of the tab name and range already displayed in *Refers to:*

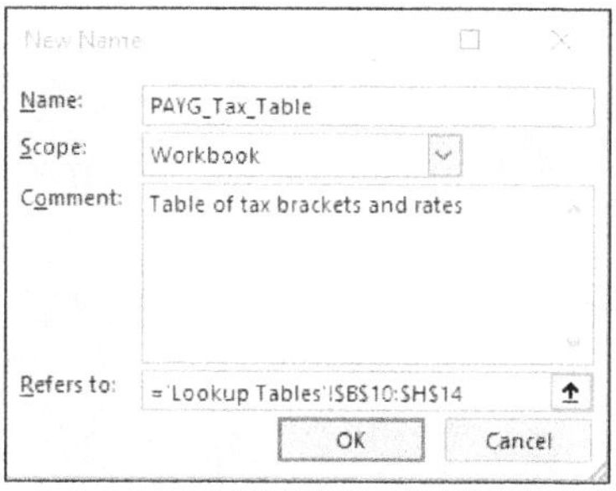

- **Enter a name** for the range (e.g., "PAYG_Tax_Table"), this is required
- **Excel - Enter a Comment** to describe the purpose of the table, not required but helps later
- **Click OK** or **Add**
  You will see the range name now appears in the top left dropdown above column A. This is because the range is still selected. This dropdown will contain your named ranges and when you select one, focus will move to the range.

Exercise 6.2 - Name the remaining tables

For this exercise, repeat for each table to define the named ranges, the following table shows the names and coordinates of all tables.

Lookup Table	Cell Coordinates	Name	Comment Excel only
PAYG Tax table	A10:H10	PAYG_Tax_Table	Table of tax brackets and rate
Other Tax payables	C26:H26	Other_Tax_Payable	Various taxes and deductions. This is the Totals line only.
Medicare Levy Threshold	B30:C30	Medicare_Levy	Threshold and rate
Pay Periods	K8:K11	Pay_Periods	How often you get paid
Misc. Lookups	K20:L26	Misc_Lookups	Various lookup values

You may have noticed some of the ranges are only one row, not the whole table, sometimes we have a single row table as for Medicare_Levy or we are only interested in the totals rows as in Other_Tax_Payable. Misc. Lookups we added an extra two rows in case you need them.

When you select the named range dropdown, you should now have the following named ranges.

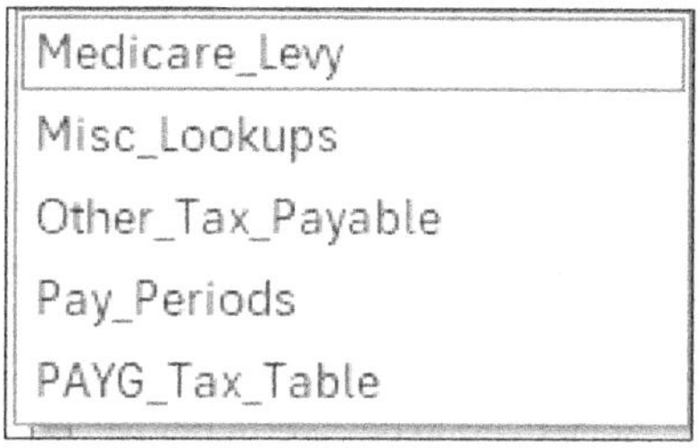

The lookup Tables worksheet should look like

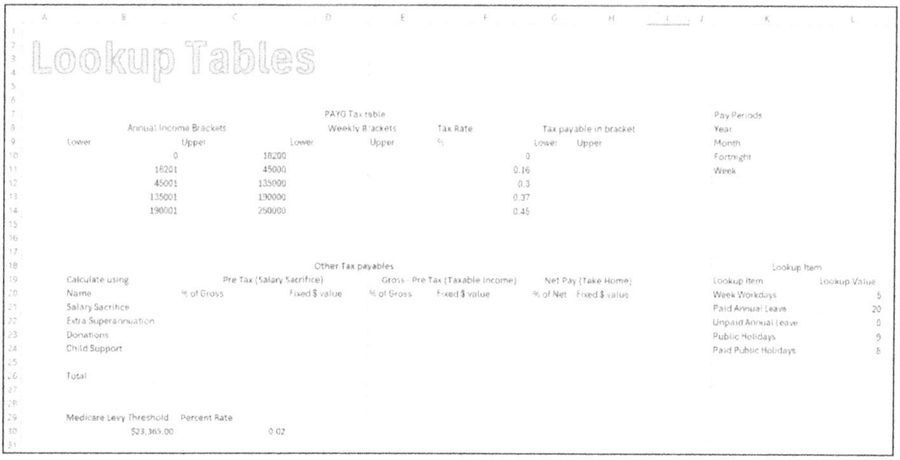

> **NOTE**: The cells currently look very plain, but we will add formatting and formulas later in the course. When we reach that point, you will have the chance to revisit and enhance this section.
>
> For now, we have established the main functionality needed to continue.
>
> When creating workbooks, prioritize functionality to ensure accurate calculations and data processing, laying a solid foundation. Once the core functions are established, focus on aesthetic and detailed improvements like formatting and styling. This approach prevents getting bogged down by visual aspects early on and ensures the workbook is both dependable and visually appealing. In this course, we will first build essential functionality, then revisit for enhancements, ensuring robust and attractive workbooks.
>
> Often before development is completed, you may realise that some things need to be changed, moved or removed resulting in any formatting you have done to be rendered ineffective or lost, for this reason we make it functional, and only then will we make it pretty.

Conclusion

By completing the Lookups worksheet, you have laid the essential groundwork for your budgeting application. The use of lookup tables and named ranges will streamline data management, ensuring accuracy and consistency throughout your workbook. These lookup tables not only automate data retrieval but also minimize errors and increase efficiency when working across various worksheets. As we move forward, you'll begin to see the benefits of this solid foundation, making your budgeting application dynamic, flexible, and easy to maintain. In the next section, we'll start using these lookup tables and named ranges in our formulas, taking the functionality of your workbook to the next level.

Quiz

Question 1: **What is the main benefit of using lookup tables in Excel?**

a) They improve the appearance of the workbook.
b) They allow for automatic data retrieval and reduce manual entry errors.
c) They increase the file size of the workbook.
d) They prevent data entry.

Question 2: **True or False: Named ranges in Excel can include spaces in their names.**

a) True
b) False

Question 3: **Which of the following is NOT an example of a named range in this chapter?**

a) PAYG_Tax_Table
b) Medicare_Levy
c) Salary_Sacrifice_Tax
d) Misc_Lookups

Question 4: **What does the cell reference "A1:B5" represent in Excel?**

a) A single cell.
b) A named range.
c) A rectangular range of cells from A1 to B5.
d) A circular reference.

Quiz Answers

1. b) They allow for automatic data retrieval and reduce manual entry errors.
2. b) False
3. c) Salary_Sacrifice_Tax
4. c) A rectangular range of cells from A1 to B5.

Self-Assessment

Key Takeaways

By the end of this chapter, you should be able to:

- Create and organize a dedicated Lookups worksheet.
- Set up lookup tables and define named ranges for efficient data management.
- Understand the importance of using lookup tables and named ranges for automation, consistency, and efficiency in Excel.

Reflective Questions

1. Have you successfully created and named the lookup tables as outlined in this chapter?
   - (Yes/No)
2. Can you explain the benefits of using lookup tables in your workbook for automation and data consistency?
   - (Yes/No)
3. Have you practiced defining named ranges in Excel, and do you understand how to use them in formulas?
   - (Yes/No)

WS 2 – Income

Introduction to the Income Worksheet

The Income worksheet is the first one we are creating, and as such, it will be more extensive and detailed. This section covers many fundamental skills and techniques, including creating headings, formatting, layout planning, and entering formulas. Mastering these skills now will make the subsequent worksheets much easier, as you will have a solid foundation to build upon.

The income worksheet in a budget is important because it helps track and plan the sources of income which form the basis of the budget. It is useful to list all income streams to ensure you have an accurate and complete picture of your income. The total income is then used by other worksheets to determine if your expenses are within your total income and help prioritize spending based on financial goals.

> **Tip for LibreOffice Users**
> Data entry, formulas, and basic formatting work the same way in LibreOffice Calc as in Excel.
> You can follow all instructions in this section directly, with only minor menu layout differences.

Creating the worksheet

If you have not already added the Income worksheet, please do so now.

- **Open Excel** and add a new worksheet.
- **Rename the worksheet** to "Income"
- **Add the heading**

Preparing the layout

It is definitely worth taking the time to plan the layout of a worksheet on paper before creating it in a spreadsheet program. Even a very rough sketch like the one below can help ensure that you have all the columns you need to get started, and the worksheet is organized and easy to read, which can make it more efficient to use.

The sketch should contain the following items

- Column letters, A to ....
- Row numbers
- Heading and column headings
- Test data, two rows is good. Calculate the values for each column and total
- Indicate where the user enters data and what is calculated
- The rough formula for each column

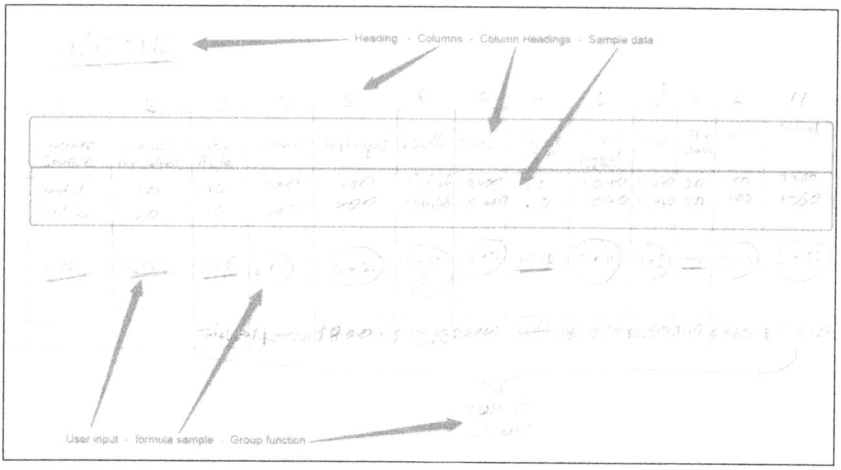

Planning on paper also allows you to experiment with different layouts and adjust before committing to a final design. Additionally, it can help you identify any potential issues or problems with the worksheet before you start entering data and formulas, which can save time and effort overall.

Once you are satisfied with the layout, you can then transfer it to the worksheet, placing the text and formulas in the appropriate cells and formatting the worksheet as needed.

By taking this step

- you will save time by getting your basic design done and finished.
- be able to think critically about your design.
    - is it clear, uncluttered and does it make sense?
    - is everything there and well grouped?
    - if you include color, are the colors easy on the eye, do they group information well? Color can be added to the spreadsheet later.

> **Note**: No matter how much you think your design through, when you start filling in formula, etc. you are very likely to think of other things to put in, take out or change. Excel is quite forgiving and if you must insert a new row, column or move sections, Excel will, in most cases, adjust any formula affected for you automatically.

Over the next paragraphs we will lay out the Income worksheet based on the hand-drawn sample above.

Setting the column headings

To transfer a layout from paper to a worksheet, you can start by adding the headings and other text to the appropriate cells in the worksheet. Once the text is in place, you can then move on to adding the formulas to the cells. This approach allows you to focus on one task at a time and ensures that the layout of the worksheet is consistent with your original design.

Start by entering the column headings. Add the columns below, the cell coordinates to place the headings are **bold**, the column text is *Italics***,** the remaining is to let you know the data type and what it is for. **Dbl-Click** on the cell and type the text in.

> **Tip**: If find you have made a typo in the heading, double-click the cell and you can edit the text.

Do not worry if the column headings are too wide for the column at this stage, we will be adjusting them.

Columns

- **B6**, *Income Source*, the column data will be *Text*.Taxable
  Where this income comes from
- **C6**, *Hours per Week*, the column data will be *Decimal*.
  The hours per week you work at this income source.
- **D6**, *Base Pay Rate*, the column data will be *Decimal*.
  The hourly rate you get paid.
- **E6,** *Taxable*, the column data will be *Text*
  Indicates if this income stream is taxable
- **F6**, *Tax-Free Threshold***,** the column data will be *Text*
  Indicates if you will be claiming the tax-free threshold on this income stream. Only one income stream per person can claim this.
- Pay period for income source
  - **G6**, *Week*, the column data will be *Decimal*.
  - **H6**, *Fortnight* **or** *Bi-Weekly*, the column data will be *Decimal*.
  - **I6**, *Month*, the column data will be *Decimal*.
  - **J6**, *Quarter*, the column data will be *Decimal*.
  - **K6**, *Year*, the column data will be *Decimal*.
- **L6**, *Superannuation Rate*, the column data will be *Decimal*.
  The percentage of base pay the employer pays for super, usually around 10%.
- **M6**, *Annual Super Amount*, the column data will be *Decimal*.
  The annual dollar amount of super.
- **N6**, *Package*, the column data will be *Decimal*.
  Annual base pay + annual super = total Package
- **O6**, *Tax week*, the column data will be *Decimal*.
  How much tax you pay on your pay per week, initially get this from your pay slip or tax office website calculator, we will be adding a VBA function to calculate this later.
- **P6**, *Take Home Week*, the column data will be *Decimal*.
  Your NET weekly pay for this income stream, your budget.
- **Q6**, *Take Home Annual*, the column data will be *Decimal*.
  Your NET annual pay for this income stream.

Your column headings should now look like this, it looks a little rough, but we will fix that shortly. For now, you can adjust your column widths by dragging on the vertical separator between the column letters.

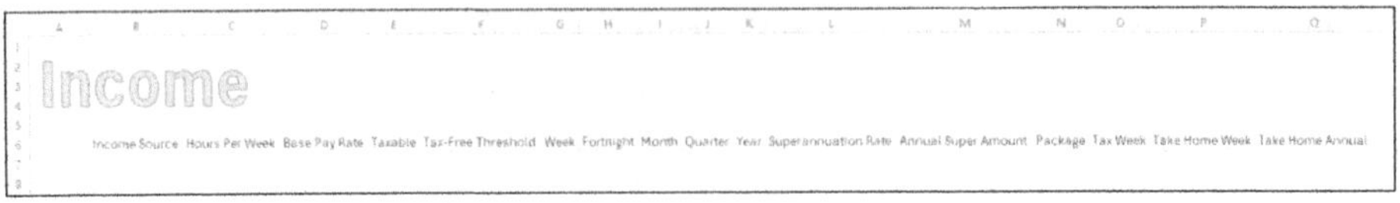

To reiterate, the idea is to just get your layout and formula first and worry about formatting later, if you get bogged down on formatting each entry as you type it, it will take much longer to create your sheet, there are ways to apply formatting to whole sections at once which we will show you.

Totals Row Heading

In order to have a clear and complete understanding of all of your income streams, a row is needed to sum all the columns above it. The total for the **Take Home Annual** column will be used as the base income for all other calculations throughout the workbook.

To help with organization, a single heading labeled **Total** should be added to the totals row in cell **F22**. We will be adding totals for columns G to K and M to Q.

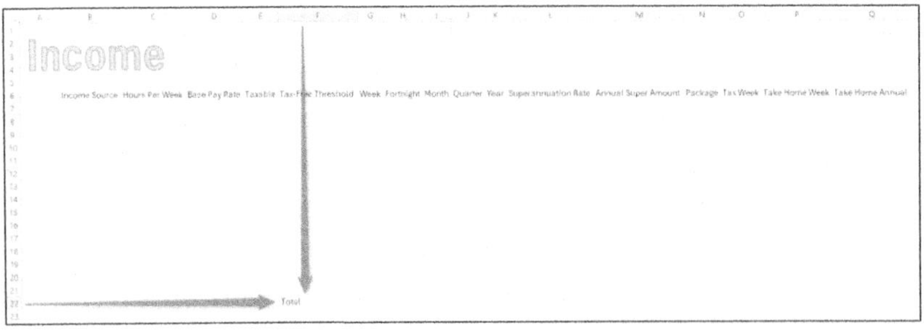

Although 15 lines for entering income details may be more than necessary, it allows for the possibility of adding more income streams in the future.

It is suggested to use the provided coordinates in order to avoid confusion as they will be referred to in many upcoming worksheets and formulas. After we have completed setting up all worksheets, we will be learning how to modify them, including adding more income rows here, be patient.

Formula

With the labels in place, we can now put the formula in to make it work.

Initial Test Data

The formula we are about to enter needs something to work with, add the following data

- **B7**, type in **Test Income**
- **C7**, type **40**
- **D7**, type **10**

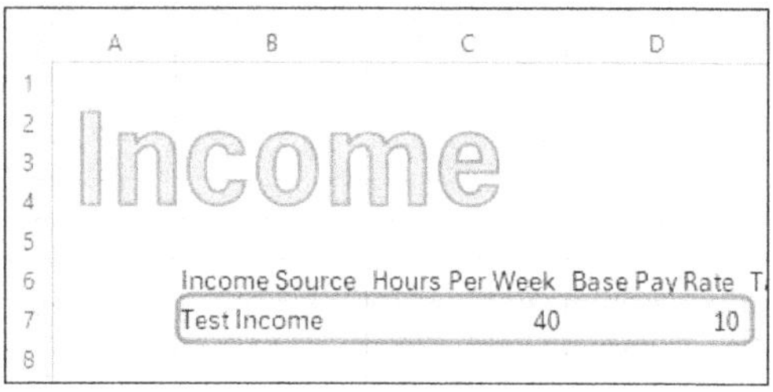

Notice we entered values divisible by 10, this makes it easier to calculate in our head as we enter the formula, we just change them to their real values later. We are now ready to enter some formula.

> **Note**: The tax related columns will not be used until later lessons, they can stay blank for now.

Week

A quite simple formula to calculate the weekly income based on the Hours per Week value * the Base Pay Rate. We will enter this formula directly.

- Dbl-Click in cell **G7,** the cursor will be blinking in the cell.
- Type the following formula directly into the cell **=C7*D7**and hit **Enter**, your formula should be as below. Notice the different colors with the referred cells matching color so you can easily see which cell the formula is referring to.

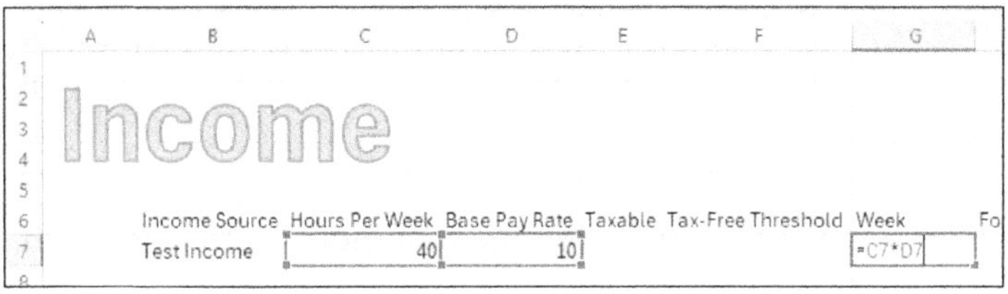

- The cell should now contain the value **400** or the value of cells C7 * D7. Also notice the selected cell coordinate and formula are displayed in the information bar above the worksheet, this is handy.

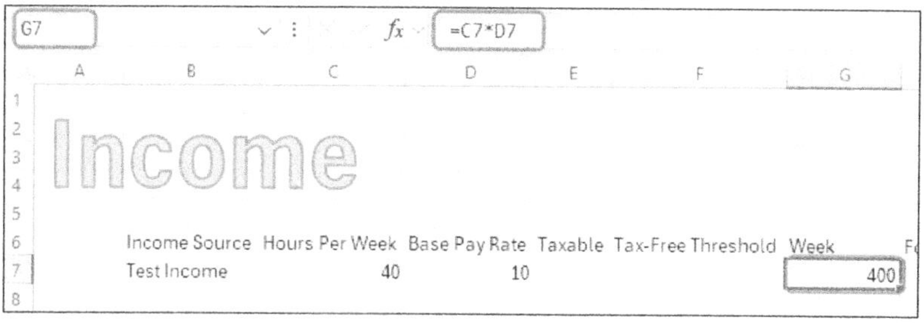

- Test it works by changing the values in C7 and D7, the value should change accordingly.
- When finished testing, put them back to 40 and 10 to keep the following formula results synchronized with the course values.

All subsequent calculations will be based on this weekly amount.

Congratulations, you have now entered your first formula, we will now move to the next one.

Fortnight or Bi-Weekly

We could type the formula in directly, but we will do something a little different to learn new techniques.

- Dbl-Click in cell **H7** to get the blinking cursor and Type = to indicate this will be a formula.
- Using your mouse, click on cell G7, you will see G7 appear in the formula in cell H7.

- Now type ***2** and press Enter; your formula and value should be

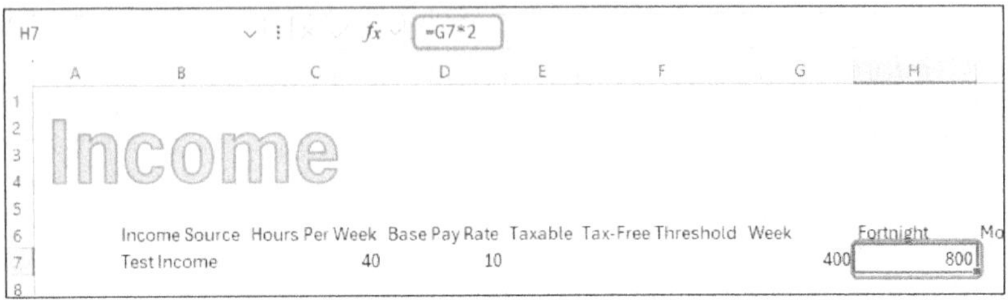

- Test it as before by changing the values in B7 and C7
- When finished testing, put B7 and C7 back to 40 and 10 respectively to keep everything synchronized while training.

Advantage: Entering formulas this way helps you avoid typing errors and ensures that you reference the correct cells. It also makes it easier to update formulas, as you can simply click on different cells to change the inputs without retyping the entire formula. This technique can save time and reduce mistakes, especially in complex spreadsheets.

That is two formulas done! You are doing great. Let's move on to the next one.

Month

The month is a little different, we need to calculate the yearly amount and divide that by 12. We will introduce the brackets here, to set the formula for Monthly Income, do the following.

- Dbl-Click in cell **I7** and enter **=(**
- using your mouse, click on cell G7, you will see G7 appear in the formula in I7

- Enter the following after ***52)/12** and press the **Enter** key, your formula should be **=(G7*52)/12**

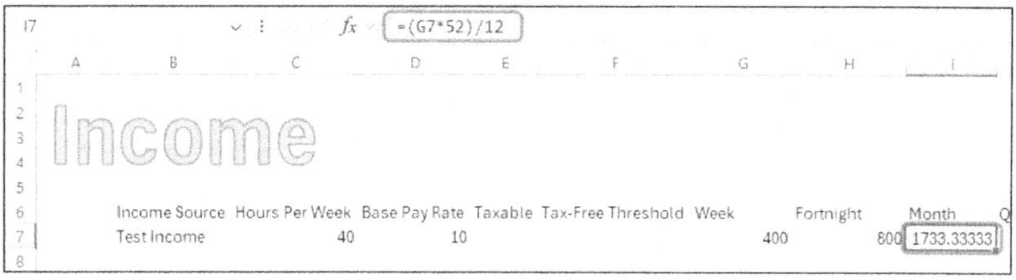

- If you get more than two decimal places as shown in the image, these will be fixed to two later when we format.

Quarter

As with month, we need to calculate the yearly amount but divide that by 4. To set the formula for Quarterly Income, do the following.

- Dbl-Click in cell **J7** and enter **=(**
- using your mouse, click on cell G7, you will see G7 appear in the formula in I7
- Enter the following after ***52)/4** and press the **Enter** key, your formula should be **=(G7*52)/4**

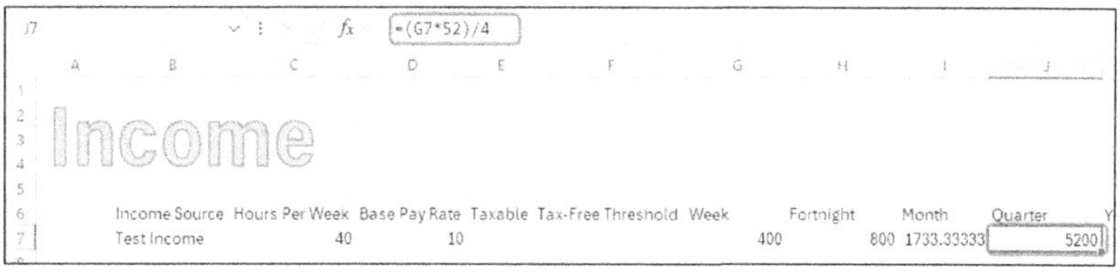

Year

The final pay period is the Yearly amount, this is weekly * 52, do the following.

- Dbl-Click in cell K**7** and Type =

- Using your mouse, click on cell G7, you will see G7 appear in the formula in K7.
- Now type ***52** and press the Enter key, your formula should be **=G7*52** Here, G7 refers to your weekly pay. The formula multiplies this by 52 to calculate annual pay.

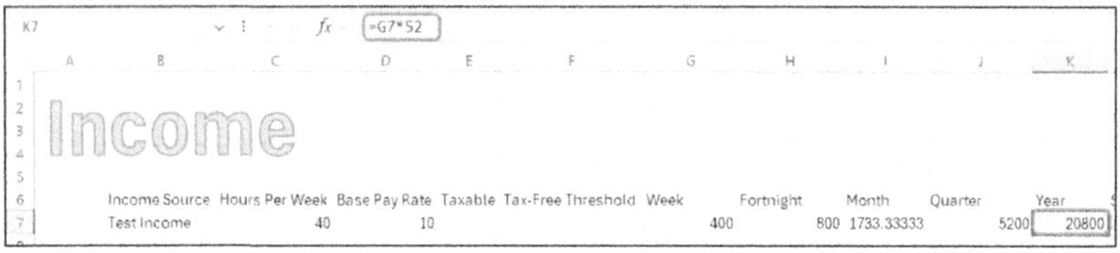

- Test it as before by changing the values in C7 and D7
- When finished testing, put C7 and D7 back to 40 and 10 respectively to keep everything synchronized while training.

Superannuation Amount

The superannuation amount is the annual dollar amount paid into your superannuation fund by your employee where applicable. This amount is calculated by multiplying the annual income by the superannuation rate. Do the following.

- Set the Superannuation Rate to 10% by typing **0.1** in cell **L7** if not already there.
  The actual superannuation rate is likely to be around 11% but 10% is easier to test with.
- **Dbl-Click** in cell M7 and Type **=K7*L7**

- and press Enter, your formula and superannuation amount should be

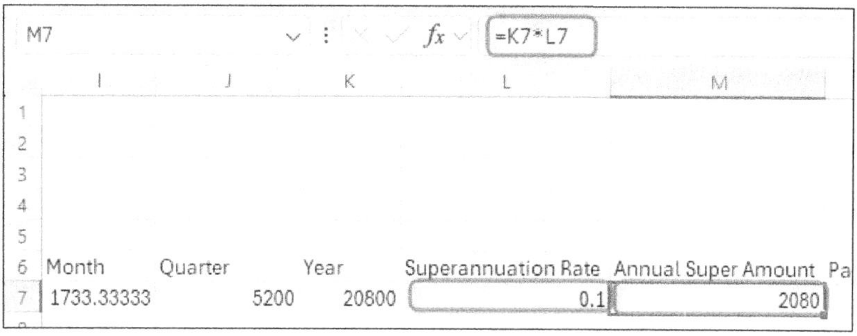

- Test as before by changing the superannuation rate in L7, also try zero (0).

When finished testing, put L7 back to 0.1 to keep everything synchronized while training.

Package

The **package** is the total **annual base pay** plus the **superannuation amount**. This is a simple addition.

- Dbl-Click in cell **N7** and Type **=K7+M7**

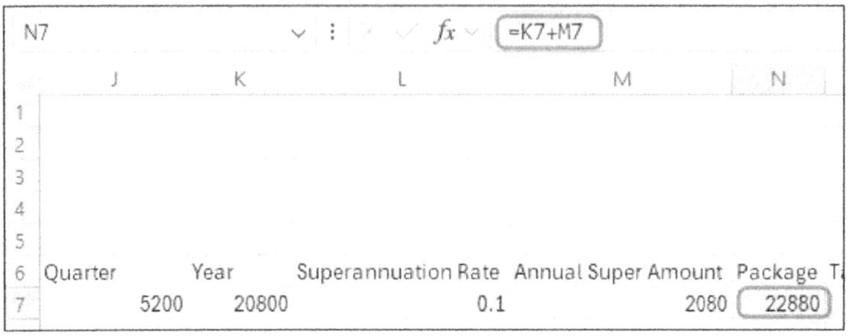

Take Home Week

The all-important question, how much do I get per week? This is the **Week Amount in G7** – the **Tax Per Week in O7**. We are not calculating the actual Tax Per Week yet, this can be done but adds a level of complexity covered later in this training course, you will need to get this figure from your pay slip or use an online tax payable calculator in your part of the world, for our purposes now, you should have an even $100.00 in cell O7.

You may be paid at a different frequency other than weekly, i.e., bi-weekly or month. We use weekly here as it is the lowest pay period and with it, we can calculate the others easily which we will do in upcoming worksheets.

- Dbl-Click in cell **P7** and Type **=G7-O7**

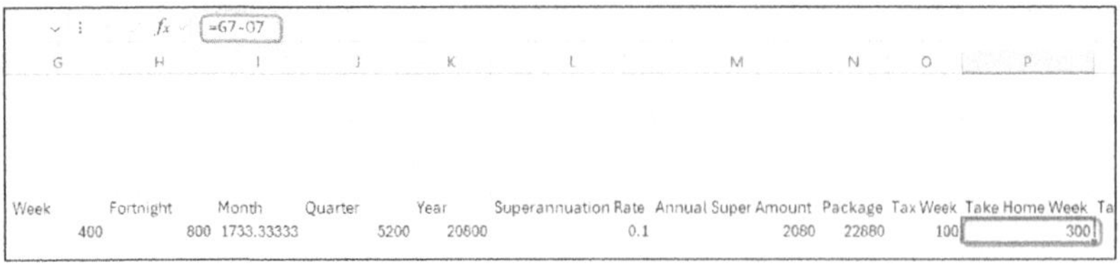

Take Home Annual

It is important to see what the actual take home finances will be available for the upcoming year to assist in planning. This is **Take Home Week P7** amount * **52**.

- Dbl-Click in cell **Q7** and Type = **P7*52**

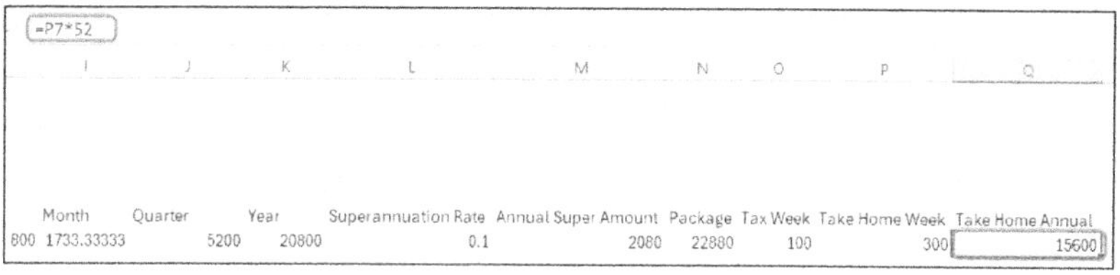

And that completes the first row of formulas, well done.

Formatting Currency cells

Now is a good time to format the currency cells, we waited until now because without data, you would not see anything.

- Select the range of cells from **D7** to **D21**
  - Click **D7**
  - Hold Shift and click **D21**
- Click the $ symbol in the **Number** options in the **Home** tab, 1 was added to cells D8:D21 so you can see the formatting.

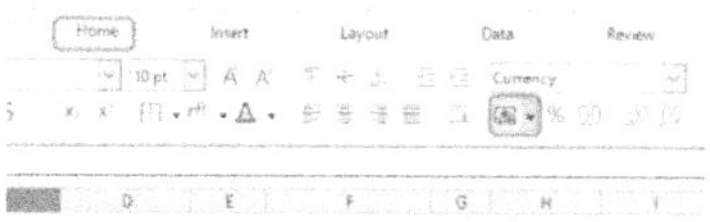

LibreOffice Calc – Select your currency

> **Note for LibreOffice Users:**
> Excel includes a currency format called Accounting, which neatly places the $ symbol on the left and the value on the right — making financial columns easier to read. LibreOffice Calc does not include this format by default, but you can recreate it using a custom number format.
>
> For step-by-step instructions, see:
> Appendix B: Creating an Accounting-Style Currency Format in LibreOffice Calc (with Locale Codes)

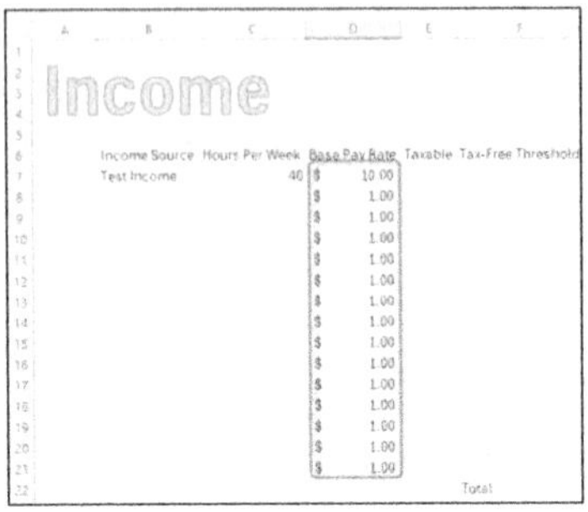

- Now do the same for the following ranges, we are including the Total row for these.
    - **G7** to **K22**
    - **M7** to **Q22**
- Adjust the column widths for the cells showing ###'s, this is Excels way of showing the number is too big to display. We added 1's in the Totals row so we can see the formatting.

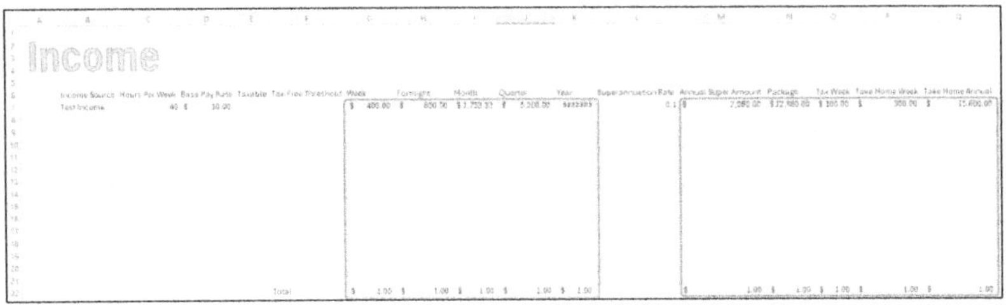

Smart Copy Cell Contents

Excel offers many features to make development and data entry easier; one feature is by smartly copying cell contents and adjusting them as it goes. We will take a little time to practice this in the Test Worksheet before coming back to our Income worksheet.

Some practice first

- Earlier you created a worksheet and named it **Test Worksheet**, click on this tab to activate it.

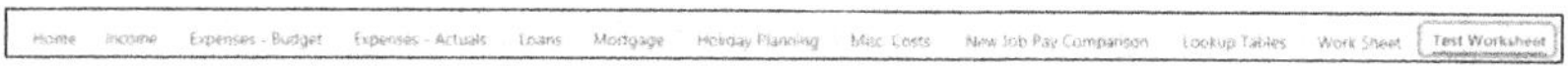

If you have not already created this sheet, do it now, it is just a blank worksheet.

- Click in cell **A1** and type in 1.1
- Click in the cell again, you will notice it has a border and a small square in the bottom right corner, hover the mouse over the square and it will turn into a cross with no arrow heads.
- While the cross is visible, click and hold your left mouse button, this will **grab** the selection.
- Drag the mouse down a few rows and let go
- The content of **A1** will be copied in all rows. LibreOfficeCalc will increase the numbers, as in the next exercise.

	A
1	1.1
2	1.1
3	1.1
4	1.1
5	1.1

Now for something smarter

- In cell **B1**, type a 1.
- In cell **B2**, type a 2
- Using the mouse, select both B1 and B2 cells; you will see the small square at the bottom right of the selection, it is always on the last row.
- Hover over it and as before, **grab** the selection, drag it down a few rows, and let go.

- You should now have consecutive numbers, 1,2,3, etc. in each of the cells.

	A	B
1	1.1	1
2	1.1	2
3	1.1	3
4	1.1	4
5	1.1	5

Useful for numbering rows and other things, right? Let us try some more.

- Cell **C1** and **C2**, enter a **5** and a **10.**
- Select, drag, and let go a few rows.
- Now you have a gap of 5 between each cell, 5, 10,15, etc.

	A	B	C
1	1.1	1	5
2	1.1	2	10
3	1.1	3	15
4	1.1	4	20
5	1.1	5	25

Excel has picked up the pattern and continued with it. Another one with dates

- In cell **D1**, enter **01-Jan-23**
- In cell **D2**, enter **02-Jan-23**
- Select both cells, grab, and drag down several rows.
- Let go the mouse button and the cells are filled with consecutive dates.

	A	B	C	D
1	1.1	1	5	01-Jan-23
2	1.1	2	10	02-Jan-23
3	1.1	3	15	03-Jan-23
4	1.1	4	20	04-Jan-23
5	1.1	5	25	05-Jan-23

You can see how useful this can be, it will also copy the cells formula if it has a formula and adjust the cell references as it copies, as a spreadsheet developer, you will appreciate the time this saves when using similar data or formula in multiple cells.

Play around with it a bit more if you like, when you are ready, go back to the Income worksheet and we will continue, let us get this formula copied.

Copying formula

- go back to the **Income worksheet.**
- Add the following data so we can see the formula has copied
    - **C8**, 10
    - **D8**, 50
    - **O8**, 120
- Starting in cell **G7**, click the cell then grab the selection with the little square in the lower right

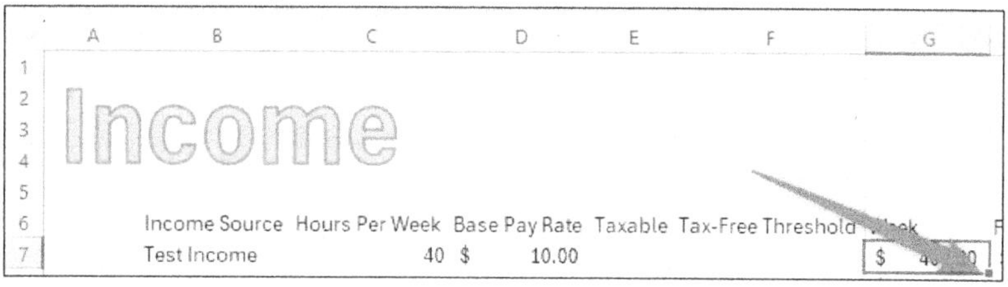

- Drag it down to cell **G21** and let go, we are not copying this formula to the Total row.
- Cell **G8** will have $500.00 in it showing the formula was copied, cells **G9** to **G21** will fill with the $ and a hyphen (from the formatting), this indicates

the formula was copied but there is no value because columns B and C are empty at this time.

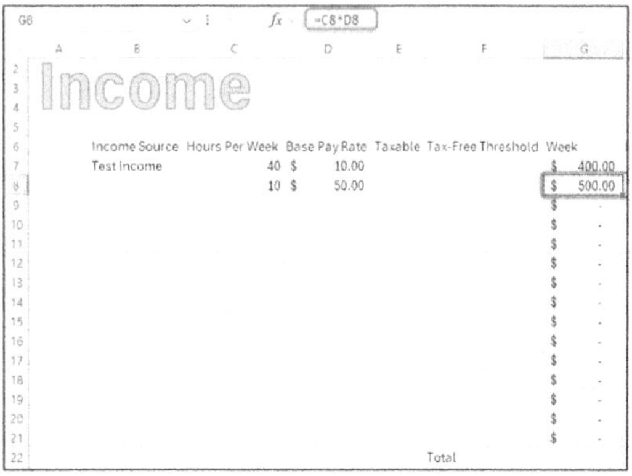

- Check each of the cells by clicking on it, the formula bar will show you the formula in the cell, as you move down each cell you will notice the Row reference has changed for each row.

You have now copied the formula for column G, we still need to do the rest, here is another trick to do more columns.

- Click in cell **H7**.
- Hold shift and click in cell **K7**, the 4 cells will be selected, and the little square is again in the bottom right corner of the selection
- As before, grab the little square and drag the selection down to **J21** and let go

- All cells will now contain a copy of the formula with the correct rows assigned

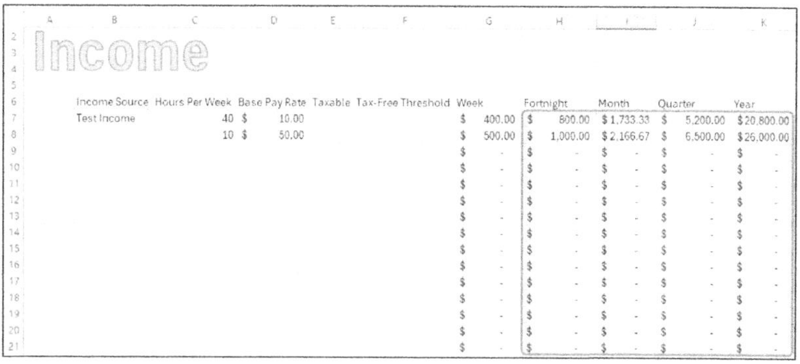

	A	B	C	D	E	F	G	H	I	J	K
2–4	Income										
6		Income Source	Hours Per Week	Base Pay Rate	Taxable	Tax-Free Threshold	Week	Fortnight	Month	Quarter	Year
7		Test Income	40	$ 10.00			$ 400.00	$ 800.00	$ 1,733.33	$ 5,200.00	$ 20,800.00
8			10	$ 50.00			$ 500.00	$ 1,000.00	$ 2,166.67	$ 6,500.00	$ 26,000.00
9							$ -	$ -	$ -	$ -	$ -
10							$ -	$ -	$ -	$ -	$ -
11							$ -	$ -	$ -	$ -	$ -
12							$ -	$ -	$ -	$ -	$ -
13							$ -	$ -	$ -	$ -	$ -
14							$ -	$ -	$ -	$ -	$ -
15							$ -	$ -	$ -	$ -	$ -
16							$ -	$ -	$ -	$ -	$ -
17							$ -	$ -	$ -	$ -	$ -
18							$ -	$ -	$ -	$ -	$ -
19							$ -	$ -	$ -	$ -	$ -
20							$ -	$ -	$ -	$ -	$ -
21							$ -	$ -	$ -	$ -	$ -

- adjust column widths if required.

Exercise

Using the method above, copy the formula for cells **M7** to **N7** down to **P21** to **Q21**

The worksheet should now look like this

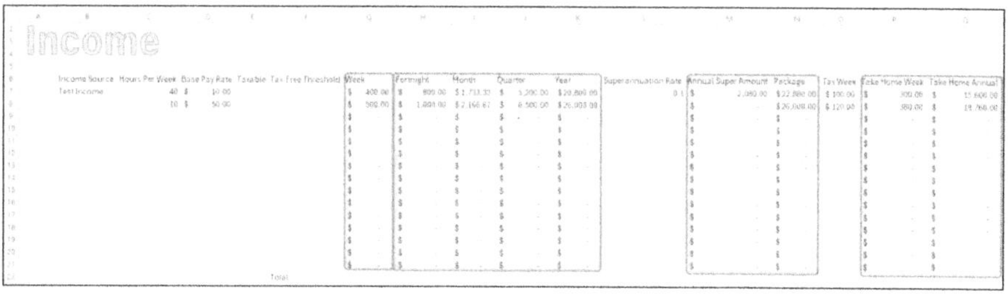

and all cells have their formula in them. Using the copy function like this saved a lot of formula entry.

> **Tip**: This might be a suitable time to save the workbook if you have not turned AutoSave on, be sure to save regularly.

The Totals Row

Now we come to the Totals row, this will sum all the columns except *Superannuation Rate* and provide a good view of your total income, especially if you have multiple income streams.

There are three ways to get the sum in the totals row for the columns, we will first do the Week in column G manually.

Manually, method 1

- Click on cell **G22.**
- Type the following formula directly into the cell =**SUM(G7:G21)** and press Enter

The cell will now display the sum of cells **G7:G21**

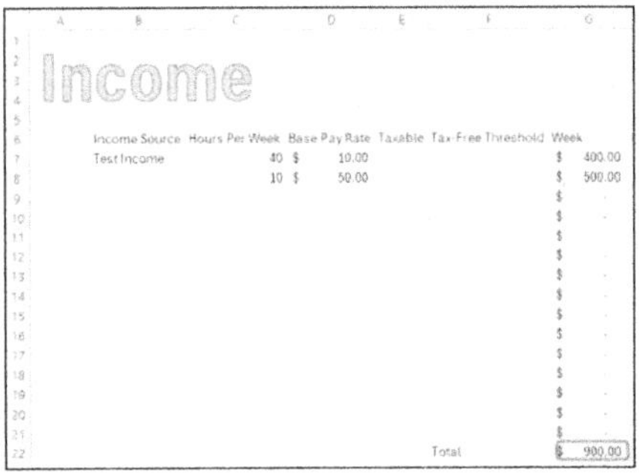

Excel may automatically copy the formula from row 21 in columns H to Q to total cells. This is a default behavior in Excel known as "AutoFill" and is designed to help save time and increase productivity when entering formulas. However, we do not want these for the total row, they are not suitable to our needs, we want the values to be summed from the column, not calculated from G22.

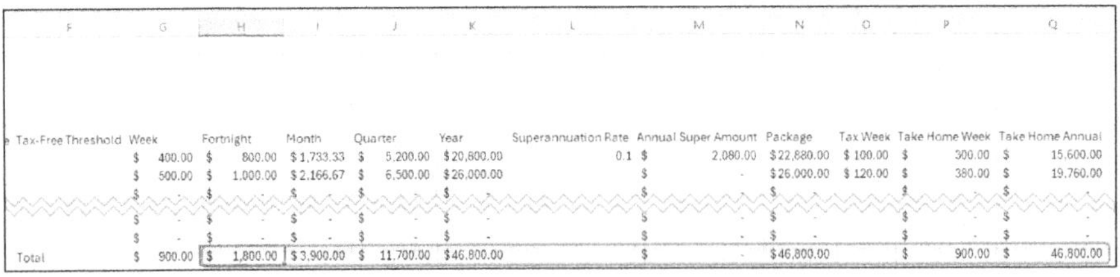

Go ahead and select cells **H22:Q22** and delete the formula by pressing the **Delete** key.

Copy Cell Formula, method 2

We will make a simple copy of the formula in cell G22.

- Click on cell G22.
- Grab the selection with the little square.
- Drag it across the row to cell K22 and let go

The cells will now show the sums for their columns from rows 7 to 21

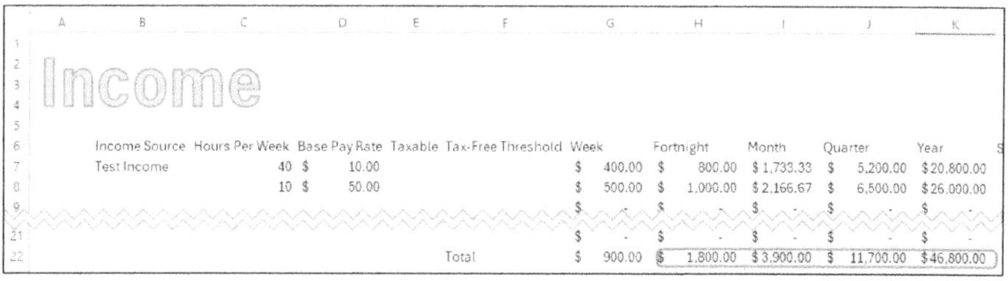

> **Note**: Using this method will also copy the formatting of the source cell, in this case D22. If you have different formats, colors, etc. in the target cells, you may want to either manually type the formula in or use the AutoSum method.

AutoSum, method 3

Autosum provides an uncomplicated way to sum columns or rows that are consecutive, as ours are without changing cell formatting. You can perform the action in a single row or column or multiples as we did for the calculation formula in the previous section.

Excel

- Click the **Home** menu in the ribbon if not already selected, this is where the AutoSum option can be found

Excel

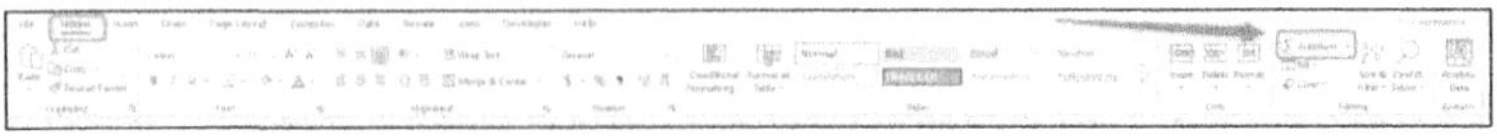

Libre

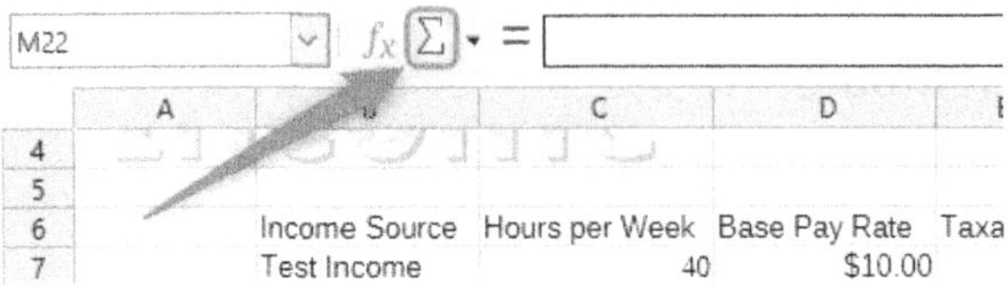

- Click Cell **M7**
- Holding the shift key,
    - **Excel**, click cell **Q22** (yes, in the totals row) this will select the entire block of cells
    - **Libre**, click cell **Q21**
- Click the **AutoSum** option in the ribbon, this puts the formula to sum each column in Totals row.
- The total cells will now display the totals

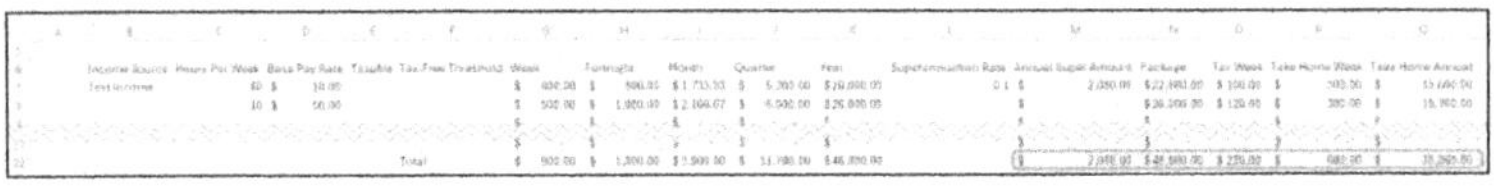

All Totals columns should now display values, except **L**, totaling the Superannuation Rate is pointless.

The worksheet should now look like

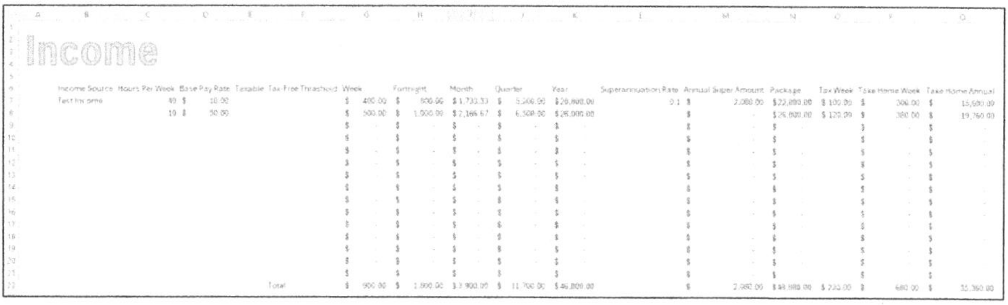

Income

Income Source	Hours Per Week	Base Pay Rate	Taxable	Tax-Free Threshold	Week	Fortnight	Month	Quarter	Year	Superannuation Rate	Annual Super Amount	Package	Tax Week	Take Home Week	Take Home Annual
Test Income	40	$ 10.00			$ 400.00	$ 800.00	$ 1,733.33	$ 5,200.00	$ 20,800.00	0.1	$ 2,080.00	$ 22,880.00	$ 100.00	$ 300.00	$ 15,600.00
	10	$ 50.00			$ 500.00	$ 1,000.00	$ 2,166.67	$ 6,500.00	$ 26,000.00		$ -	$ 26,000.00	$ 120.00	$ 380.00	$ 19,760.00
					$ -	$ -	$ -	$ -	$ -		$ -	$ -		$ -	$ -
					$ -	$ -	$ -	$ -	$ -		$ -	$ -		$ -	$ -
					$ -	$ -	$ -	$ -	$ -		$ -	$ -		$ -	$ -
					$ -	$ -	$ -	$ -	$ -		$ -	$ -		$ -	$ -
					$ -	$ -	$ -	$ -	$ -		$ -	$ -		$ -	$ -
					$ -	$ -	$ -	$ -	$ -		$ -	$ -		$ -	$ -
					$ -	$ -	$ -	$ -	$ -		$ -	$ -		$ -	$ -
					$ -	$ -	$ -	$ -	$ -		$ -	$ -		$ -	$ -
					$ -	$ -	$ -	$ -	$ -		$ -	$ -		$ -	$ -
					$ -	$ -	$ -	$ -	$ -		$ -	$ -		$ -	$ -
					$ -	$ -	$ -	$ -	$ -		$ -	$ -		$ -	$ -
					$ -	$ -	$ -	$ -	$ -		$ -	$ -		$ -	$ -
					$ -	$ -	$ -	$ -	$ -		$ -	$ -		$ -	$ -
				Total	$ 900.00	$ 1,800.00	$ 3,900.00	$ 11,700.00	$ 46,800.00		$ 2,080.00	$ 48,880.00	$ 220.00	$ 680.00	$ 35,360.00

Conclusion

By completing the Income worksheet, you've established the foundation for tracking your sources of income in the budgeting application. This worksheet plays a crucial role in determining if your expenses align with your income and in calculating other financial goals. You've learned key skills, such as planning your layout, creating column headings, and using formulas to calculate your weekly, bi-weekly, monthly, quarterly, and annual income, as well as superannuation and tax. As we continue, these values will be integrated into future worksheets, and you'll build on the skills you've mastered here to further develop your budgeting application.

Quiz

1. **What is the purpose of the "Take Home Week" column in the Income worksheet?**
   a) To calculate the weekly taxable income.
   b) To determine the weekly net pay after tax.
   c) To calculate annual income.
   d) To track the hours worked per week.

2. **Which formula calculates the annual income based on weekly income in the Income worksheet?**
   a) =G7/52
   b) =G7*52
   c) =G7+52
   d) =G7-52

3. **True or False: The totals row in the Income worksheet should sum all the columns, including the Superannuation Rate column.**
   a) True
   b) False

4. **What does the formula =K7+M7 calculate in the Income worksheet?**
   a) Weekly income plus annual superannuation amount.
   b) Annual base pay plus the superannuation amount (total package).
   c) Monthly income plus tax payable.
   d) Fortnightly income plus the superannuation rate.

Quiz Answers

1. **What is the purpose of the "Take Home Week" column in the Income worksheet?**
   Answer: b) To determine the weekly net pay after tax.

2. **Which formula calculates the annual income based on weekly income in the Income worksheet?**
   Answer: b) =G7*52

3. **True or False: The totals row in the Income worksheet should sum all the columns, including the Superannuation Rate column.**
   Answer: b) False – There is no reason to sum the percentages

4. **What does the formula =K7+M7 calculate in the Income worksheet?**
   Answer: b) Annual base pay plus the superannuation amount (total package).

Self-Assessment

By the end of this chapter, you should be able to:

- Create and organize the Income worksheet, including adding column headings.
- Enter and use formulas to calculate weekly, monthly, quarterly, and annual income.
- Understand how superannuation and tax impact the overall budget.
- Use techniques like copying formulas and AutoSum for efficiency.

Self-Check Questions:

1. Have you created the Income worksheet and tested the layout by entering formulas for income calculations?
   - (Yes/No)

2. Can you correctly calculate weekly and annual income using the formulas provided in the chapter?

  - (Yes/No)

3. Have you practiced copying formulas and using AutoSum for efficient totals calculation in Excel?
    - (Yes/No)

Next we will start formatting the worksheet.

Formatting the worksheet

Formatting the worksheet, i.e., setting colors, column widths, text bolding, is an often overlooked but exceptionally important part of developing your worksheet applications. Why is it so important? Because it is likely that you will be working in the workbook for hours on end and for that reason, it needs to look good, be pleasant to work in and be functional. If the layout is difficult, it will be confusing to use, if the colors are too harsh or too contrasty, you may get eye strain, headaches or tiredness. You owe it to yourself to make the experience as pleasant as possible. Here are some pointers.

- If you are going to be the only person using the workbook, then you can really format it how you like, but if others are going to be using it, their experience with the workbook, including layout and formatting will determine if they continue to use it, make it pleasant to use for all, including yourself.
- Use pastel colors, these are more pleasant to look at over long periods of time. Brighter colors will put more strain on the eyes, make the user tired or even cause headaches.
- Do not have too many formats such as
    - Limit fonts to two or three sizes only with the majority of text the same size. Avoid too much small font text, below 10 points.
    - Bold only items that require highlighting.
    - Limit the color scheme to as few colors as possible, remember, pastels.

- Use a single color to use throughout the workbook identify data entry cells, this makes it easier for the user to find these. We will be using pastel yellow.

> **Note**: this is also important because later, we will be learning how to lock the worksheets down to prevent accidental overwrite of formula, having a single data entry color will make it easier to identify cells we want to remain unlocked.

- Do not have too many thick borders.

Let us start with formatting the worksheet.

Setting word wrap

By default, word wrap is turned off for all cells in the worksheets. If you have cells that are expected to display more text, such as larger headings or descriptions, or even notes, you may wish to have the text wrapped to multiple lines within the cell. You can then adjust the row height and column width to display it as you wish.

We have four headings at this stage that are too wide for the column content and are good candidates to wrap words, they are **C6, F6, L6** and **M6**. You could set each one individually, but we are going to set them all at the same time, here is how to do it.

- Click on cell **C6** and then while **holding down the Ctrl key** on the keyboard, **click** on **F6, L6** and **M6** in turn. This will select the four cells and whatever operation we perform next will be applied to all four.
  You can see they are all selected because they have changed color, the

last one you selected will have a double border, and the row and column coordinates will be highlighted

> **Note**: Because the cells we wanted to select are not all adjacent to each other, we used **Ctrl** to assist in selecting, Ctrl allows gaps between selections. Had they all been adjacent, say we wanted to select all cells between C6 and L6, then we would have used the **Shift** key to assist, we could have selected C6 then holding Shift down while clicking on L6 would have selected every cell between those two cells.

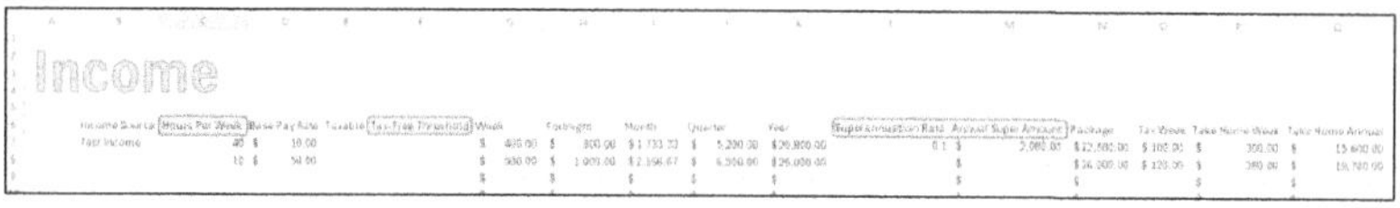

- Right-Click in any of the selected cells and from the **context menu**, *the menu that pops up,* select **Format cells**

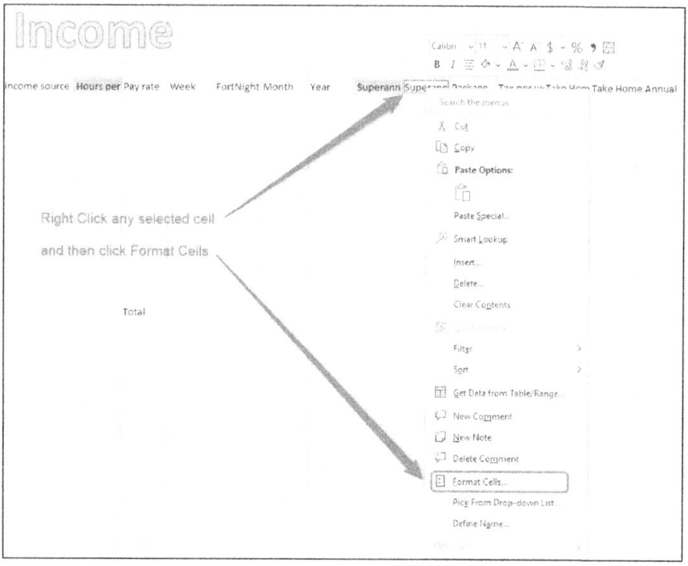

- The Format Cells dialog window will open

- Select the **Alignment Tab** and check the **Wrap text** check box and click **OK** to close the **Format cells** dialog window.

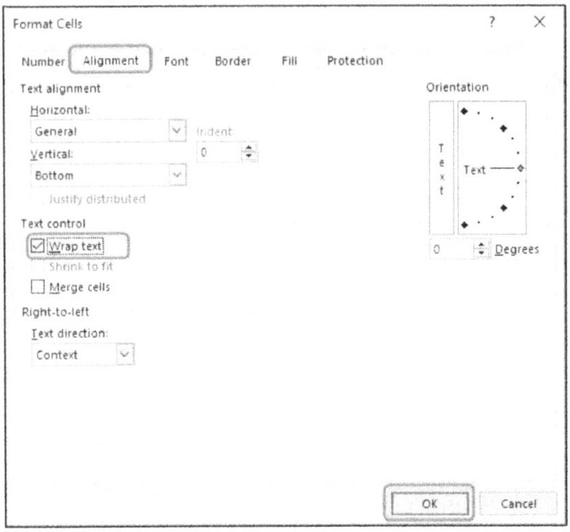

You have now set the four cells to wrap the text to display multiple rows within the cell. This could have been any number of cells and rows.

You may now need to adjust the row height and column widths to display the text correctly if Excel did not do it for you. Let us do this anyway.

Setting row height

To set the row height to display the heading over two lines within the cell do the following.

- Click on the row heading for row **6,** this is our target line, but it can be any single or multiple rows. This puts the row headings into focus to be modified.

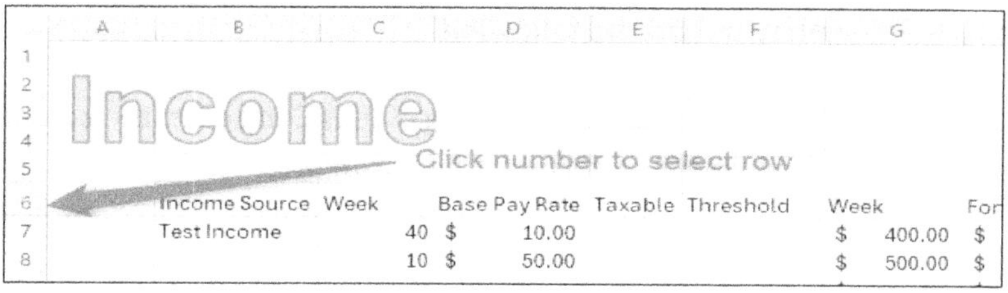

- **Hover** the cursor over the line **below the 6** until you see the cursor change to

- Click the **left** mouse button to **grab** it and then **drag** the mouse **down**, the line height will expand. Let go of the mouse button when the line is tall enough and the line height will stay at the new height.

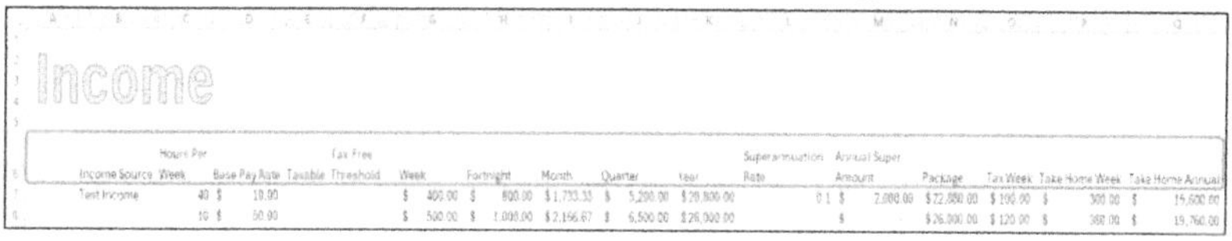

When first adjusting the height, make it a little larger than you really need so you can see the effects when you change the column width. You can make a final adjustment once the column width is set.

Setting column width

After setting word wrap. You will likely need to adjust the width of the columns to properly display the data. When setting a columns width you will consider guiding you

- Cell label
- Cell contents
- Cell Formatting, bold and larger text need more room
- Screen width and number of columns

To set the column width do the following.

- Click the top column heading for column **C** to select the column and to get the headings into focus for adjustment.
- **Hover** the cursor over the line **to the right of column C** until you see the cursor change to 
- Click the **left** mouse button to **grab** it and then **drag** the mouse **left or right**, the column width will expand or shrink as required

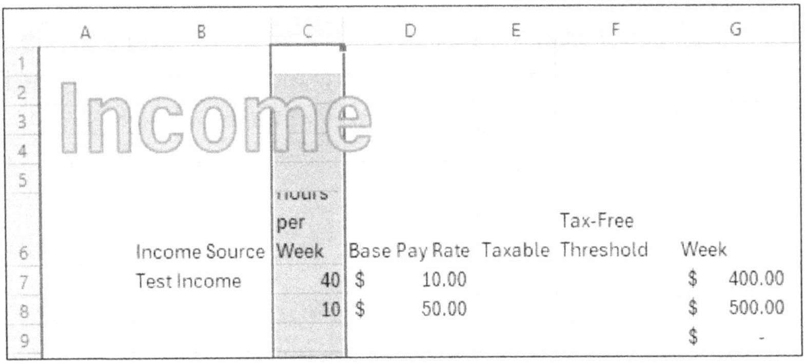

- Let go of the mouse button and the row width will stay at the new width.
- Repeat for columns **F, L** and **M.**
- Your worksheet should now look like

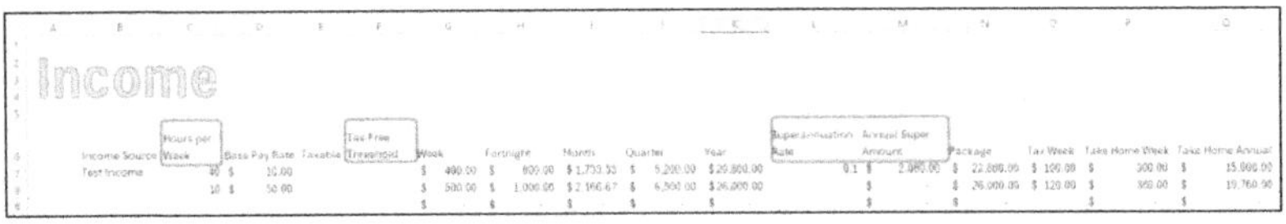

Your final widths are determined on what you perceive looks best for the text you displayed in both headings and data cells. The word Superannuation in column L is wide, and the data is narrow at three characters, you may want to change it to Super and make the column narrower. This depends on personal taste; how much other data is on the sheet and if screen space is a premium for your specific application, monitor size.

Multi word column headings may not wrap at the ideal location, see column C6 heading, this would be better split after **Hours** so **per Week** appears on second row. To fix this

- Double Click on the cell to select it and make the cursor visible, **C6** in this example
  You will see the cursor flashing
- Click where you want it to split, before the word **per**
- Press **Alt + Enter**, this will force it to split where the cursor is, see below image

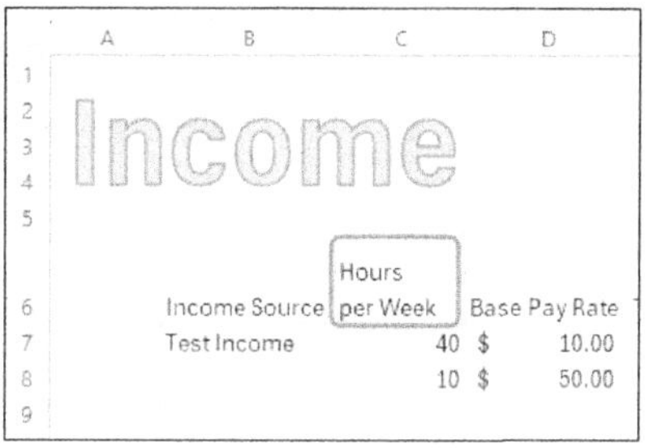

Exercise

Adjust the widths of the remaining columns so all headings are visible, consider how wide the data will be in each column and if the headings are split at the right place. Hint, you might even have other columns that need to be word wrapped. Your final column layout should be something like this.

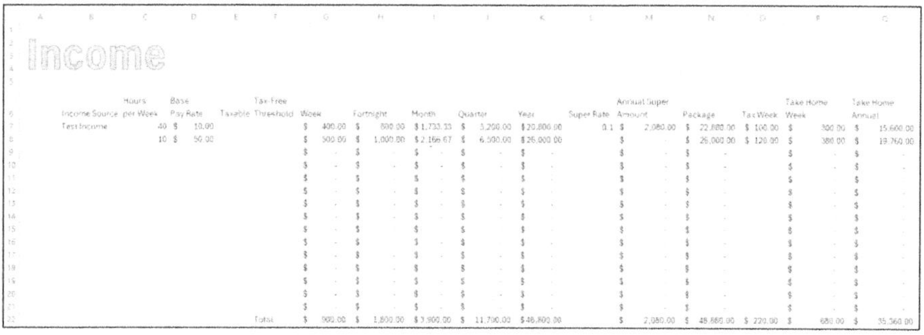

Setting font size

We will be leaving all font sizes to the standard size except for the worksheet heading, which we have already adjusted and the Total cells for **Take Home Week** and **Take Home Annual** cells, we want these to stand out using a larger font.

To adjust the font size of cells P22 and Q22 do the following.

- Select both **P22** and **Q22** by holding the **Ctrl** Key down and click on each cell in turn

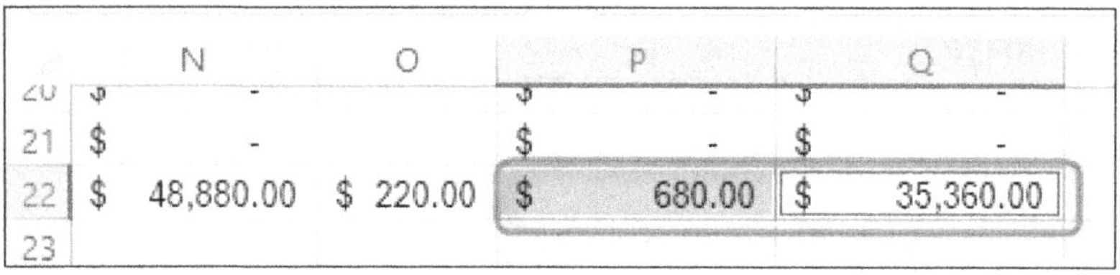

- Change the font size to **18** by right-click the cells and the font adjustment will show above the context menu

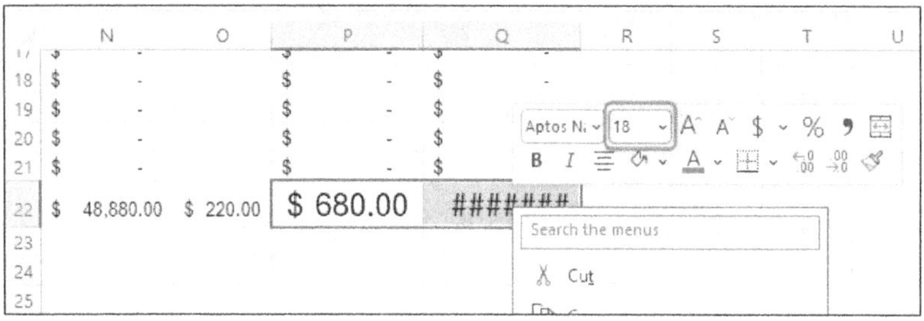

- Adjust the column widths if required, remember, these two numbers could be large and may need some room to grow.

The worksheet cells P22 and Q22 should now look like below.

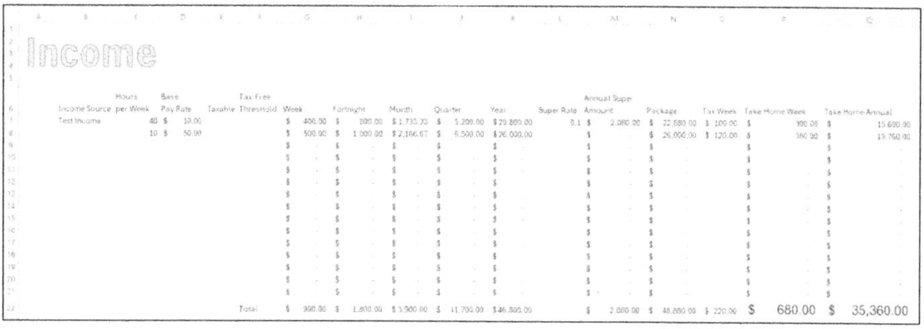

Setting bold text

Use Bold text to make something stand out from the rest of the text, in the worksheet we will make the headings and the totals bold.

To set the text to bold, do the following (we will do it all in one go by selecting two ranges of cells)

- Left click in cell **B6** to select it and holding down the **Shift key**, click on cell **Q6**, the range of cells will be highlighted
- Now hold down the **Ctrl** key, click in cell **G22**, the cell will be selected
- Now hold down the **Shift** key, click in cell **Q22**, the range will be selected, we now have two selected ranges and what we do next will affect all selected cells.
- Click the **Bold** icon in the ribbons **Font** menu

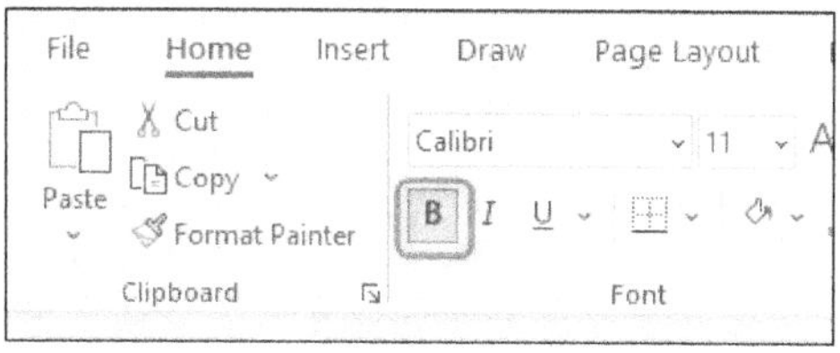

- all highlighted cells should now be Bold.
- Examine the headings and data, you may need to adjust column widths as bold text is a little wider than normal text. The sheet should now look like

Income

Income Source	Hours per Week	Base Pay Rate	Taxable	Tax-Free Threshold	Week	Fortnight	Month	Quarter	Year	Super Rate	Annual Super Amount	Package	Tax Week	Take Home Week	Take Home Annual
Test Income	40	$ 10.00			$ 400.00	$ 800.00	$ 1,733.33	$ 5,200.00	$ 20,800.00	0.1	$ 2,080.00	$ 22,880.00	$ 100.00	$ 300.00	$ 15,600.00
	10	$ 50.00			$ 500.00	$ 1,000.00	$ 2,166.67	$ 6,500.00	$ 26,000.00		$	$ 26,000.00	$ 120.00	$ 380.00	$ 19,760.00
					$ -	$ -	$ -	$ -	$ -		$ -	$ -		$ -	$ -
					$ -	$ -	$ -	$ -	$ -		$ -	$ -		$ -	$ -
					$ -	$ -	$ -	$ -	$ -		$ -	$ -		$ -	$ -
					$ -	$ -	$ -	$ -	$ -		$ -	$ -		$ -	$ -
					$ -	$ -	$ -	$ -	$ -		$ -	$ -		$ -	$ -
					$ -	$ -	$ -	$ -	$ -		$ -	$ -		$ -	$ -
					$ -	$ -	$ -	$ -	$ -		$ -	$ -		$ -	$ -
					$ -	$ -	$ -	$ -	$ -		$ -	$ -		$ -	$ -
					$ -	$ -	$ -	$ -	$ -		$ -	$ -		$ -	$ -
					$ -	$ -	$ -	$ -	$ -		$ -	$ -		$ -	$ -
					$ -	$ -	$ -	$ -	$ -		$ -	$ -		$ -	$ -
					$ -	$ -	$ -	$ -	$ -		$ -	$ -		$ -	$ -
					$ -	$ -	$ -	$ -	$ -		$ -	$ -		$ -	$ -
				Total	$ 900.00	$ 1,800.00	$ 3,900.00	$ 11,700.00	$ 46,800.00		$ 2,080.00	$ 48,880.00	$ 220.00	$ 680.00	$ 35,360.00

Setting cell borders

Grid Lines

The cell lines you see onscreen at the moment are the Excel Gridlines; these are not borders. They are light shades of grey and are there to assist you. You can hide these when you have finished developing the spreadsheet to give a cleaner look to your worksheet by toggling the **Gridlines** option in the **View** menu.

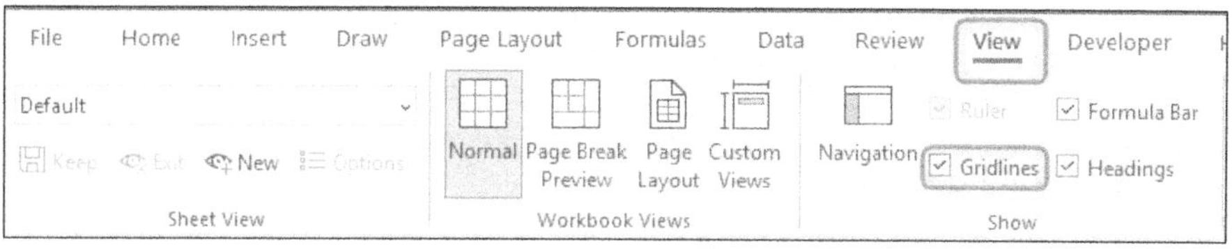

Try it and clear the checkbox, it looks so clean, doesn't it? Be sure to check it again before continuing, it just helps to have them on when designing worksheets, you can clear it later.

Now let us continue setting the borders.

To separate the individual cells so their contents remain easy to read, we will now set the borders for all the cells in our grid. Again, we will do this in one operation. These are darker than the grid lines and will not go away when you hide the gridlines.

Do the following to set the cell borders.

- Click on cell **B6.**
- Holding down the **Shift** key, click cell **Q22**, the entire grid will be selected
- From the Home, Font menu in the Ribbon, click the small down arrow in the Border selector

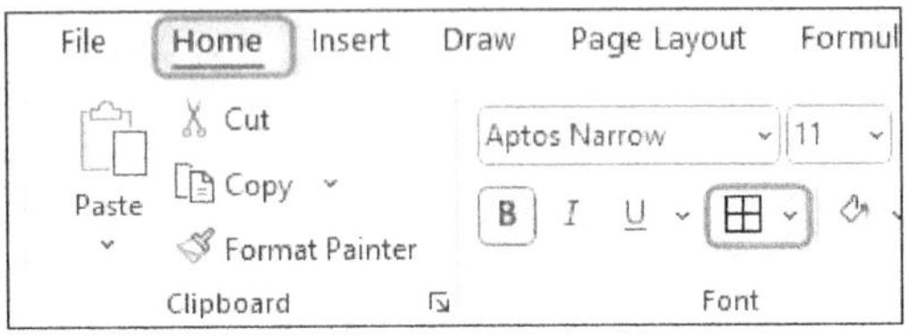

- Select **All Borders**

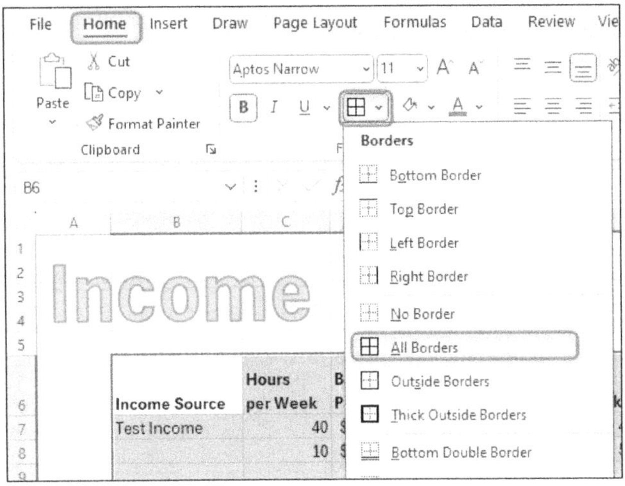

Every cell in the range will now have a border, here is what the worksheet will look like, with gridlines off. As you can see, there are a lot of options for the borders, you can play around with them to get it exactly right.

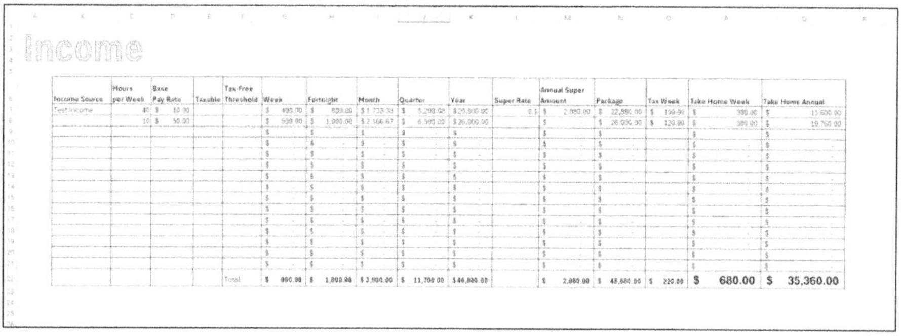

Income

Income Source	Hours per Week	Base Pay Rate	Taxable	Tax-Free Threshold	Week	Fortnight	Month	Quarter	Year	Super Rate	Annual Super Amount	Package	Tax Week	Take Home Week	Take Home Annual
Test Income	40	$ 10.00			$ 400.00	$ 800.00	$ 1,733.33	$ 5,200.00	$ 20,800.00	0.1	$ 2,080.00	$ 22,880.00	$ 100.00	$ 300.00	$ 15,600.00
	10	$ 50.00			$ 500.00	$ 1,000.00	$ 2,166.67	$ 6,500.00	$ 26,000.00		$ -	$ 26,000.00	$ 120.00	$ 380.00	$ 19,760.00
					$ -	$ -	$ -	$ -	$ -		$ -	$ -		$ -	$ -
					$ -	$ -	$ -	$ -	$ -		$ -	$ -		$ -	$ -
					$ -	$ -	$ -	$ -	$ -		$ -	$ -		$ -	$ -
					$ -	$ -	$ -	$ -	$ -		$ -	$ -		$ -	$ -
					$ -	$ -	$ -	$ -	$ -		$ -	$ -		$ -	$ -
					$ -	$ -	$ -	$ -	$ -		$ -	$ -		$ -	$ -
					$ -	$ -	$ -	$ -	$ -		$ -	$ -		$ -	$ -
					$ -	$ -	$ -	$ -	$ -		$ -	$ -		$ -	$ -
					$ -	$ -	$ -	$ -	$ -		$ -	$ -		$ -	$ -
					$ -	$ -	$ -	$ -	$ -		$ -	$ -		$ -	$ -
					$ -	$ -	$ -	$ -	$ -		$ -	$ -		$ -	$ -
					$ -	$ -	$ -	$ -	$ -		$ -	$ -		$ -	$ -
					$ -	$ -	$ -	$ -	$ -		$ -	$ -		$ -	$ -
				Total	$ 900.00	$ 1,800.00	$ 3,900.00	$ 11,700.00	$ 46,800.00		$ 2,080.00	$ 48,880.00	$ 220.00	$ 680.00	$ 35,360.00

Setting Fill Colors

Often, the Fill Color of cells are used to separate and highlight grouped information. What you choose for your color scheme is entirely up to you but try to keep in mind the following.

- Keep colors to softer pastel colors for eye comfort.
- Bright colors after a while cause eye strain, headaches and make using the worksheet unpleasant.
- Not too many colors, they should help, not distract.

Other than reserving **pastel yellow** for user input cells throughout this course, you can set your colors as you please. Reserving the yellow for user input is just to make it consistent and avoid confusion throughout the course, you can change it later if you wish. Let us get started.

In the Income worksheet, you will be able to enter data in the cell ranges **B7:F21**, **L7:L21** and **O7:O21**. To make these obvious and easy to find, we will set their color to a pastel yellow, we will do this for ALL user input cells in upcoming worksheets.

To set the three ranges for the user input cell colors, do the following.

- Click on cell **B7**, hold down the **Shift** key and click **F21**, the block will be selected
- Hold down the **Ctrl Key** down, click cell **L7**, L7 will now be selected
- Hold down the **Shift** key and click on **L21**, the L7:L22 range will now be selected as well
- Hold down the **Ctrl Key** down, click cell **O7**
- Hold down the **Shift** key and click on **O21**, the O7:O22 range will now be selected as well

All three blocks are now selected; the next operation will be applied to all selected cells.

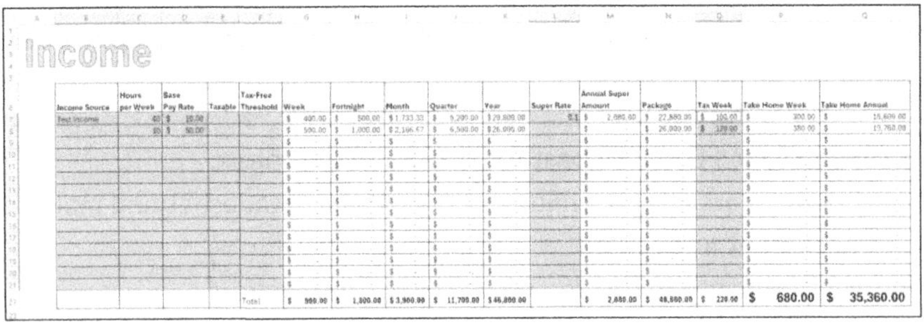

- Excel
    - From Home, Font Menu in the Ribbon, click the down arrow on the **Fill Color** tool

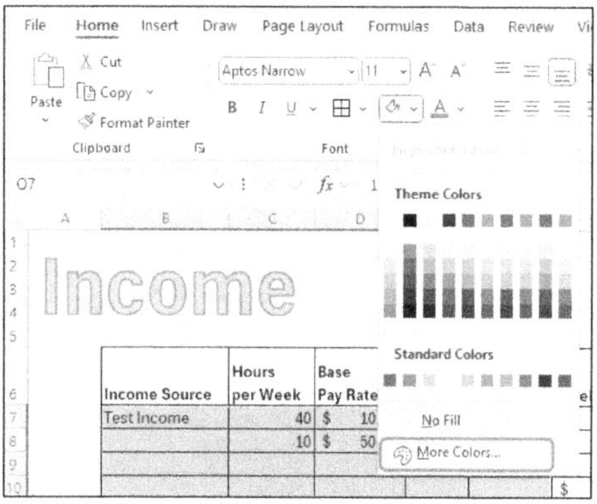

- This will open the color palate, select the Yellow closest to the center and click OK

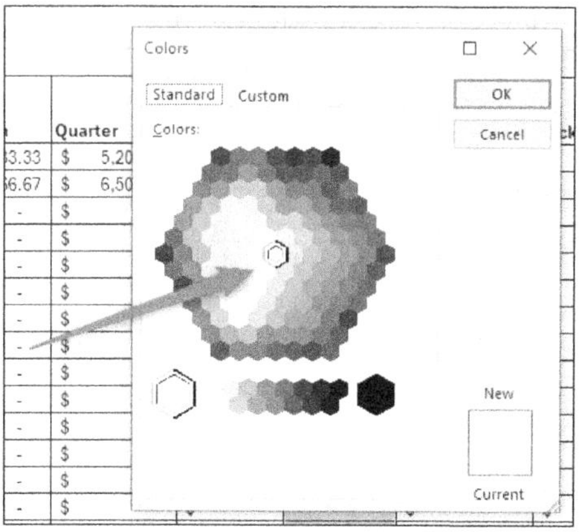

- This will set the cell colors and also put the color in the Recent Colors for easier access later

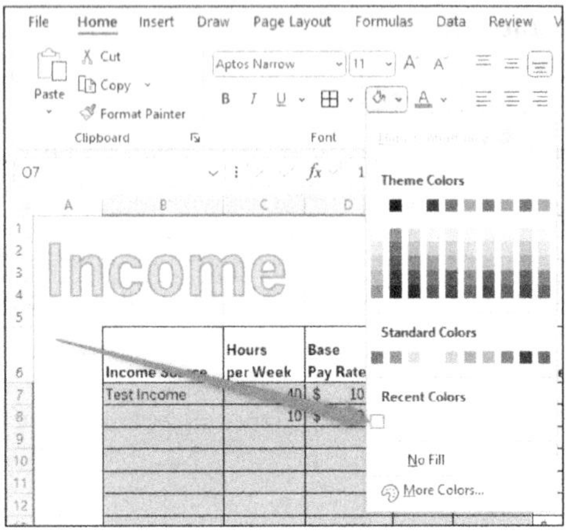

- LibreOffice Calc
  - From Home, Font Menu in the Ribbon, click the down arrow on the **Fill Color** tool

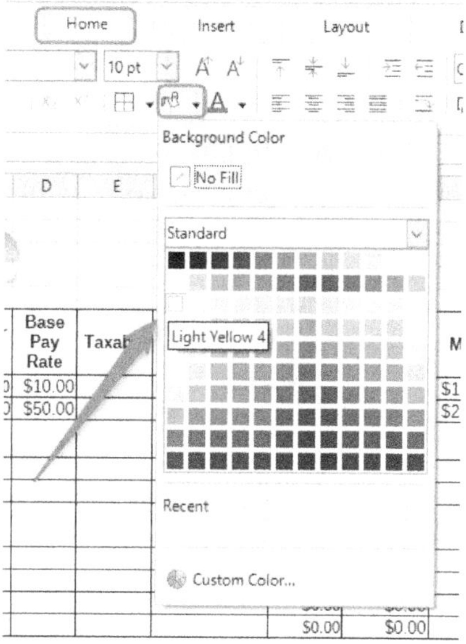

- Select the yellow, all selected cells will now be yellow as shown below. Set the remaining cells in the grid to colors of your choice, but not the yellow, here is mine

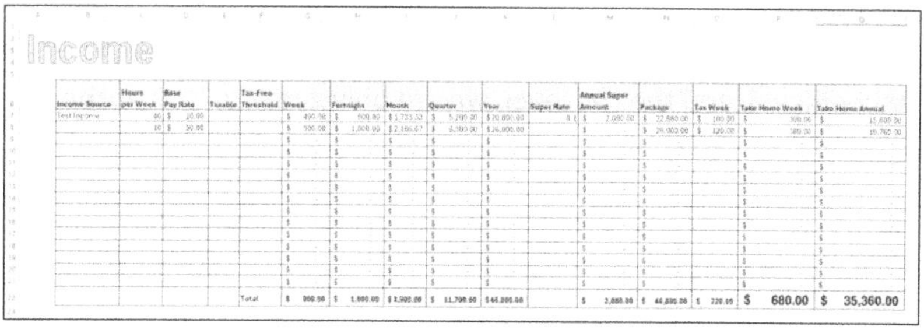

Setting forecolors

Use different forecolors to highlight data, in the Income worksheet we are only going to highlight two cells with a different font color, they are cells **P22** and **Q22**, our income totals, essential information that we want to see immediately.

You can set them to whatever color you like, keep in mind red is often used to highlight negative numbers, so a nice green or something. Do the following.

- Select both cells **O21** and **P21**, you have had a lot of selection practice now.
- From the **Font Menu** in the Ribbon, click the down arrow on the **Font Color** tool and select the color you want to assign, these do not need to be pastel, make them bright so they stand out. As you move around the colors, the cells will change so you can preview the colors.

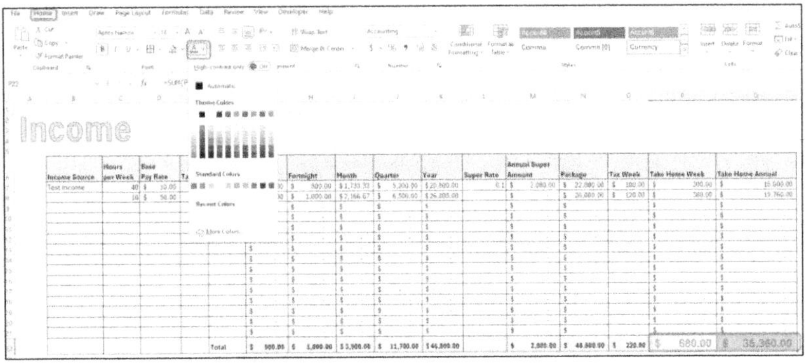

Now it is starting to look good, time for setting protection.

Setting protection

Setting protection in a workbook can be done at the workbook level, the worksheet level, and the cell level, we are only going to look at the cell level for now, we will get to the worksheet and workbook later.

Protection is achieved by assigning passwords at the worksheet and workbook level, the purpose is to

- protect your work from prying eyes, this is sensitive information
- protect the formula, these may be propriety
- protect the formulas from being overwritten which could render the workbook useless
- define where users can enter or change data

Note: Nothing you do below will take effect until you lock the worksheet

By default, all cells will be locked when you set worksheet or workbook level protection, this is great, but we do not want all cells to be locked, we want some to be editable by the user so they can enter data, all our yellow cells.

All other cells should remain locked to protect the formula and layout from being overwritten. Fortunately, Excel allows us to designate which cells we want to remain unlocked; this is how we do it.

First, we need to ensure everything on the worksheet is set to its default state, locked, in case you have changed it before.

First time through you will not have made changes to security, go through these steps anyway so you know how to reset the worksheets cell protection.

a. Select ALL cells in the worksheet by clicking the top/left of the worksheet, see image below, this will select the entire worksheet

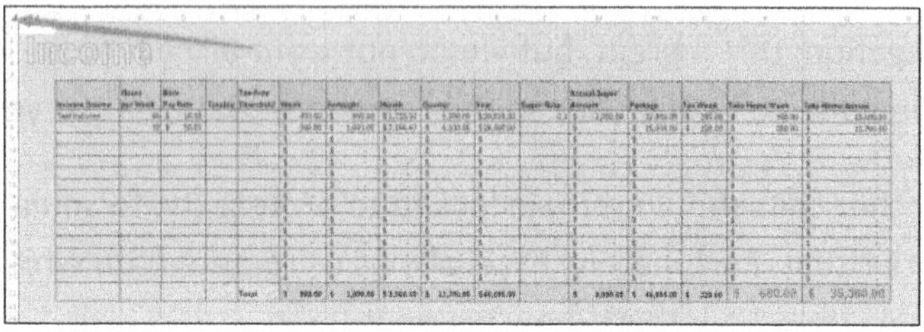

b. Right click on any cell and from the menu, select **Format Cells**, the Format Cells popup will open

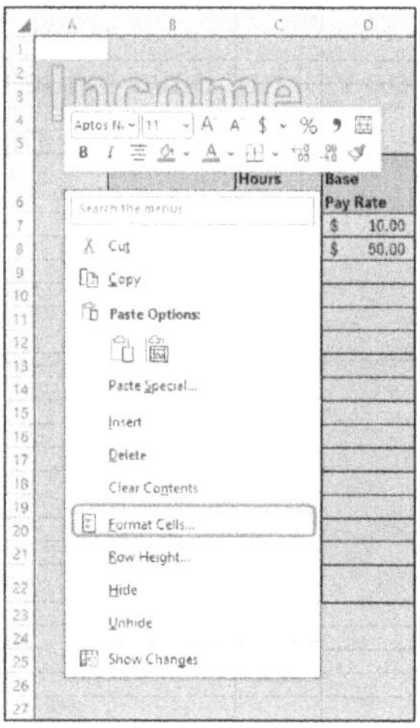

c. Select the **Protection tab,** check **Locked** if not already checked, this will set the entire worksheet to be locked and click **OK** to close the popup.

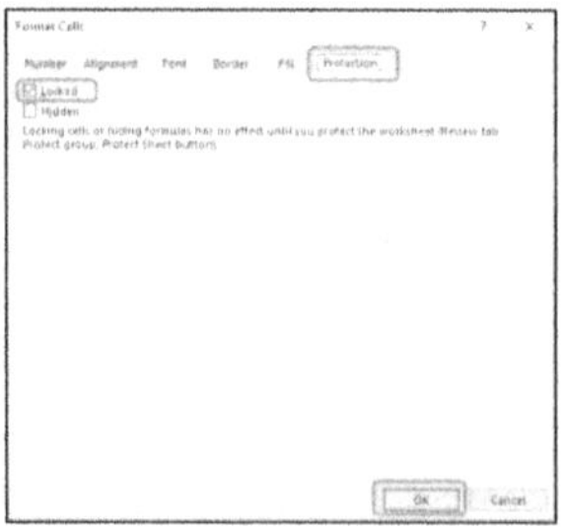

This will ensure all cells in the worksheet are in their default state, locked. Now we can set the yellow input cells to unlocked

2. Select all of the yellow cells as you did when setting the color.
3. Right click on any of the selected cells and from the menu, select **Format Cells**. When the Format Cells popup opens, select the **Protection tab.**
4. Uncheck **Locked**, this will set the yellow cells to be unlocked and editable when the worksheet is locked.

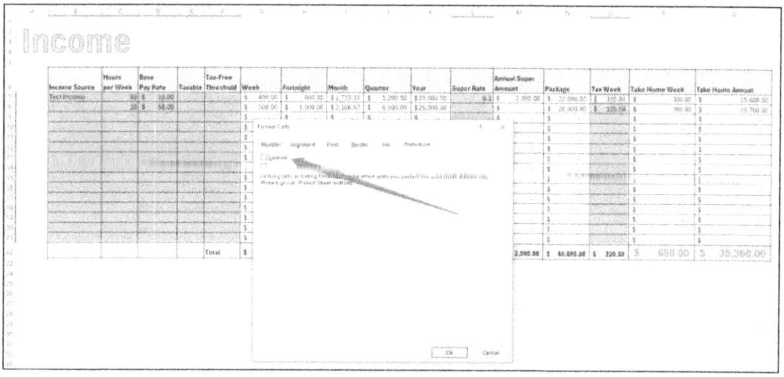

Testing the protection

Now that you have set which cells to lock and to remain unlocked, see if it worked by doing the following.

- Save the worksheet and make a copy of it, be sure to always keep an unlocked copy of the workbook and worksheets somewhere safe, if you forget the password, you will not be able to get access to it.

- Right-Click on the **Income Tab** and select **Protect Sheet**

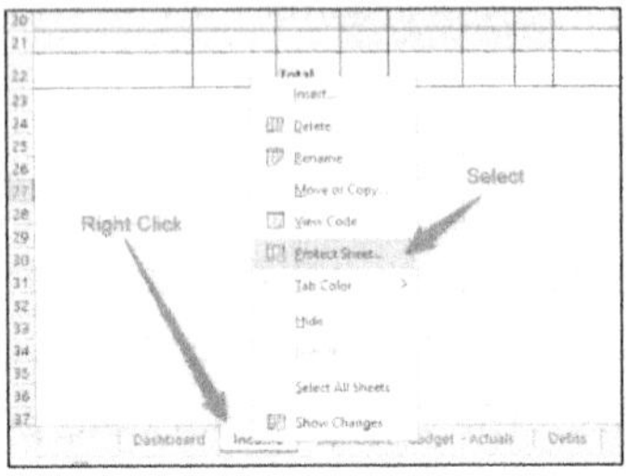

- Enter a password, as we are testing here, use something simple like **abcd** for now

- Click **OK**, you will be prompted to enter the password again, do it and click **OK** to lock the worksheet.

To try it

- Click in any cell other than the yellow ones, try and enter some data. You will get the following message

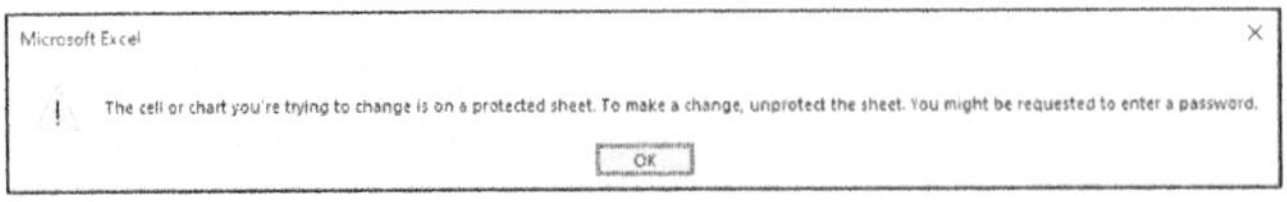

- Click in a yellow cell, try, and enter some data. The data will be accepted by Excel.

- Finish off by unprotecting the worksheet by **Right Click** on **Income** tab, select **Unprotect Sheet** and enter the password **abcd** so we can continue development. The cell lock setting will remain as you set them.

> **Note**: If you choose not to enter a password, the sheet will still be locked. You can unlock it anytime without needing a password. This is a good option if you're not very worried about security and just want to make sure your formulas are not accidentally changed.

Setting Data Validation

Data validation protects your data by restricting the type of data that can be entered into specific cells. This will ensure data integrity by not allowing you to enter invalid characters such as an alpha character into a cell requiring a number. It can be used to restrict cells to one of several datatypes, including Date, Time, Decimal, Whole Number, Maximum Text Length and for numbers, within a specified range.

If a user enters an invalid character or out of range into a cell that any formulae references, the formula will not work correctly. The worksheet will be locked later so you only need to set data validation on the User Input cells, the yellow ones.

To set data validation in Microsoft Exceland LibreOffice Calc, follow these steps:

- Select the cells for which you want to set the validation, select **B7:B21**
- Go to the Data tab and click on Data Validation.

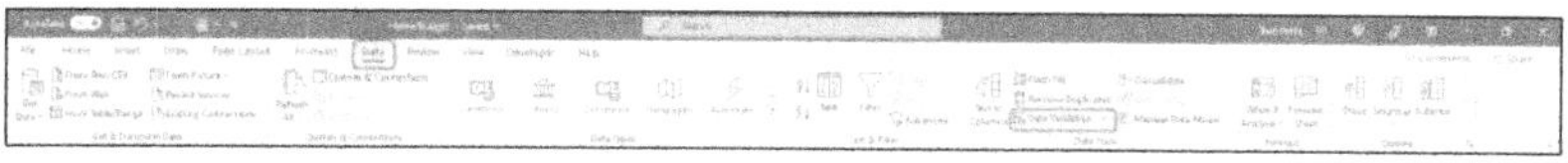

- **Excel** - In the Data Validation dialog box, choose the type of validation you want to set (e.g., whole number, decimal, list, etc.). The data types of the columns were mentioned when the headings were set. Cells B7:B21 are to contain text values so select **Text Length.**

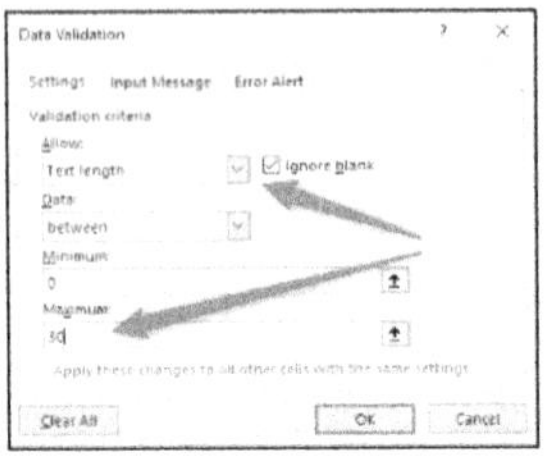

- **LibreOffice Calc** – Right-Click on any of the selected cells and choose Data Validation from the popup menu.

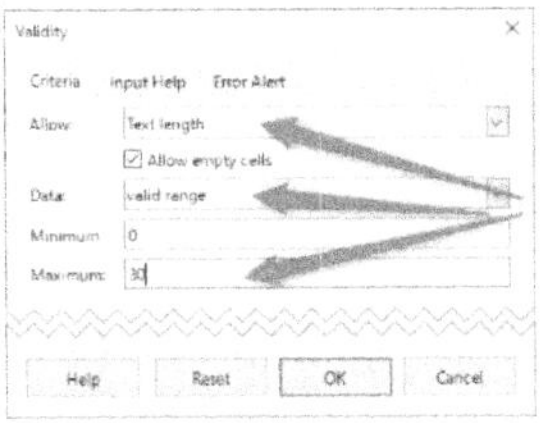

- Set Minimum to 0 and Maximum to 30
  What is available to you will depend on the data type you selected for **Allow**.

- Optionally, add an input message and an error alert to provide instructions or warnings when focusing on the cell.

- **Input message**, if set will be displayed when user selects the cell

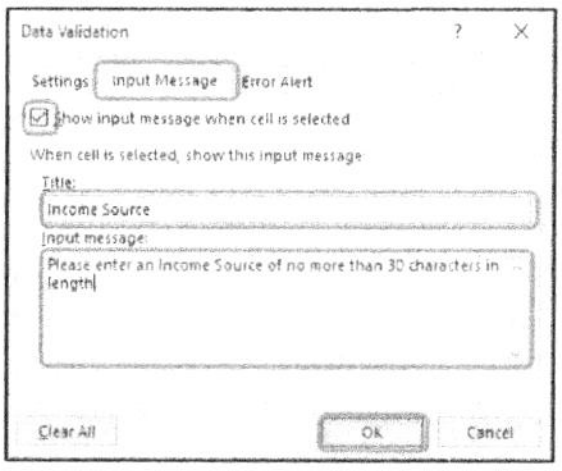

- **Error message**, if set if user puts data in that does not meet the rule you set in the Settings tab

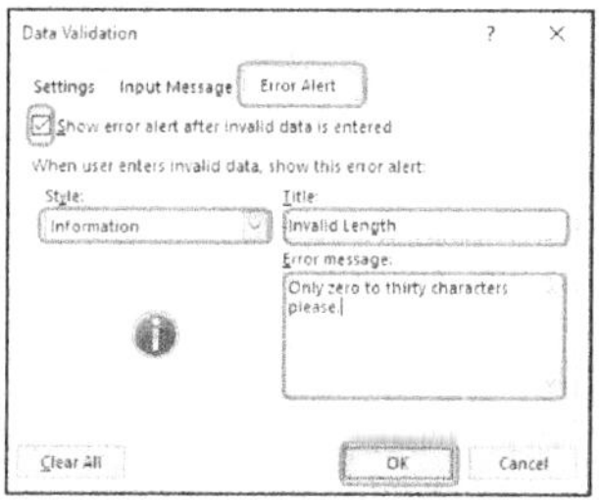

- Click OK to apply the validation and try it out

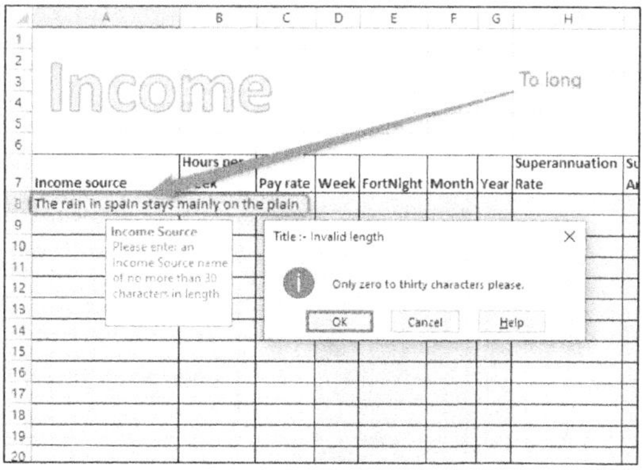

It is worth taking the time to set data validation, especially if other people will be using your spreadsheet.

Exercise

Set the data validation, Input message and Error messages for the remaining User Input cells, cell details below. Of course, you can adjust the values in Notes for Min and Max. Because over-time cannot always be relied on, set the hours to the basic hours of the job, i.e., 38 or 40. This way your budget will work with those hours, and any overtime is a bonus.

Cell Range	Data Type	Min	Max	Notes For while you are setting these up, you can of course set what you need and enter your own messages
B7:B21	Text Length	0	30	Limit length of text to Max characters
C7:C21	Decimal	0	60	Hours should be how many paid hours per week
D7:D21	Decimal	0	50,000	Using 50k in case you get odd income like royalties (more on this later)
E7:F21	List			Check Ignore blank or Allow empty cells Check In-cell dropdown Type Y,N on separate lines in Source or Entries
L7:L21	Decimal	0	0.2	20% super is a lot, but you can change if you need more
O7:O21	Decimal	0	50,000	To cover odd income tax if required

Helper Calculators

Helper calculators play a crucial role in ensuring the accuracy and comprehensiveness of your budget. They allow you to break down and standardize various forms of income and expenses, making them easier to manage and incorporate into your budget worksheet. The following are two essential helper calculators you will create:

- **Base Pay calculator**
  Hourly pay rates may include superannuation. To accurately calculate your base rate for use in the worksheet, we will now create a small helper calculator.

  This calculator will help you determine your base pay by excluding superannuation, ensuring that you have a precise figure to work with.

- **Weekly Breakdown Calculator**
  Income does not always fit into the standard hourly rate/hours per week model and cannot easily be broken down into a weekly amount.

  Such income may include monthly, yearly, royalties, or other irregular amounts that you may want to include for budgeting purposes.

  To convert these into a weekly amount so they can be entered into the worksheet, we will now create a small helper calculator.

Create Helper Calculators

By now you have learned enough skills to add these calculators yourself.

- Create them exactly as shown in the image below including the formatting and use the same locations.

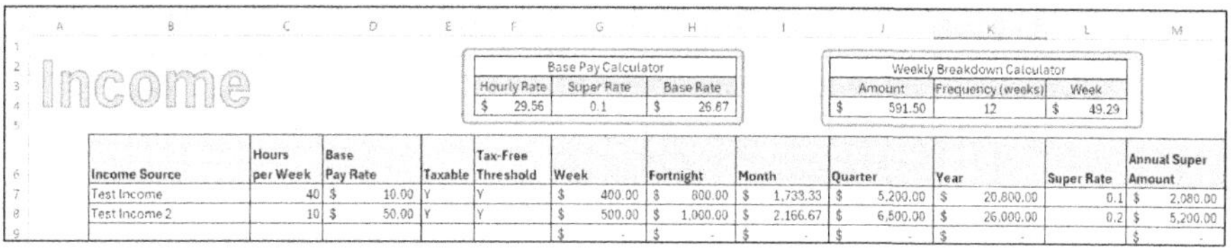

Income

Base Pay Calculator		
Hourly Rate	Super Rate	Base Rate
$ 29.56	0.1	$ 26.67

Weekly Breakdown Calculator		
Amount	Frequency (weeks)	Week
$ 591.50	12	$ 49.29

Income Source	Hours per Week	Base Pay Rate	Taxable	Tax-Free Threshold	Week	Fortnight	Month	Quarter	Year	Super Rate	Annual Super Amount
Test Income	40	$ 10.00	Y	Y	$ 400.00	$ 800.00	$ 1,733.33	$ 5,200.00	$ 20,800.00	0.1	$ 2,080.00
Test Income 2	10	$ 50.00	Y	Y	$ 500.00	$ 1,000.00	$ 2,166.67	$ 6,500.00	$ 26,000.00	0.2	$ 5,200.00
					$ -	$ -	$ -	$ -	$ -		$ -

Hint: Create the first then copy/paste to make the second then change the labels and formula

- The formula are as follows
  - Base Rate
    - **H4**, =F4/(1+G4)
    - This calculation determines the base pay rate by dividing the value in cell F4 (total pay including superannuation) by one plus the value in cell G4 (superannuation rate), effectively extracting the superannuation component.
  - Week
    - **L4,** =IF(K4=0, "", J4/K4)
    - This formula checks if **K4** is zero or blank. If it is, the formula returns a blank result (""), and if not, it performs the division **J4/K4.** This check stops the #DIV/0 error.

Below are some test values to test your formula

Base Pay Calculator		
Hourly Rate	Super Rate	Base Rate
$ 29.56	0.1	$ 26.87

Weekly Breakdown Calculator		
Amount	Frequency (weeks)	Week
$ 591.50	12	$ 49.29

How to use the Helper Calculators

- **Base Pay Calculator**
  - **Enter the hourly rate** (including superannuation).
  - **Enter the super rate**, e.g., 11% should be entered as 0.11.
  - The **base rate** will be calculated. Enter this value in **column D** on the row you are working in.
- **Weekly Breakdown Calculator**
  - **Enter the amount you will receive**.
    - If the amount varies, enter the lower possible amount to ensure the budget is calculated conservatively. Any extra received will be a bonus.
  - **Enter the frequency in weeks**.
    - Round down if the number of weeks is not precise. For example, for quarterly payments, enter 12 weeks.
  - Enter the **weekly amount** into the **Base Pay Rate**.
  - Enter **1 in Hours per Week**.
    - This tells the spreadsheet to use this average amount in the budget.
    - If you want to include superannuation for this income, you can enter the calculated weekly amount into the base pay calculator, enter the result in **column D**, and pay the difference into your super fund.

Finishing the worksheet

Final Adjustments

- **Formatting**:
  - Ensure that all text and data are properly aligned and formatted for readability.
- **Column Widths**:
  - Adjust column widths to ensure all data fits neatly within the cells without truncation.
- **Colors**:

    - Verify that the color scheme is consistent and easy on the eyes. Highlight input cells in yellow for clarity.
- **Turn Off Gridlines**:
    - Go to the **View** tab.
    - Uncheck the **Gridlines** option to turn off gridlines.
- **Check All Input Cells**:
    - Select the yellow input cells.
    - Right-Click (R-Click) on the selected cells.
    - Choose **Format Cells**.
    - Go to the **Protection** tab.
    - Ensure the **Locked** checkbox is unchecked to keep these cells unlocked.

You are now ready to secure the worksheet

Secure the worksheet

Finally, we lockdown the worksheet to protect it from accidental erasure of the formulae.

- Right Click on the **Income Tab**
- Select **Protect Worksheet**
- Enter a password, as we are evaluating here, you can use something simple like **abcd** for now

  You may choose not to use a password while you are still working through the course, but if you do be sure to always keep an unlocked copy of the workbook and worksheets somewhere safe, if you forget the password, you will not be able to get access to it.

- Click **OK**, you will be prompted to enter the password again

- Enter the password again and click **OK.**

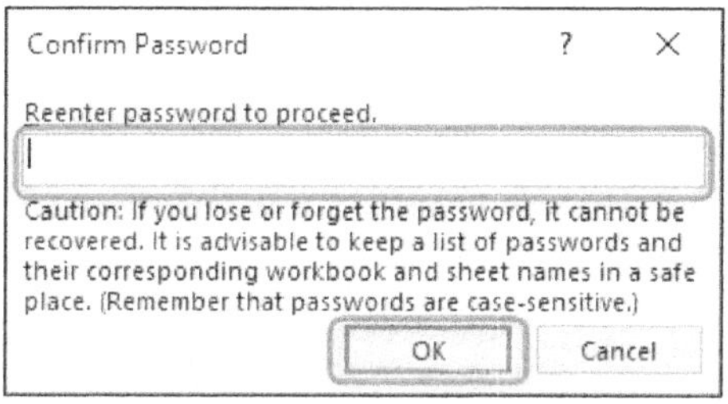

- The worksheet is now locked.

The Income worksheet is now complete.

The values in **P22** and **Q22** will be used throughout the rest of the workbook for all budget calculations.

You have finished the Income sheet but now we have to finish the lookup tables, you have learned the skills to finish it.

Finish the Lookup Tables worksheet

You have now learned how to set formulas, format the worksheet and set security. These are vital throughout the remainder of this course, and in general so to get a little more practice, in this exercise you, go back to the Lookup Tables and set the formatting, formulas and security.

- Formatting
  - Set the input cell color, yellow, as shown in the following image, you can set the remaining colors as you like, remember, pastels.
  - Set currency cells to currency format
  - Set percentage cells to decimal
  - Set cell alignment as shown below, left, centre, etc. Time to make it pretty, and readable.

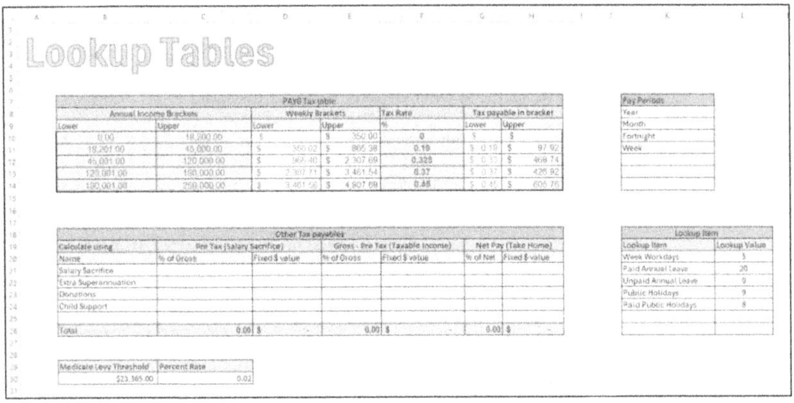

- Formula, only the *PAYG Tax Table* and *Other Tax Payables* requires formula
  - *PAYG Tax Table*
  - **Weekly Brackets**

    These break down the annual ranges to weekly ranges which are more meaningful to most people, enter them as follows
    - D10, =**B10/52**
    - E10, =**C10/52**
      - Using the drag techniques learned earlier, select both cells and drag the formula down to cell row 14
  - **Tax Payable in Bracket**

    These calculate the minimum and maximum amount payable in each range
    - G10, =**B10*F10**

            - This is likely to always be 0. This is slightly different to the formula in rows 11 to 14 as they refer back to the previous row and we cannot do that here.
        - H10, =**(E10-D10)*F10**
            - drag the formula down to cell row 14
        - G11, =**(B11-C10)*F11**
            - Notice this subtracts the previous rows upper weekly amount (C10) from the current rows lower amount (B11), this gives the actual dollar of pay in the bracket so we can calculate the amount payable.
            - drag the formula down to cell row 14
        - H11, =**(E11-D11)*F11**
            - Subtracts the lower value in bracket, D11 from the top value, E11 gives the maximum dollar amount of pay in the bracket so we can calculate the amount payable.
            - drag the formula down to cell row 14

    - *Other Tax Payables*
        - C26, **=SUM(C21:C25)**
        - Select and drag C26 to H26 to copy the formula to other columns

- Security
    - Unlock the input cells

Conclusion

In this chapter, you have learned how to create and format an income worksheet, which is crucial for tracking and planning your budget. Here are the key points covered:

1. **Importance of the Income Worksheet**:
    - The income worksheet helps track and plan sources of income, providing a complete picture of your financial situation.
    - It forms the basis for other worksheets to determine if your expenses fit within your total income.
2. **Creating and Formatting Headings**:
    - You learned how to create a prominent heading using WordArt and how to copy and paste it across multiple worksheets to save time and ensure consistency.
    - Proper formatting of headings makes your worksheet more readable and visually appealing.
3. **Preparing and Laying Out the Worksheet**:
    - Planning your worksheet layout on paper before creating it in Excel ensures that all necessary columns are included and organized.
    - You transferred the planned layout to the worksheet, entered text and formulas, and formatted the worksheet for clarity.
4. **Entering and Copying Formulas**:
    - You entered various formulas to calculate weekly, fortnightly, monthly, and yearly income, as well as superannuation and total packages.
    - Using Excel's features, you learned how to copy these formulas efficiently to other rows, saving time and reducing errors.
5. **Formatting for Readability and Usability**:
    - Setting appropriate row heights, column widths, font sizes, and colors enhances the usability of the worksheet.
    - Proper formatting helps prevent eye strain and makes the worksheet more pleasant to work with.
6. **Helper Calculators**:
    - You created helper calculators for calculating base pay excluding superannuation and for converting irregular income into a weekly amount.

    - These calculators simplify the process of entering accurate income data into the worksheet.
7. **Final Adjustments and Securing the Worksheet**:
    - Ensuring all text and data are properly aligned and formatted, turning off gridlines, and highlighting input cells for clarity.
    - You learned how to unlock input cells, apply data validation, and finally secure the worksheet to protect it from accidental changes.

By completing these steps, you have built a comprehensive and functional income worksheet that serves as a strong foundation for your budget planning. You are now ready to proceed with entering your actual income data and continuing with the next parts of your budget workbook.

Congratulations on completing the Income worksheet!

Quiz

1. **Why is proper formatting important in a worksheet?**
   a) It reduces the file size.
   b) It ensures the formulas work correctly.
   c) It makes the worksheet easier to use and pleasant to work with over long periods.
   d) It prevents errors when copying data.

2. **What is the recommended way to adjust the layout when working with multi-word headings in a column?**
   a) Use smaller font sizes.
   b) Use word wrap or insert a manual line break with "Alt + Enter."
   c) Increase the column width significantly.
   d) Use bold text for all headings.

3. **Which cell formatting technique is recommended for identifying input cells in the worksheet?**
   a) Use bright colors like red or green.
   b) Use thick borders around input cells.
   c) Use pastel yellow fill to mark input cells for clarity.
   d) Use bold text for all input cells.

4. **What does data validation help prevent in a worksheet?**
   a) Incorrect font size being applied.
   b) Entering invalid data types into specific cells.
   c) Rows from being deleted.
   d) The formatting from being changed.

Quiz Answers

1. c) It makes the worksheet easier to use and pleasant to work with over long periods.
2. b) Use word wrap or insert a manual line break with "Alt + Enter."
3. c) Use pastel yellow fill to mark input cells for clarity.
4. b) Entering invalid data types into specific cells.

Self-Assessment

By the end of this section, you should be able to:

- Understand the importance of formatting in creating user-friendly and visually appealing worksheets.
- Use Excel features like word wrap, manual line breaks, and column width adjustments to enhance readability.
- Apply consistent formatting, such as font size, colors, and borders, to make the worksheet more functional and pleasant to use.
- Set data validation to control what type of information can be entered into specific cells.

Self-Check Questions:

1. Have you successfully formatted the income worksheet, including adjusting column widths, row heights, and applying consistent colors?
    - (Yes/No)
2. Can you explain why pastel colors and limited font sizes are recommended for long-term usability of a worksheet?
    - (Yes/No)
3. Have you applied data validation to your input cells, ensuring that only the correct data types can be entered?
    - (Yes/No)

WS 3 - Expenses - Budget

The Expenses – Budget worksheet is crucial for managing your finances. By listing all your expected expenses, you can compare them against your income and ensure you are living within your means. It also helps in identifying areas where you can cut costs and prioritize spending based on your financial objectives.

When completed, the final **Expenses – Budget** worksheet will look like

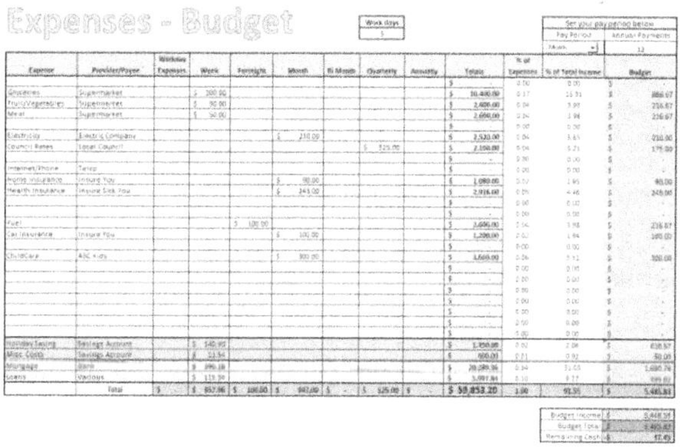

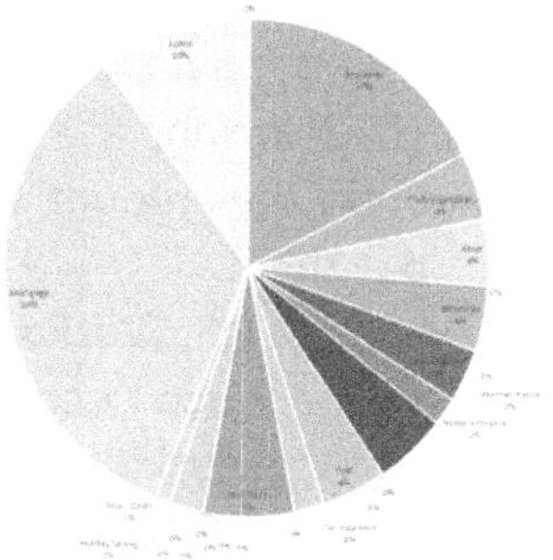

Let's get started.

Worksheet and Heading

If you have not yet created the **Expenses – Budget** worksheet and heading please create them now.

Preparing the Layout

Over the next few paragraphs, we will be laying out the worksheet's components. Because you have had a lot of practice formatting, we will also do some formatting as we go.

Budget Column headings

The headings will define the columns that will contain the information for the budget. Columns **B to J** will contain the input cells, columns **K to N** will contain formula.

Start by entering the column headings as described below.

- B6, **Expense**
  Type of expense, i.e., rent, food, electricity, etc.
- C6, **Provider/Payee**
  who is it paid to
- The following are where you enter the amount you pay the expense, enter the amount in the column that best represents the frequency you pay them.
  - D6, **Workday Expenses**
    such as coffee, lunch, snacks, transport, etc. purchased each workday
  - E6, **Week**
  - F6, **Fortnight**
  - G6, **Month**
  - H6, **Bi Month**
  - I6, **Quarterly**
  - J6, **Annually**
- K6, **Annual Total**
  Totals the row to an annual amount.
- L6, **% of Expenses**
  Percentage of total expenses
- M6, **% of Total Income**
  percentage of total income
- N6, **Budget**
  Budgeted amount for period in weeks

When the column headings are added, go ahead, and

- set the text bold
- set a background color for the cells. Remember, you can select all the cells in the row from columns B6:N6 and set them all at the same time.
- Adjust the column widths

Column Totals line

As with the totals line in the Income worksheet, we only need to set one label for the Totals row. Columns B and C are used for text so no total is required for them, columns D to N will be displaying numeric information, each of these will require total columns.

We will be putting the totals in row 35 for now. We only need one heading in the totals row, add it now.

- C35, **Total**

You can now go ahead and set the background for cell C35 and its font style. Use the Format Painter tool to copy the formatting in cell C6 to C35 by doing the following.

- Click cell **C6** to select it.
- Select the **Format Painter** option in the **Home, Clipboard** menu item on the ribbon.
- Click cell **C35**, to copy the formatting to **C35**.

You can also format the Totals cells from **D35:N35** by doing the following.

- You may want to add some temp data in cells **D35:N35** so you can see the formatting.
- Click in cell **C35**, we want to copy this cells format.
- Select the **Format Painter** option in the **Home, Clipboard** menu item on the ribbon.
- Hold down the shift key and click in **D35** and while holding down the left mouse button drag to **N35** and let go

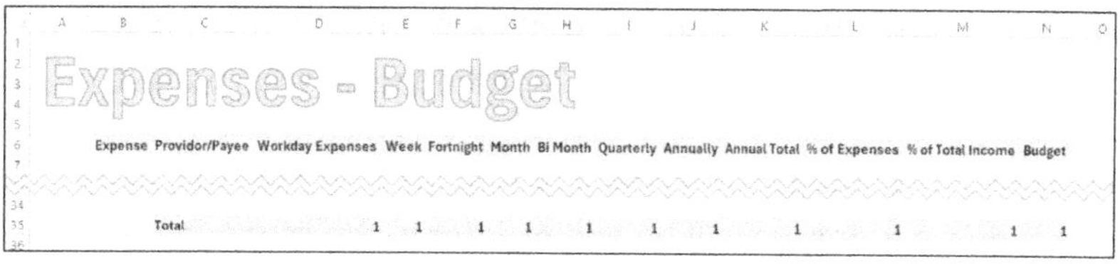

- Format cells **D7:K35** and cell **N7:N35** to currency format by
    - You may want to add some temp data in random cells in the **D7:N35** range so you can see the formatting.
    - Click in cell **D7**, hold down the Shift Key and click in cell **K35** to select the range of cells.
    - Then holding down the **Ctrl** key, click on cell **N7** and drag down to **N35**, you will now have two blocks selected
    - Click **Home/Number/$** on the ribbon to make all cells accounting format.

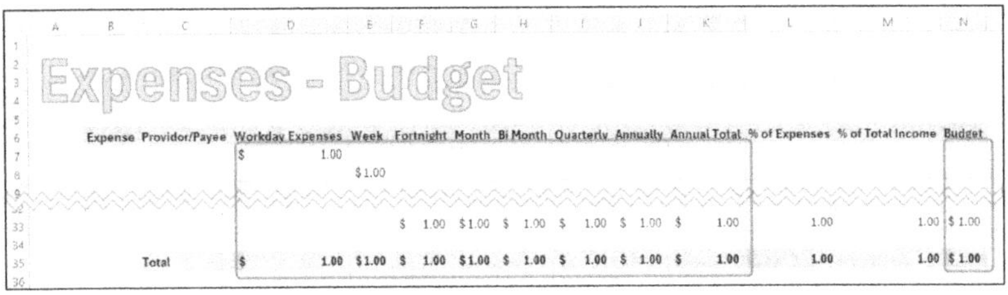

Now we move on to the formatting the input sections.

Data Input cells

The input cells are **columns B to J**.

Columns B and C contain text to describe the expense item and to whom it is paid. The text in these cells will be entered once, you will of course add and remove them as required.

Columns D to J contain the dollar amounts paid with each column representing the frequency the item is paid, i.e., weekly, month, etc. The values in these cells will be adjusted as you adjust the dollar amounts in your budget.

The expense rows range from **row 7 to row 30** with **Rows 31 to 34** reserved for special expense items we will be adding later in the course as we set up their relevant worksheets. Rows **31 to 34** are NOT input cells, they will get their values from other worksheets but need to be included here as part of your budget, this will become clearer later.

Format the **columns B7:C30** first, do this by

- Select the **range B7:C30** by clicking B7 and dragging your selection down to C30 and letting go of the mouse.
- Click the **Fill Color** option on the **Font menu** in the ribbon.
- Select a slightly different shade of yellow to indicate it is an input field but also to make it stand apart from the main input area where you will be entering the dollar values. You may need to use the **More Colors** option.

Now format the main input area by

- Select the range from **D7:J30** as before.
- Select the **Fill Color** option from the **Font menu.**
- Select the shade of Yellow used to indicate input.

Now format the Totals column, **Columns K7:K30**

- Select the range from **Columns K7:K30**
- Select the **Fill Color** option from the **Font menu.**
- Select a light shade of Green.

Now format the Special Expense Area, **B31:K34** by

- Select the range from cells **B31:K34**
- Select the **Fill Color** option from the **Font menu.**
- Select a light shade of Blue.

Now format **Columns L7 to N34.**

- Set any Fill Color for **columns K7:K30**
- Set any Fill Color for cells **L7:M34**
    - You could leave these white
- Set any Fill Color for cells **N7:N34**

Setting the background colors has removed the grid guide lines from view, now is a good time to add the grid lines.

- Select range **B6:N35**
- Open the Borders dropdown in **Home, Font**
- Select **All Borders**

The Expenses – Budget page will now look similar to the following.

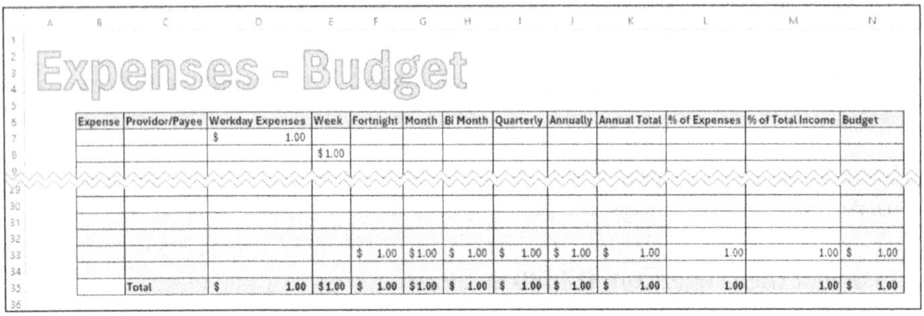

Expenses - Budget

Expense	Providor/Payee	Workday Expenses	Week	Fortnight	Month	Bi Month	Quarterly	Annually	Annual Total	% of Expenses	% of Total Income	Budget
		$ 1.00										
			$1.00									
				$ 1.00	$1.00	$ 1.00	$ 1.00	$ 1.00	$ 1.00	1.00	1.00	$ 1.00
	Total	$ 1.00	$1.00	$ 1.00	$1.00	$ 1.00	$ 1.00	$ 1.00	$ 1.00	1.00	1.00	$ 1.00

Special Expense Items

The special expenses in rows 31:34 is defined a little later in the course, however as they are not input fields, we need to set their labels now.

- **B31**, Holiday Saving
- **C31**, Saving Account
    - You could have several Loans so there may be various creditors.
- **B32**, Misc. Costs
- **C32**, Savings Account
    - These are items you will try and budget for, car repairs, house maintenance, etc.
- **B33**, Mortgage
- **C33**, Lender
    - You could have several mortgages so there may be various creditors.
- **B34**, Loans
- **C34**, Various

At this stage you can remove any temp data you placed in the sheet to see formatting, the worksheet should now look like this

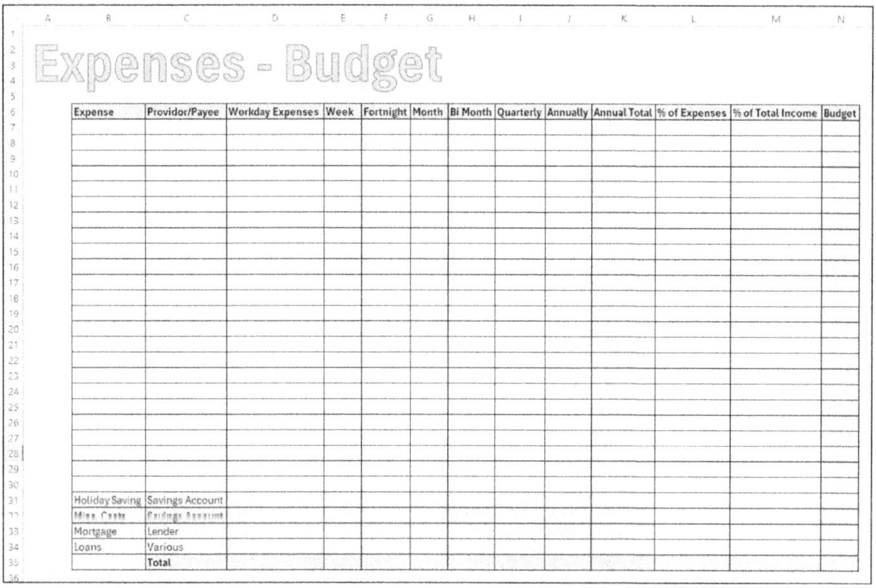

We will come back to this later to finish these rows when we have created the source worksheets for them.

Totals and Budget columns

These columns will show your totals and budget for each item you enter, they tell you how much you need annually to cover the expense and how much you must set aside each pay day to ensure you have enough to pay for the item. To be able to calculate these values, we need to know how often you get paid and how many days per week you work (for some items only). Because these can vary, we will

> **Note**: You could code the value directly into your formulas however when your pay period changes, for instance if you change your job, you will need to locate and change them all. By using a lookup value, you can reference the cell holding the value in your formula and if it changes, you only change the single cell value.

create a lookup value we can reference in the formula in the next section, we will put this in now.

Annual Pay Days

- In cell **M4**, enter the label, **Annual Pay Days**
- For cell **M5** do the following
  - Set the Fill Color to your input color, yellow.
  - Enter how many times a year you get paid.
    - Week, 52
    - Fortnight, 26
    - Month, 12
  - Center the cell contents
  - Set the borders
  - Set the background color of **M4** and set font bold

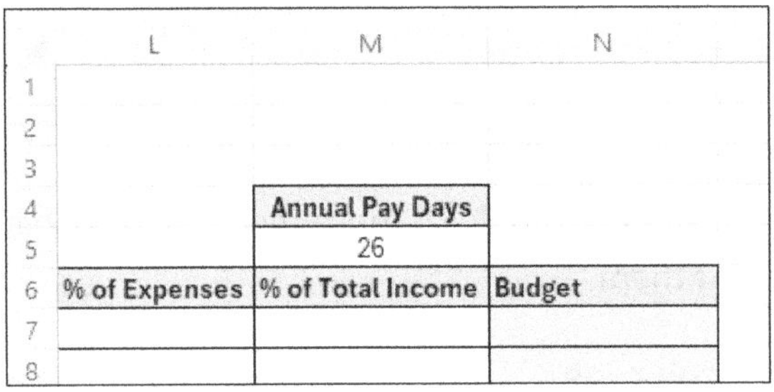

Work Days

Some calculations in the worksheet are based around how many days are worked per week, because this can also vary, rather than hardcoding the value, usually 5, into the formulae. We can set up a cell to hold this value and make the formula reference it, exactly the same as for the Annual Pay Days you just added,

- In cell **K4**, enter the label, **WorkDays**
- For cell **K5** do the following
  - Set the Fill Color to your input color, yellow.

- Center the cell contents
- Enter how many days per week you work, **5**

	J	K	L	M	N
1					
2					
3					
4		Workdays		Annual Pay Days	
5		5		26	
6	Annually	Annual Total	% of Expenses	% of Total Income	Budget
7					
8					

Once setup and the formulas are created, you will only need to adjust these two values as required to recalculate the budget.

Security - Unlocking the input cells

Now that we have finished the layout of the sheet, this is a suitable time to set the security on the input cells by setting them as unlocked. Let us unlock them by

- Select all cells from **B7:J30**
- Right Click anywhere in the selection
- Select **Format Cells**
- Select **Protection** tab.
- Clear the **Locked** check box.
- Click **OK** to close the popup window.

Exercise – Set security for Lookup cells

Set the security for cells **K5** and **M5** to unlock.

That is it, you have now unlocked the input cells, let us move on to the formula.

Creating the formula

Before we begin, in this section we will not be setting formula in the cells in the **D31**:**J34** range, we will come back to them later, we have a special purpose for this area.

In this section we will learn to

- add formula.
- reference cells in other worksheets within our formula
- reference lookup cells for formula values
- lock column and row co-ordinates with a formula

Let's start.

The input cells

The yellow input cells in the range **B7**:**J30** do not have formula.

Totals Row

The **Totals** row, from **D35**:**N35** sums the column values, exactly as the income sheet did, in fact, apart from the actual cells involved, the formulas are identical.

The formula for cell **D35** is ***=SUM(D7:D30)***, this tells Excel to sum all the value from C7:D30 and put the value in this cell, D35. We have already covered how to enter the formula for a single cell; we will now enter a simple totals formula for an entire block of cells using the **AutoSum** function to demonstrate a special feature of AutoSum.

AutoSum needs to know which columns to do a total formula for, it examines the data in the cells and uses this to determine if to put in a SUM formula, we can do this by entering a numeric value in the first row of the block for the columns we want to sum, AutoSum will use this to determine the type of data.

- Enter a 1 in cells **D7:K7** and **N7**

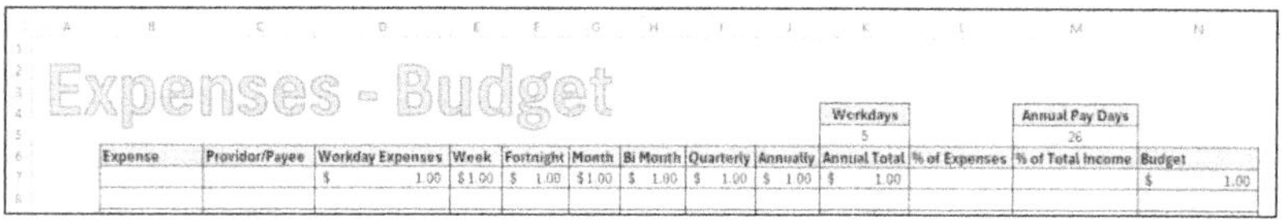

- Click cell **D7** to select the cell.
- Whilst holding down the **Shift** key, click cell **N35**, this will select the full range from **D7:N35**. Columns L and M will also be selected; they will be ignored because they have no value in the first row.
- **Excel**, Click **AutoSum** in **Home, Editing** section of the ribbon.

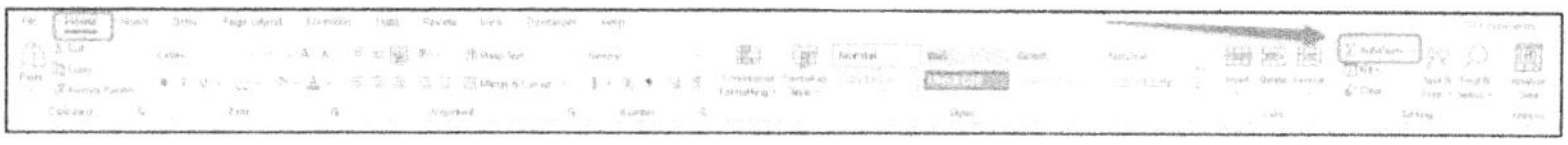

- **LibreOffice Calc**, Click **AutoSum** on the formula bar toolbar

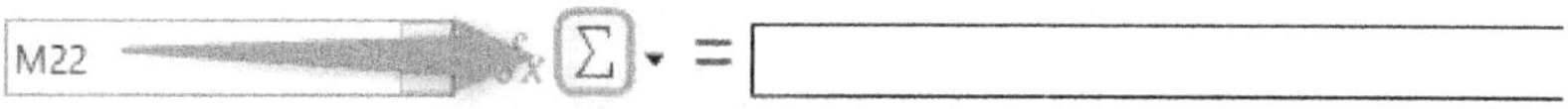

- Clicking Autosum will put a SUM() formula in the last row of the section for each of the columns in the selection that have a numeric value, the formulas column reference will be adjusted for each of the columns.

You should now see the Totals showing for each of the columns where you put a 1. Cells L35 and M35 are blank because there was no numeric value. This is a big time saver when creating or editing worksheets.

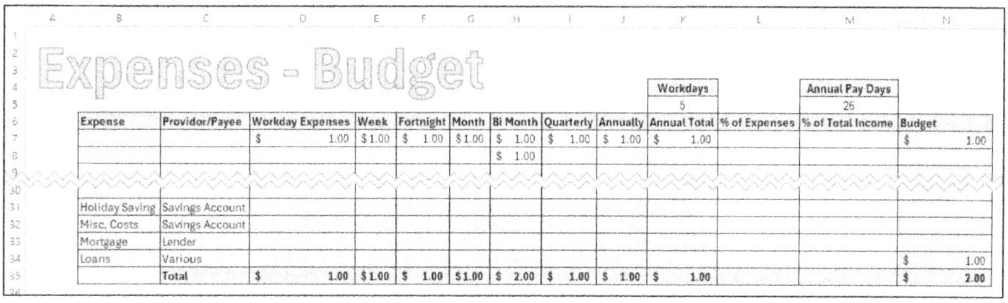

Evaluating the formula

Test the formula is working by entering values several of the cells in the D7:N35 range, the sums of the columns will change to show in the new totals. When you are done testing, delete all of test values you may have entered in the range **D7**:**N35**. Remember, you can select the whole range and press **Delete**, always check your selection twice before you delete.

Note: **Ctrl-Z** will undo your recent changes.

Annual Totals Column

The annual totals column will, for each row, total up all the values in the columns **D** to **J** to an annual value for the item. As each of the columns represents a different period, we need to perform a calculation on the values to convert them to an annual amount. We will break this formula down so you can see how it goes together.

In preparation for entering the formula, enter a **1** in cell **D7,** if the formula is entered correctly then **K7** will display 260.

The formula for cell **K7** is ***=(D7*(52*$K$5)) + (E7*52) + (F7*26) + (G7*12) + (H7*6) + (I7*4) + J7***

> **Note**: (52*$K$5) is referencing the Workday in K5, we are going to copy this formula, and we do not want this reference to change so we use the $'s to lock them.

Cell referenced	***Time period***	***Formula Calculation***	***Test result***	***Explanation***
D7	***Workday***	*(D7*(52*$K$5))*	260	Calculates the daily workday costs to an annual value. The values in this column will be items such as coffee, lunch, and other daily expenditure items. The workdays per week are represented by the value of $K$5 and are multiplied by 52 for a full year.
E7	***Week***	***(E7 * 52)***	52	Weekly values, multiplies the value by 52 to get the full year value
F7	***Fortnight***	***(F7 *26)***	26	Fortnightly values, amount multiplied by 26 to get the full year value
G7	***Month***	***(G7 * 12)***	12	Month values (calendar month), values are multiplied by 12 to reach the annual amount
7	***Bi Month***	***(H7*6)***	6	Every second month, values multiplied by 6 to reach the annual amount
I7	***Quarterly***	***(I7*4)***	4	Every three months, values multiplied by 4 to reach the annual amount
J7	***Annually***	***J7***	1	Annual value used in formula as displayed; there is no calculation

the **Test Result** for **K7** in the table below The breakdown is.

Each of its own is not that complex and all we are doing is join them all together with a + between each, enter the following formula in cell **K7.**

K7 fx =(D7*(52*$K$5))+(E7*52)+(F7*26)+(G7*12)+(H7*6)+(I7*4)+J7

Expenses - Budget

Workdays	Annual Pay Days
5	26

Expense	Providor/Payee	Workday Expenses	Week	Fortnight	Month	Bi Month	Quarterly	Annually	Annual Total	% of Expenses	% of Total Income	Budget
		$ 1.00							$ 260.00			
Holiday Saving	Savings Account											
Misc. Costs	Savings Account											
Mortgage	Lender											
Loans	Various											
	Total	$ 1.00	$ -	$ -	$ -	$ -	$ -	$ -	$ 260.00			$ -

Evaluating the formula

Be sure to test the formula by entering a 1 in each of the cells D7:J7, ensure only one cell at a time has a 1 in it. You will have values in both the Annual Total column (K7) and the Totals row (K35) changing as you enter and change values; ensure they are correct by matching the Cell number with the Test Result in the above table.

Copy the formula.

When you are satisfied, go ahead and copy the formula in **K7** to all cells in the **K8**:**K34** range, remember, select the **K7** cell and drag it down using the small square on the bottom right of the selection frame.

Evaluate all rows again before moving on.

When the formula is copied, you can test each individually, add a 1 in all cells as shown below, the **Annual Total** in the totals row should be 361.

Leave these temp values in for now, we will continue to use them.

Expenses - Budget

Workdays	Annual Pay Days
5	26

Expense	Providor/Payee	Workday Expenses	Week	Fortnight	Month	Bi Month	Quarterly	Annually	Annual Total	% of Expenses	% of Total Income	Budget
		$ 1.00							$ 260.00			
			$1.00						$ 52.00			
				$ 1.00					$ 26.00			
					$1.00				$ 12.00			
						$ 1.00			$ 6.00			
							$ 1.00		$ 4.00			
								$ 1.00	$ 1.00			
									$ -			
									$ -			
Holiday Saving	Savings Account								$ -			
Misc. Costs	Savings Account								$ -			
Mortgage	Lender								$ -			
Loans	Various								$ -			
	Total	$ 1.00	$1.00	$ 1.00	$1.00	$ 1.00	$ 1.00	$ 1.00	$ 361.00			$ -

Exercise

Often when creating worksheets, you may realise you left something out and need to go back and add it in. Earlier, we set the formula in the Totals row (36) to sum up the columns. However, we intentionally omitted columns L and M from the exercise to demonstrate how AutoSum automatically selects columns to total. Now we need to include columns L and M and have their formulas in place to ensure completeness. To set the summing formula.

- Enter any numeric value in columns **L7** and also in column **M7**.
- Select from **L7:M35**.
- Click AutoSum in the Editing group on the ribbon.
- The totals of the columns should be displayed in **L35:M35**.

% Of Expenses

This column shows the percentage each item is of your total expenses, this helps you see the impact each item has on your budget.

The **Annual Total** is cell **K35**, this is used to calculate the percentage.

The formula for cell **L7** is **=(K7/$K$35)** go ahead and type it into cell **L7**

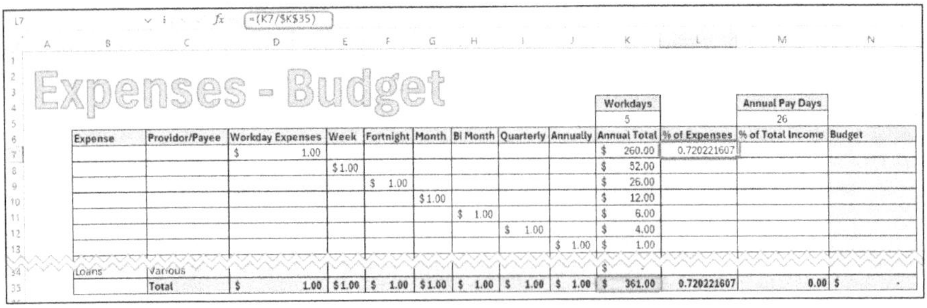

Let us break it down.

- =
  - tells Excel this is a formula.
- **(K7/$K$35)**

  - is in brackets to force them to be calculated first, as there are no other calculations in the formula, brackets are optional.
  - This is dividing the Annual Total value for the item (K7) by the sum of all item's annual totals in cell K35, this will return a percentage.
  - We are using the $ symbols to lock in the K35 cell coordinate as we do not want that changed when we copy the formula to the other cells in column K.

To make the value more human-readable, we can format it as a percentage. It is easier to read 72.02% than 0.720221607 as a percentage value. By formatting the cell as a percentage, we can display the value as 72.02%.

To format the cell as percentage.

- Select cell **K8.**
- Click on the % symbol in the Number menu on the ribbon.
- You will need to click the Increase Decimal symbol a couple of times to allow decimals if you do not Excel will round off the value, if the decimal part is
  - below .5 Excel will round down.
  - .5 or more Excel will round up.
  - You can have as many decimal places as you like, two are accurate enough for the budget..

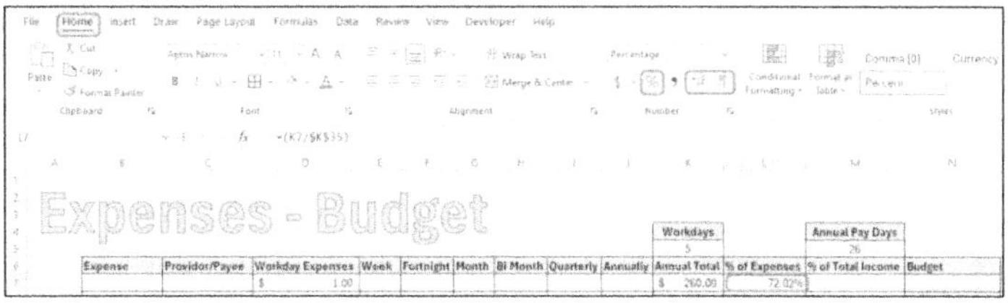

Testing and Copying the formula

Put some values in each of the columns in the C8:J8 range and evaluate the percentage calculated correctly, when you are satisfied the result is correct, copy the formula and format in **L7** to the cells from **L9** to **L34** by using the drag method to copy the formula and the cells formatting.

Because this column shows percentages from a common source, the total in L35 will always come to 100%. This is a good time to format L35 and M35 as percentages, select both cells and set formatting as you did just now for L8

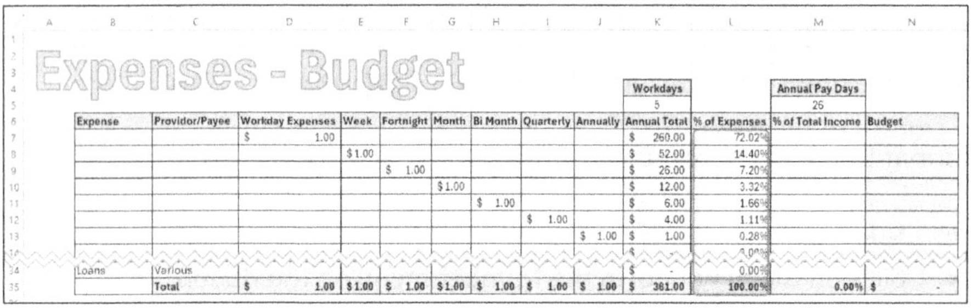

Expenses - Budget

Workdays: 5

Annual Pay Days: 26

Expense	Provider/Payee	Workday Expenses	Week	Fortnight	Month	Bi Month	Quarterly	Annually	Annual Total	% of Expenses	% of Total Income	Budget
		$ 1.00							$ 260.00	72.02%		
			$1.00						$ 52.00	14.40%		
				$ 1.00					$ 26.00	7.20%		
					$1.00				$ 12.00	3.32%		
						$ 1.00			$ 6.00	1.66%		
							$ 1.00		$ 4.00	1.11%		
								$ 1.00	$ 1.00	0.28%		
Loans	Various								$ -	0.00%		
	Total	$ 1.00	$1.00	$ 1.00	$1.00	$ 1.00	$ 1.00	$ 1.00	$ 361.00	100.00%	0.00%	$ -

% Of Total Income

The percentage of Total Income is particularly useful as it shows how much of your expendable income any specific expense item demands. We will be learning how to reference a value on another worksheet, specifically the Income worksheet.

The formula for cell **M7** is

- **Excel**
    - **=(K7/Income!$Q$22)**
- **LibreOffice Calc**
    - **=(K7/$Income.$Q$22)**

, go ahead and type it in the relevant formula exactly as shown

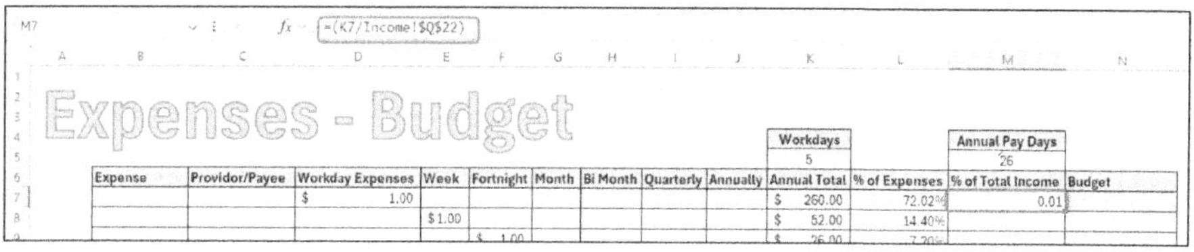

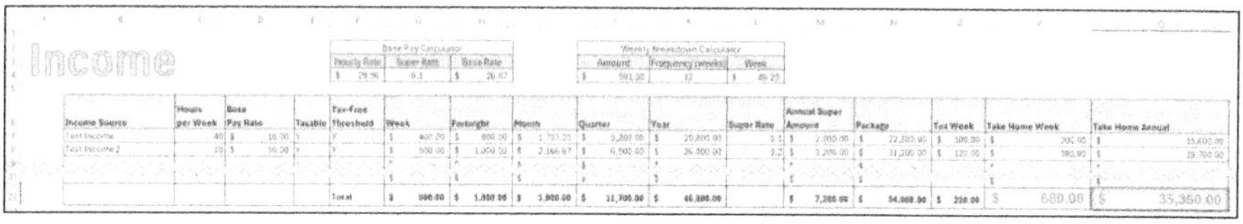

The formula instructs to divide the value in cell **K7** by the value in cell **Q22** from the worksheet named **Income**.

In **Excel**, the cell is referenced with worksheet name (**Income**) and the locked cell coordinate (**$Q$22**) separated by an exclamation (**!**) - **Income!$Q$22.**

In **LibreOffice Calc**, cell references use a slightly different format. The worksheet name (e.g., **$Income**) and the locked cell address (e.g., **$Q$22**) are separated by a period, like this: **$Income.$Q$22**.

Cell **Q22** represents the total **Take Home Annual** income across all income sources. This calculation will yield the annual percentage of the total income that is represented by the value of cell **K7**.

The use of dollar symbols before the column (Q) and row (22) references ensures that the cell coordinate ($Q$22) remains unchanged when we copy the formula to other cells.

Go ahead and copy the formula to the other cells in column M ranging from **M8**:**M35**

Evaluating the formula

Enter the values shown below in the input cells and check if the calculated results in column M are correct.

Expenses - Budget

									Workdays		Annual Pay Days	
									5		26	
Expense	**Providor/Payee**	**Workday Expenses**	**Week**	**Fortnight**	**Month**	**Bi Month**	**Quarterly**	**Annually**	**Annual Total**	**% of Expenses**	**% of Total Income**	**Budget**
		$ 20.00							$ 5,200.00	81.25%	14.71%	
			$11.00						$ 572.00	8.94%	1.62%	
				$ 12.00					$ 312.00	4.88%	0.88%	
					$13.00				$ 156.00	2.44%	0.44%	
						$ 14.00			$ 84.00	1.31%	0.24%	
							$ 15.00		$ 60.00	0.94%	0.17%	
								$ 16.00	$ 16.00	0.25%	0.05%	
									$	0.00%	0.00%	
Loans	Various								$ -	0.00%	0.00%	
	Total	$ 20.00	$11.00	$ 12.00	$13.00	$ 14.00	$ 15.00	$ 16.00	$ 6,400.00	100.00%	18.10%	$ -

Note: the total value in cell M35 represents the total percentage of your income the expenses consumed. Ideally this value should not go over 100%.

Budget

The budget column, this column will tell you how much money you need to set aside in each pay period as defined in cell **M5** to service this expense.

- The formula is **=K7/$M$5**, go ahead and enter it in cell **N7**
    - This is taking the annual total in cell **K7** and dividing it by the amount of pay days you receive per year as defined in cell **M5**.
    - To easily validate the formula is correct, change the number of paydays in cell **M5** to 10, the result in **N7** will be 1/10th of the value in cell **K7**. Leave the **M5** value as 10 for now to make further validation easier, you can change it back later.
- Go ahead and copy the formula to the other cells in column **N** ranging from **N8:N34**

Expenses - Budget

Workdays	Annual Pay Days
5	10

Expense	Providor/Payee	Workday Expenses	Week	Fortnight	Month	Bi Month	Quarterly	Annually	Annual Total	% of Expenses	% of Total Income	Budget
		$ 20.00							$ 5,200.00	81.25%	14.71%	$ 520.00
			$11.00						$ 572.00	8.94%	1.62%	$ 57.20
				$ 12.00					$ 312.00	4.88%	0.88%	$ 31.20
					$13.00				$ 156.00	2.44%	0.44%	$ 15.60
						$ 14.00			$ 84.00	1.31%	0.24%	$ 8.40
							$ 15.00		$ 60.00	0.94%	0.17%	$ 6.00
								$ 16.00	$ 16.00	0.25%	0.05%	$ 1.60
									$ -	0.00%	0.00%	$ -
Loans	Various								$ -	0.00%	0.00%	$ -
	Total	**$ 20.00**	**$11.00**	**$ 12.00**	**$13.00**	**$ 14.00**	**$ 15.00**	**$ 16.00**	**$ 6,400.00**	**100.00%**	**18.10%**	**$ 640.00**

Final budget breakdown

In this section, we will set up cells to display the totals and calculate the remaining cash. The first two cells will gather information from other cells and worksheets and the third cell will use these values to calculate the remaining cash. This will tell you at a glance if your income meets your expenses, particularly valuable information to know, enter the following for each of the cells.

- **Payday Income**, the budget income is taken from the Income worksheet and is how much we have to work with.
  - **M37**, Enter the label, *Payday Income.*
  - **N37,** Enter the following formula.
    - **=Income!Q22/M5** for *Excel* or **=$Income.Q22/M5** for *LibreOffice Calc*
      - This is telling Excel or LibreOffice Calc to use the value located in cell Q22 on the **Income** worksheet
      - /M5 is telling Excel to divide that amount by Annual Pay Days in cell M5, the result is the amount of money we have for our budget

- **Total Budget**, this is the value in **N35**, it is here so the values used in the calculations below are easier to see. Sometimes you may need to duplicate values, so you do not have to go searching for them.
  - **M38**, label is *Total Budget*
  - **N38**, enter the following formula.
    - **=N35**
      - Simply copying the value from N35, total expenses

- **Remaining Cash**, the most important number, how much cash we have left.
  - **M39**, label is *Remaining Cash*
  - **N39**, enter the following formula.
    - **=N37-N38**

      We are subtracting the *Total Budget* from *Payday Income* to get the remaining cash available to you after all expenses are met.

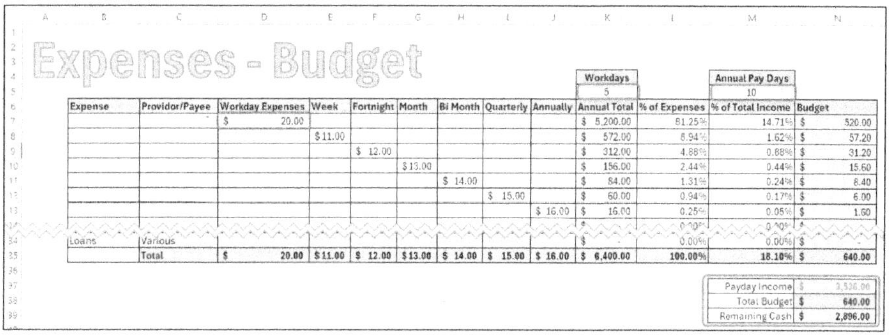

We will format these soon, continue on.

Conditional Formatting

Conditional Formatting is a feature that enables you to apply specific formatting to cells depending on the cell's value or the value of another cell or formula. This functionality proves particularly valuable in highlighting values that fall outside a predetermined range. In our worksheet, we aim to identify whether two important cells surpass specific thresholds. These cells are as follows:

- **M35**, Total for **% of Total Income**
    - Ideally, the value in the highlighted area should not exceed 100%, or even a lower threshold such as 90% or any other value that holds significance for you.
- **N39**, **Remaining Cash**
    - We definitely want to know if this goes below zero.

Starting with cell **M35**, set Conditional Formatting by

- Click on cell **M35** to select it.
- From the **Home** menu on the **ribbon**, select **Conditional Formatting**

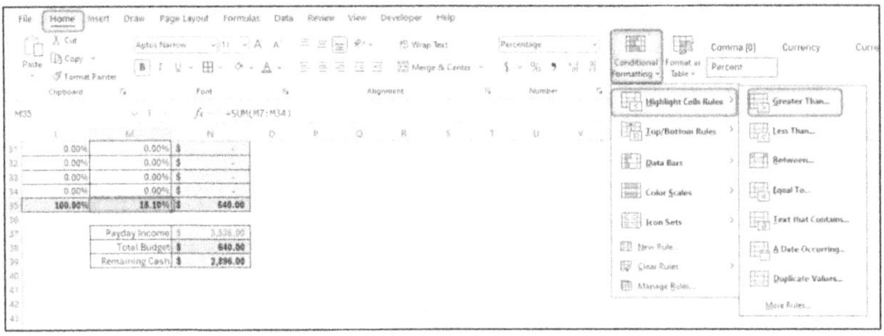

- **Excel**, Click **Highlight Cells Rules** and then **Greater Than**. An input window will open

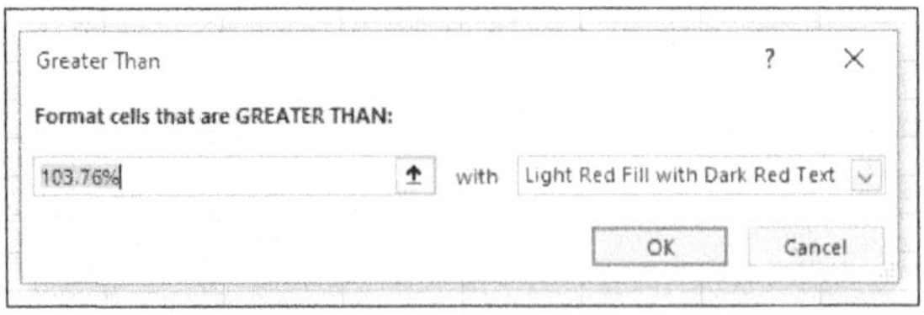

- **LibreOffice Calc**, Click **Highlight Cells Rules** and then **Greater Than**. An input window will open

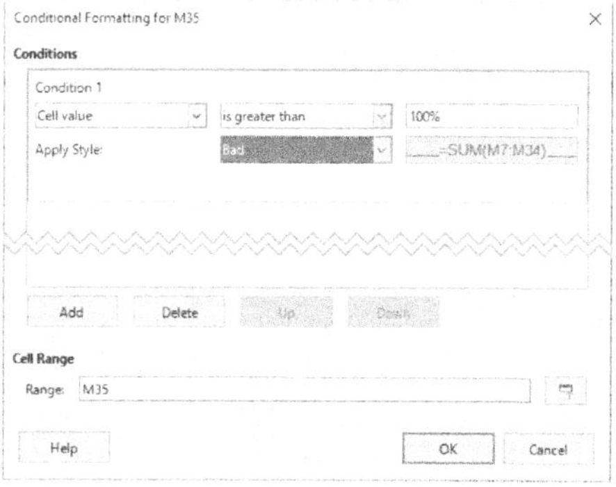

- The current value of cell **M35** will be displayed in the window, change this to **100%**, if you prefer a lower value such as 85% or 90%, put that in.
- In the dropdown to the right, select **Light Red Fill with Dark Red Text** or any other formatting option. Libre, select **Bad** you will see the preview to the right.
- Click OK.
  - o If the cell value is already over 100%, the cell displays the conditional formatting selected otherwise it will look the same.

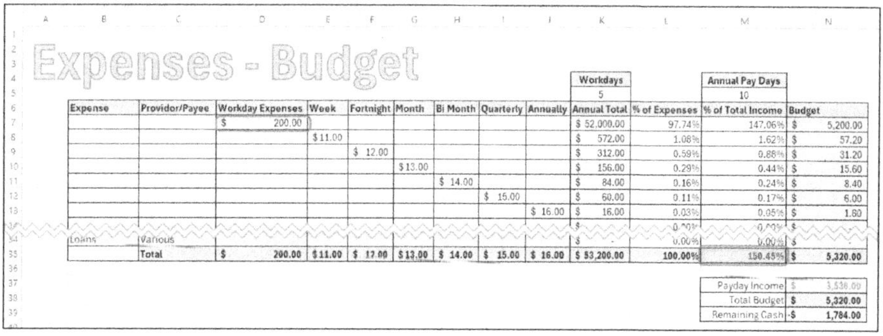
Expenses - Budget

Expense	Providor/Payee	Workday Expenses	Week	Fortnight	Month	Bi Month	Quarterly	Annually	Annual Total	% of Expenses	% of Total Income	Budget
		$ 200.00							$ 52,000.00	97.74%	147.06%	$ 5,200.00
			$11.00						$ 572.00	1.08%	1.62%	$ 57.20
				$ 12.00					$ 312.00	0.59%	0.88%	$ 31.20
					$13.00				$ 156.00	0.29%	0.44%	$ 15.60
						$ 14.00			$ 84.00	0.16%	0.24%	$ 8.40
							$ 15.00		$ 60.00	0.11%	0.17%	$ 6.00
								$ 16.00	$ 16.00	0.03%	0.05%	$ 1.60
Loans	Various								$ -	0.00%	0.00%	$ -
	Total	$ 200.00	$11.00	$ 12.00	$13.00	$ 14.00	$ 15.00	$ 16.00	$ 53,200.00	100.00%	150.45%	$ 5,320.00

Workdays: 5
Annual Pay Days: 10

Payday Income	$ 3,536.00
Total Budget	$ 5,320.00
Remaining Cash	-$ 1,784.00

Evaluate the formatting works by

- If a large value (200) is entered in the WorkDay column D7, causing the total to exceed 100%, the formatting will be changed to red to indicate this discrepancy.
- Change the value back (20) and it will revert to its normal formatting.

Exercise

- The conditional formatting for cells N39 follows the same process as we just did for cell M35, with the difference that we will select "Less Than" and enter a value of 0 (zero). Make this change and test it.

The cells should now look like this, adjust the value in D7 again to test.

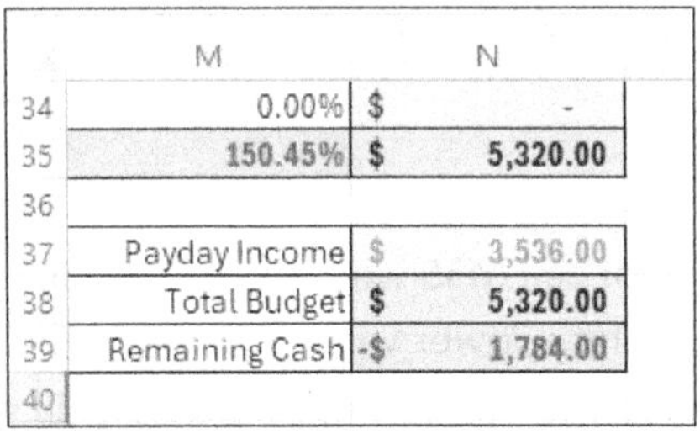

	M	N
34	0.00%	$ -
35	150.45%	$ 5,320.00
36		
37	Payday Income	$ 3,536.00
38	Total Budget	$ 5,320.00
39	Remaining Cash	-$ 1,784.00
40		

Set the formatting for **N37** and **N38** as you like and set the borders. And be sure to set the value in D7 back to 20.

You will use this little summary a lot as it brings together your total income for the pay period, how much your expenses are for the same period and how much you have left over for your own use.

Pie Chart

To provide a visual representation of the budget breakdown, we can add a pie chart to the worksheet. The pie chart will require two ranges of information to display correctly:

- Labels: These will be derived from the Expenses column, ranging from B7:B34.
- Values: These will be obtained from the Annual Total column, ranging from K7:K34.

Let us proceed with creating the chart using these ranges.

Tip for LibreOffice Users
When inserting charts in LibreOffice Calc, the Chart Wizard steps will look slightly different from those shown in Excel screenshots.
However, the available chart types and customization options are the same.
Simply follow the prompts to select your chart type, data range, and formatting.

Creating the pie chart - Excel

Follow these steps.

- Resize your screen so you can see the data area as well as a good space to the right to add your chart, use the magnification tool in the bottom/right of the screen
- Select the **Insert** menu from the ribbon and select the **Insert Pie or Doughnut Chart** icon in the *Charts* section, a menu will open, select the **2-D Pie Chart** option

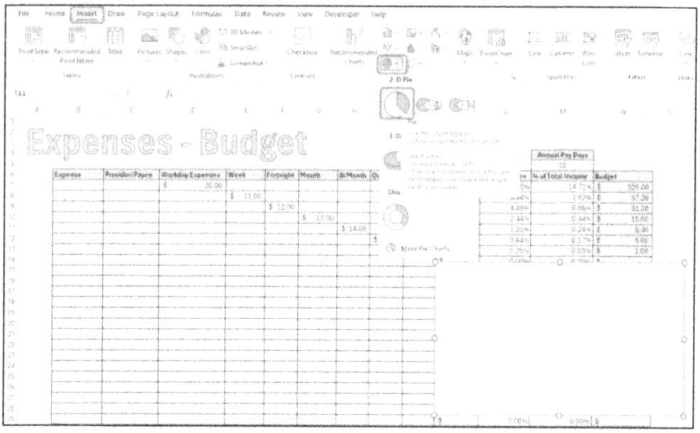

- You will now have a blank rectangle on your screen; this will be your Pie Chart when we have set it up. Drag it over to the area you want the chart, position, and resize it as desired.

- Now we can start setting it up,
    - Click on the pie charts square, the ribbon will now display the chart options, click on **Select Data**, the *Select Data Source* window will open.

- Click **Add** in the *Legend Entries (Series)* window. You will see a round chart appear although nothing in it yet and the *Edit Series* window will open

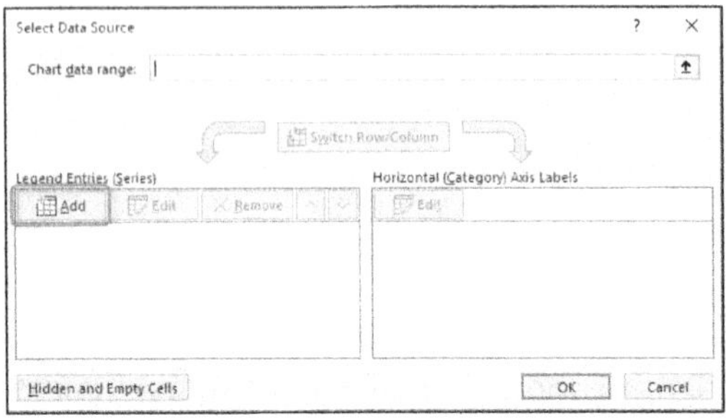

- Click in the *Series Name* input box and then click cell K6, **Annual Total**. This will set the series name to Annual Total

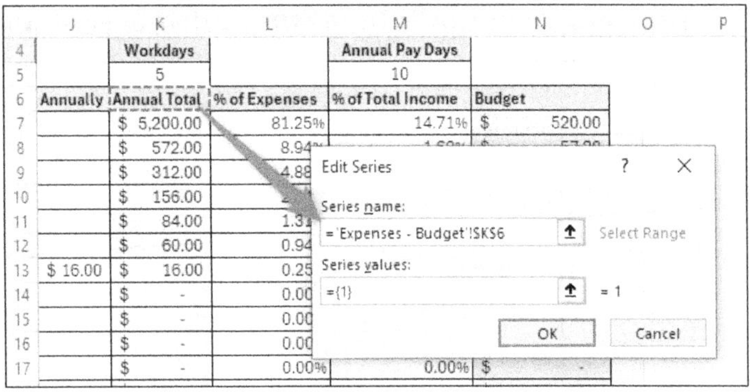

- Now click in the *Series Values* box, select the text in it, and delete it so the box is blank. Once done, click in cell **K7** and drag all the way down to **K34**. This will select the value range for the chart. The chart should now change and display several slices with a number and a percentage, we will fix the labels now, go ahead and click OK to close the window and you will be returned to the Select Data Series window, notice the chart is now displaying.

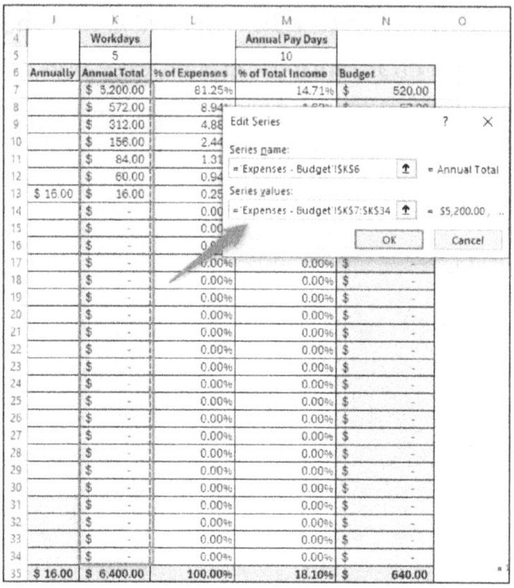

- You are back in the Select Data Series window, you will notice the left pane has Annual Total and the right pane has a series of numbers, 1 to 28.

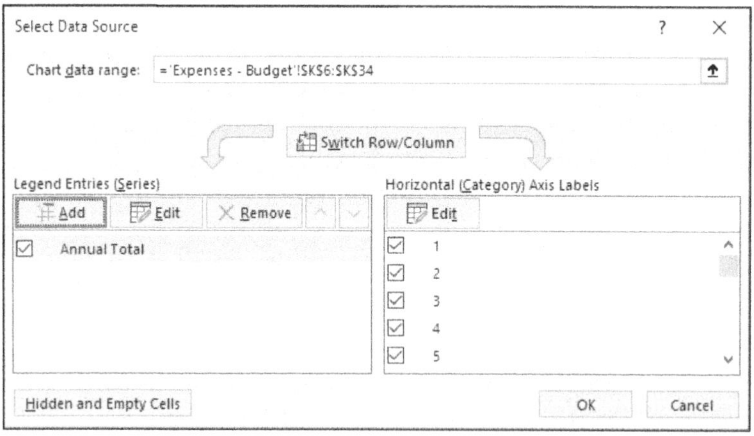

- The numbers are the default labels, we need to tell Excel what to use as labels, do the following.
  - If Column B is not visible, use the slider to get it in view
  - If you do not have Expense labels in place yet, add some now

- In the right pane, click **Edit**, a single input box will open, **Axis label range.**
- Click in Axis label range and then click in cell **A8** and drag all the way down to **A35** and let go the button, the range will be displayed in the box and the chart will change to show the labels, labels are now set, click **OK**

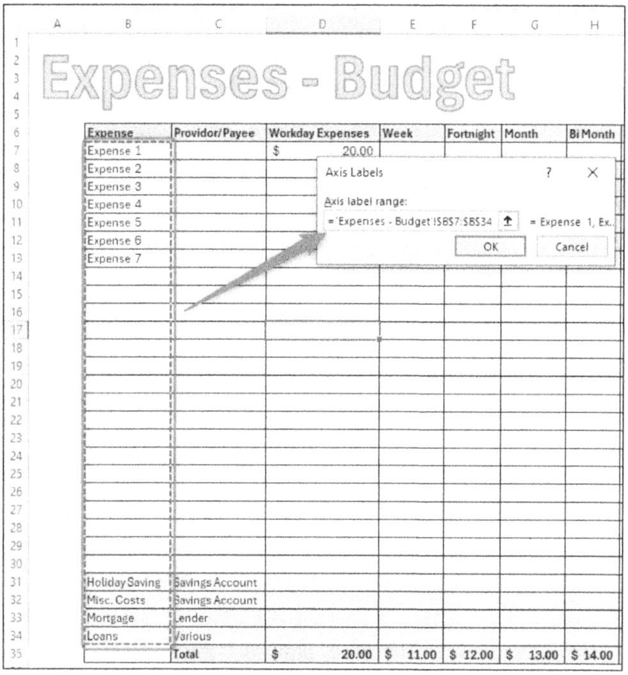

- The window now shows your labels, click OK to close the window
- Your chart is finished in that it will now display the data, but we need a few things to make it look better such as
    - Remove the legend, labels are easier
        - Click on the legend and press Delete
    - Display labels and value with the pie slices
        - Click on a pie slice
        - Right click and select **Format Data Labels**
          The right panel will open with your options
        - Select the following
            - Category Name

- Value
- Outside End

There are many options to format your chart, way too many to get into here. Save your work and play around with the various formatting options until you have it just how you want it.

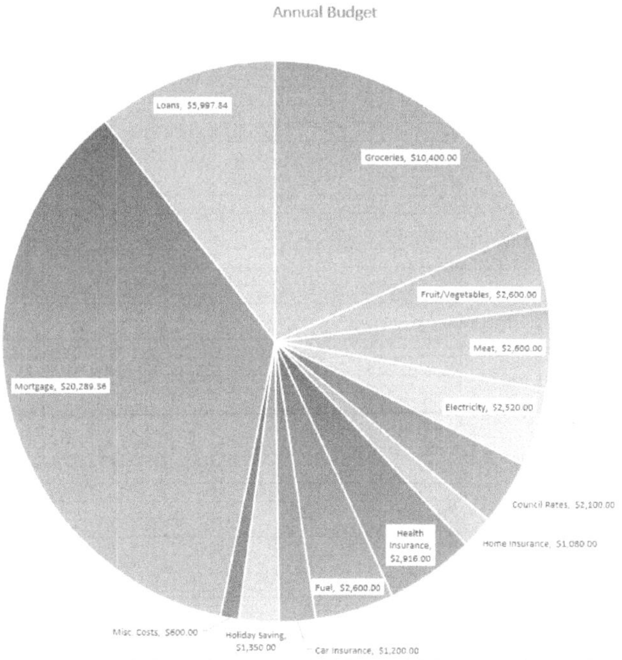

As you change the labels and values in the data input area of the worksheet, the chart will update dynamically.

> **Note**: We created this chart using quite a manual process so we could learn the different components of the chart. When we create the Dashboard worksheet, we will create another chart in a much simpler process.

Creating the pie chart - LibreOffice Calc

Follow these steps.

- Resize your screen so you can see the data area as well as a good space to the right to add your chart, use the magnification tool in the bottom/right of the screen
- Select all cells from **K7** to **K34**
- Open Chart Wizard **Insert -> Chart**
  The Chart Wizard will open on step 1. Chart Type. Select **Pie** and leave it on the first option
- Select **2. Data Range**, if you had selected K7:K34 then this range will be in the *Data range* box Data series in Columns will be selected, if so, move to next step. If not enter the following in the **Data range** box and select **Data series in columns**

  $'Expenses - Budget'.$K$7:$K$34

- Select **3. Data Series**, You should see

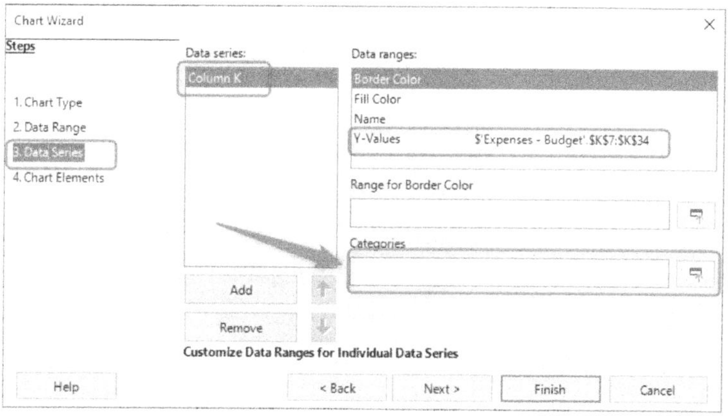

We now want to set the Categories (Labels), we will get these from **B7:B34**, notice these line up with the values in K.

- Click the icon to the right of the *Categories* box, s **Select Range for Categories Are** box pops up, to set the rang, Click and Hold **B7** and drag down to **B34**, the range will be inserted for you, the range is...if you want to manually enter it

$'Expenses - Budget'.$B$7:$B$34

- Select **4. Chart Elements**, Enter the title **Annual Total** you can enter a subtitle if you want but not necessary, Clear the **Display Legend** tick box.
- Click **Finish.** Then chart will be displayed, move it to where you want it, resize it.
- *Right Click* on the chart, select the option **Insert Data Labels**, immediately the chart will display $ value as labels.
- *Right Click* on the chart again, this time select **Format Data Labels**, the format window will open.
- *Click* on the **Data Labels** tab, **Value as number** will be checked, check **Category** as well and click **OK.** This will display the Expense and Value as the labels.

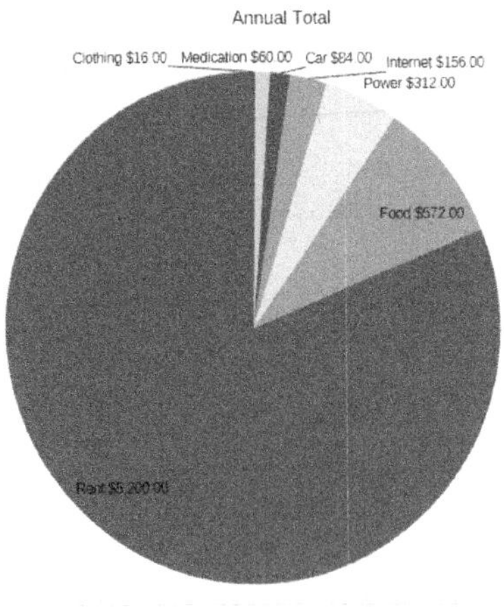

There are many options to format your chart, way too many to get into here. Save your work and play around with the various formatting options until you have it just how you want it.

Putting in real data

Now it is time to enter the real data into the Expenditure-Budget worksheet. Please take your time and input all the necessary information, including your daily coffee, lunch, snacks when at work, and any other expenses.

Keep in mind that if you have more items to enter than the currently available rows permit, please limit your entries to the existing rows for now. This will ensure that the cell references used throughout the remainder of the workbook remain consistent.

Towards the end of the course, in the section *Modifying and Enhancing Worksheets,* we will cover the topic of inserting rows and how to add formulas for the new rows. We will also discuss which parts of Excel automatically adjust when new rows are added. At that point, you can make room and add more items as needed

Conclusion

In this chapter, you have developed the **Expenses - Budget** worksheet, an essential tool for tracking and managing your personal or household finances. By listing and categorizing your expenses, you can ensure that your financial goals are realistic and aligned with your income. You have also learned how to break down expenses by payment frequency, calculate their annual impact, and assess how much of your total income each expense consumes. In addition, the pie chart offers a visual representation of your expenses, making it easier to see where your money is going. This worksheet is not only useful for managing daily costs but also serves as a vital tool for making long-term financial decisions. You now have the skills to format, secure, and calculate important financial data, ensuring that your budgeting is clear, accurate, and adaptable.

Quiz

1. **What is the purpose of the Expenses - Budget worksheet?**
   a) To track income streams.
   b) To organize and manage all your expenses based on payment frequency.
   c) To format cells with colors and borders.
   d) To create a pie chart.

2. **What formula is used in the Annual Total column to calculate yearly expenses based on different payment frequencies?**
   a) =SUM(D7:J7)
   b) =(D7*(52*$K$5)) + (E7*52) + (F7*26) + (G7*12) + (H7*6) + (I7*4) + J7
   c) =SUM(K7/N7)
   d) =K7/$K$35

3. **How does the "Percentage of Total Income" formula reference another worksheet?**
   a) By using a reference to the same worksheet.
   b) By using conditional formatting.
   c) By referencing a locked cell from the **Income** worksheet.
   d) By using the SUM function.

4. **What does Conditional Formatting allow you to do in the Expenses - Budget worksheet?**
   a) Automatically calculate totals.
   b) Highlight cells based on specific criteria, such as percentages over 100% or remaining cash below zero.
   c) Format cells based on payment frequencies.
   d) Apply pie charts to budget categories.

Quiz Answers

1. b) To organize and manage all your expenses based on payment frequency.
2. b) =(D7*(52*$K$5)) + (E7*52) + (F7*26) + (G7*12) + (H7*6) + (I7*4) + J7
3. c) By referencing a locked cell from the **Income** worksheet.
4. b) Highlight cells based on specific criteria, such as percentages over 100% or remaining cash below zero.

Self-Assessment

By the end of this chapter, you should be able to:

- Organize and list expenses in the worksheet by category and frequency.
- Apply and copy formulas to calculate totals, percentages, and budgeted amounts.
- Format cells with colors, borders, and protection to enhance usability and security.
- Use Conditional Formatting to highlight critical budget values.
- Visualize your expenses with a dynamic pie chart.

Self-Check Questions:

1. Have you entered all your expenses in the worksheet, and does the Annual Total column calculate correctly for all entries?
    - (Yes/No)
2. Can you interpret the percentages in the "Percentage of Total Income" column and ensure they reflect accurate proportions of your expenses?
    - (Yes/No)

3. Have you tested the Conditional Formatting feature to ensure it highlights cells when certain thresholds are exceeded (e.g., over 100% for total expenses)?
    - (Yes/No)

WS 4 - Expenses – Actuals

Worksheet and Heading

If you have not yet created the **Expenses – Actuals** worksheet and heading please add the worksheet and heading now before proceeding.

Integrating Expenses and Budget Data into the Expense-Actuals Worksheet

Because we have already set out our expenses and budget in the *Expenses – Budget* worksheet, we can use this data for the *Expenses-Actuals* worksheet by setting ranges and inserting them here. This will allow us to seamlessly integrate existing information, ensuring consistency and accuracy in our financial planning. We can then add additional columns, formulas, and formatting as required to complete the worksheet. Let us get started by creating the two ranges we need.

Begin by clicking the *Expenses – Budget* tab to move focus to the budget worksheet

Expenses

We want to include the current headings for Expense and Provider/Payee for all expenses, so our target range is **B6:C34**, we are including the headings in this range.

- Select range **B6:C34**
- *Excel*, Right Click anywhere in the select and select **Define Name**
- *LibreOffice Calc,* **Data -> Define Name**
- Enter **Expenses** in Name box
- Leave *Scope* as *Workbook for Excel* or *Document (Global) for LibreOffice Calc*
- *Excel only*, add a *Comment* so we can see what it is for in future development (it is unlikely you will remember), such as *"Expense and Provider/Payee details for all expenses"*
- Click **OK** or **Add**

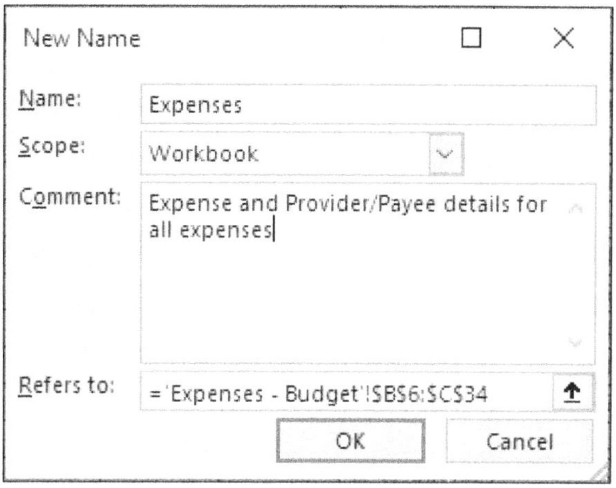

Budget

We want to include the current Budget amount, so our target range is **N6:N34**

Follow the same steps as for Expenses, the following are the details you need

- Range - **N6:N34**
- Name - **Budget**
- Leave *Scope* as default
- Excel, add a *Comment*, such as *"Budgeted amounts for each expense category"*
- Click **OK** or **Add**

Check both ranges are set properly by clicking anywhere in the worksheet and then select the ranges from the dropdown above the A column, as you select them, the range should be highlighted.

> **Note for LibreOffice Users**
> In Excel, these named ranges are used directly to mirror the data into the Expenses – Actuals worksheet.
> LibreOffice Calc doesn't support that method, so we'll link the cells manually instead. Still, defining these ranges is great practice — and you may use them in your own workbooks later.

By defining these named ranges for Expenses and Budget, we can easily reference and include this data in other worksheets. Let's do that now.

Add Budget to Actuals worksheet - Excel

Now we will add them to the *Expenses – Actuals* worksheet.

Begin by clicking the *Expenses – Actuals* tab to move focus to the worksheet.

Expenses

Now we have the *named ranges* setup we can include them in the *Expenses – Actuals* worksheet, do the following.

There are two ways to include a named range on the worksheet, we are inserting two named ranges so we will show both methods.

- Click on the **Expenses – Actuals** worksheet tab to move focus to the worksheet
- Method 1 – for Expenses named range
    - Click in cell **B6**
    - Start by Typing **=expenses**
    - At some point, a small popup will display filtering to objects beginning with what you have typed, **Expenses** should be one of them
    - Double-Click on the **Expenses** in the list, you will see **=Expenses** appear in the cellPress **Enter**, the range values will appear, they are unformatted at this stage

> **You could have continued typing** =expenses and only when you have typed the complete word, pressing Enter would Excel put it in. *Pressing enter early or using the arrow keys to highlight Expenses in the list and pressing enter will not work.*
>
> Also, Ignore the zero's that may be showing where there are blanks in the source data, we will fix them in formatting.

Budget

- Method 2 – for Budget named range
  - Click in cell **D6**
  - Click on the **Formulas** tab on the ribbon, locate the **Defined Names** group
  - Click the arrowhead on option **Use in Formula** to open the list of named ranges
  - Select **Budget**, Excel will put *=Budget* in the cell
  - Press **Enter**, the range will appear
  - Method 1 is easier.

Notice everything is lined up, this is because we carefully selected the ranges, including the column headings. Adjust the column widths so everything is visible, we will now add more column headings. Any changes to these in the **Expenses – Budget** worksheet will automatically be reflected here, try it.

> **Note**: You cannot edit the details in the linked named range, these are for display only, you can of course use the details in formula which we will get to soon.

Add Budget to Actuals worksheet – LibreOffice Calc

LibreOffice Calc does not support Excel-style array formulas like {=Expenses}. Instead, you can manually link each row to ensure changes in the Budget sheet are always shown in Actuals.

1. Go to the **Expenses – Actuals** sheet.
2. In cell **B6**, type:
   ='Expenses - Budget'.B6
3. Press Enter.
4. Use the **fill handle** to drag the formula down to B34.
5. Repeat for columns **C** and **D**, using the same process:
   - C6 → *='Expenses - Budget'.C6*
   - D6 → *='Expenses - Budget'.**N6*** NOTE: This is referring the N6 not D6

These cells will now always display the *Category, Provider and Budget* values from the Budget sheet — even if you edit them later.

Column headings

We need to add three more columns, start with the headings in the following cells

- **E6,** *Actual*
    - The amount actually spent
- **F6**, *Variance*
    - The difference between the budgeted amount and the actual amount.
- **G6**, *Comment*
    - Additional notes or explanations related to the expense or variance.

That completes the heading, let us now set up the formula

Formula

The Variance column has the only formula in the worksheet, let us get that in now

- Click in cell **F7**
- Type in **=ROUND(D7-E7,2)**
    - This formula calculates the variance by subtracting the actual amount (E6) from the budgeted amount (D6) and then rounds the result to two decimal places.
- Copy **F7** to range **F8:F34**

And that is all the formula for the worksheet, test it by entering values in the Actuals column, if you enter the following when compared to the budget amount

- Lower amount (you spent under budget, great)
    - Variance will be a positive value showing the amount saved
- Same amount (on budget)
    - Variance will be zero

- Higher amount (you went over budget)
  - Variance will be a negative value showing how much over budget you went

Now we have done the formula, we will move on to formatting the sheet

Formatting

You can set your formatting how you like later, use the colors below for now

Standard

Set the formats on the following cell ranges

- Colors and styles
  - **B6:G6**, Gray fill, bold, centered
  - **B7:C34**, Text, Light Blue fill
  - **D7:D34**, Accounting, Lighter Blue fill
  - **E7:E34**, Accounting, Light Yellow (input)
  - **F7:F34**, Accounting, leave as no fill
  - **G7:G34**, Text, Light Yellow (input)
- Removing zeros in columns B and C
  - Select **B7:C34**
  - Right-click and choose **Format Cells**.
  - Go to the **Number** tab, then select **Custom**.
  - In the **Type** field, enter the following custom format:
    - ;;;@ (3 semi-colons and an ampersand)

> **Note:** The custom format ;;;@ works by specifying how to display numbers:
>
> First semicolon (;): Skips formatting for positive numbers.
>
> Second semicolon: Skips formatting for negative numbers.
>
> Third semicolon: Skips formatting for zero values, leaving them blank.
>
> @: Displays text as-is.
>
> This format hides any numbers (including zeros) and only displays text. If you need to display a number, spell it.

- Borders (using the borders dropdown in ribbons Home/Fonts)

- **B6:G34**, All Borders
- **B6:G34**, Thick Outside Border (Excel)
- **B6:G6**, Thick Outside Border (Excel)

That completes the standard formatting for the worksheet.

> **Note**: Accounting format put the $ sign to the left and the values to the right, any zero value will display a hyphen.

Conditional

The Variance column shows how you are tracking the budget, we want an easy way of seeing what is on or under budget, but more importantly, what is over budget. We can use conditional formatting to change the font color, if the value is zero or positive then we can display the value in green font, if the value is negative, we can display in red font. Let us set the conditional formatting, we will require two tests

- Set On or Under Budget formatting (Green)
  - Click in cell **F7**
  - **Excel**
    - On the ribbon, click on **Home/Styles/Conditional Formatting**
    - Select **New Rule**, *New Formatting Rule* window will popup
    - Select the second option, **Format only cells that contain**, the bottom section of window will change
    - Click on dropdown where it shows *between* and select **Greater than or Equal to**, the input boxes to the right should change to a single box
    - Enter a zero (0) in the box
    - Click the **Format** button, the *Format Cells* window will popup
    - Click on **Font** tab
    - The Color dropdown will say Automatic at the moment, click on it to open the color selections

        - Select a darker shade of Green, it will be easier to read, check the preview provided
        - When you have the perfect shade of Green selected, click **OK** and then **OK**. The window will close and if the value in **F7** is 0 or more, it will change to Green
    - **LibreOffice Calc**
        - On the ribbon, click on **Home/Conditional/Manage**
        - Select **Add**, New *Conditional Formatting for X##* window will popup
        - Top 3 boxes, enter ***Cell Value***, ***is greater than or equal to***, ***0*** ← *zero*
        - Apply Style = ***Good***
- Set Over Budget formatting (Red)
    - Click in cell **F7**
    - **Excel**
        - On the ribbon, click on **Home/Styles/Conditional Formatting**
        - Select **New Rule**, *New Formatting Rule* window will popup
        - Select the second option, **Format only cells that contain**, the bottom section of window will change
        - Click on dropdown where it shows *between* and select **less than**, the input boxes to the right should change to a single box
        - Enter a zero (0) in the box
        - Click **Format** button, the *Format Cells* window will pop up
        - Click on **Font** tab
        - The Color dropdown will say Automatic at the moment, click on it to open the color selections
        - Select a darker shade of Red, it will be easier to read, check the preview provided
        - When you have the perfect shade of Red selected, click **OK** and then **OK**. The window will close and if the value in **F7** less than 0, it will change to Red
    - **LibreOffice Calc**
        - On the ribbon, click on **Home/Conditional/Manage**

- Select **Add**, New *Conditional Formatting for X##* window will popup
- Top 3 boxes, enter ***Cell Value***, is ***less than***, ***0*** *←zero*
- Apply Style = ***Bad***

○

Testing the conditional formatting

Test it by entering values in **E7** that are less than, equal to and greater than the value in **D7**, the text color should change accordingly.

Now the conditional formatting is set, copy the **F7** to the remainder of the column, **F8:F34** using the drag square in bottom/right corner of selection box, this will copy the formula and all formatting.

You will need to redo the thick border around the entire block, F34 will lose its bottom border.

Finish formatting

Now you can finish of the formatting and protection if not already done

- **D7:D34**, Light Blue background, Accounting, Cell Protection **on**
- **E7:E34**, Yellow background, Accounting, Cell Protection **off**
- **F7:F34**, Accounting, Cell Protection **on**
- **G7:G34**, Yellow background, Text, Cell Protection **off**

Keeping records

We could have included the Actual, Variance, and Comment columns in the Budget worksheet, but we have other plans that require them to be in their own worksheet. At the end of every budgeting period, after you have filled in the Actuals and Comments, you will want to archive the worksheet so you can reference it later. You will not need everything displayed in the Budget sheet for the archive, just the main information. Later in the course, we will set up an easy-to-use archiving feature to facilitate this process.

Conclusion

In this chapter, you successfully created the **Expenses - Actuals** worksheet, allowing you to track actual expenses and compare them to your budgeted amounts. By integrating named ranges from the **Expenses - Budget** worksheet, you ensured consistency in your financial data and avoided duplication of effort. You also added conditional formatting to quickly highlight variances, making it easier to see whether you're over or under budget.

Key skills you practiced:

- Using named ranges to integrate data between worksheets.
- Applying formulas to calculate variances.
- Formatting worksheets with custom formats, including hiding zeros and using conditional formatting for variance analysis.
- Structuring your data to make it easily referenceable in future reports and archives.

This chapter equips you with the tools to efficiently track your spending and ensure your budget stays on target.

Quiz

1. **What does the formula =ROUND(D7-E7, 2) do in the Expenses - Actuals worksheet?**
    - a) Adds the actual expense to the budgeted amount.
    - b) Subtracts the actual expense from the budgeted amount and rounds the result to two decimal places.
    - c) Multiplies the budgeted amount by the actual expense.
    - d) Divides the actual expense by the budgeted amount.

2. **How can you hide zeros in a cell range using a custom format?**
    - a) Set the cell format to Accounting.
    - b) Apply the custom format ;;;@.
    - c) Use conditional formatting to hide zeros.
    - d) Enter "0" in the custom format field.

3. **What type of values are highlighted in red by conditional formatting in the Variance column?**
    - a) Values greater than or equal to zero.
    - b) Negative values.
    - c) Zero values.
    - d) Text values.

4. **What is the benefit of using named ranges like "Expenses" and "Budget" across worksheets?**
    - a) It automatically creates links between worksheets.
    - b) It allows easier reference and ensures consistent data.
    - c) It prevents the need for data validation.
    - d) It removes formatting restrictions.

Quiz Answers

1. b) Subtracts the actual expense from the budgeted amount and rounds the result to two decimal places.
2. b) Apply the custom format ;;;@.
3. b) Negative values.
4. b) It allows easier reference and ensures consistent data.

Self-Assessment

1. **Main Learning Points:**
    - You learned how to create and apply **named ranges** for efficient cross-worksheet referencing.
    - You applied **conditional formatting** to visually highlight budget variances, improving worksheet usability.
    - You practiced adding formulas like ROUND to calculate variances and prevent rounding errors.
    - You explored methods to customize and format worksheets, including how to hide zero values.
2. **Self-Check Questions:**
    - Can you explain how the named range "Expenses" improves data consistency between worksheets?
    - How would you apply conditional formatting to highlight positive variances in green and negative variances in red in another context?
    - How does the formula =ROUND(D7-E7, 2) help ensure your variance calculations are accurate?

WS 5 - Loans

Many individuals take out Loans to finance significant purchases such as cars, boats, furniture, and more, which may be financially unattainable otherwise. In this next worksheet, we will focus on listing your Loans and their associated repayment amounts. This will allow you to gain a comprehensive understanding of all your current loans, excluding your mortgage.

We will also establish a link between the Loans worksheet and the Budget worksheet. This connection will enable you to incorporate your Loan repayments into your overall budget, ensuring a holistic view of your financial situation. By integrating this information, you will have a more accurate representation of your expenses and can make informed decisions regarding your budgeting and loan management. Let us proceed with creating the Loans worksheet and establishing the necessary links to the Budget worksheet.

Worksheet and heading

If you have not already created the **Loans** worksheet and heading, please create them now.
IF you have, click the **Loans** tab to activate the worksheet.

Column Headings

The columns will be laid out like the budget worksheet in that you will have two columns for Loan and creditor, 6 columns for payment frequency and one column for total.

Let us get the headings in place.

- Headings will go in row 6, cells B to I, please enter the following.
  - B6, **Purpose of Loan**
    - The purpose of the Loan, i.e., Car, Boat.
  - C6, **Week**
    - If repayments are weekly, enter the amount paid here.
  - D6, **Fortnight**

        - If repayments are fortnightly (every other week), enter the amount paid here.
    - E6, **Month**
        - If repayments are monthly, enter the amount paid here.
    - F6, **Bi-Monthly**
        - If repayments are made every two months, enter the amount paid here.
    - G6, **Quarterly**
        - If repayments are quarterly, enter the amount paid here.
    - H6, **Annually**
        - If repayments are annually, enter the amount paid here.
    - I6, **Annualized Total**
        - Total paid in one year

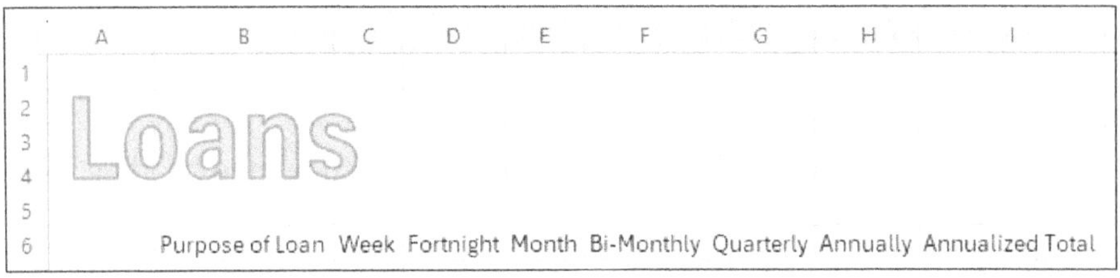

Formula for columns M, N and O

The formula in these three columns will provide you with the information you need to get a good overview of the Loans you currently service. Let us begin entering the formula.

- **Column I**, Annualized payments
  This represents the total amount you will pay each year for the loan. It uses a formula to calculate the amounts entered for the loan repayments.
    - The formula for cell **I7** is = **(C7*52) + (D7*26) + (E7*12) + (F7*6) + (G7*4) + H7**
      You have seen this in the other worksheets, the formula is adding the weekly, fortnightly, monthly, etc. columns to achieve the annual

amount.

Enter this formula into cell **I7**

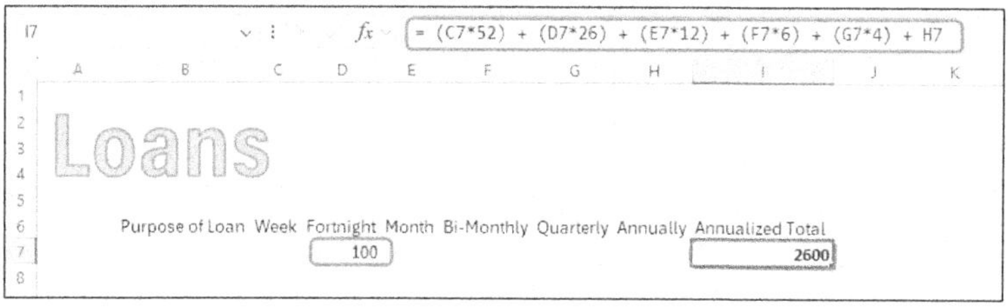

Selecting cell **I7**, copy the formula to cells **I8:I24** by using the drag/copy method with

the small square on the bottom/right of the selection

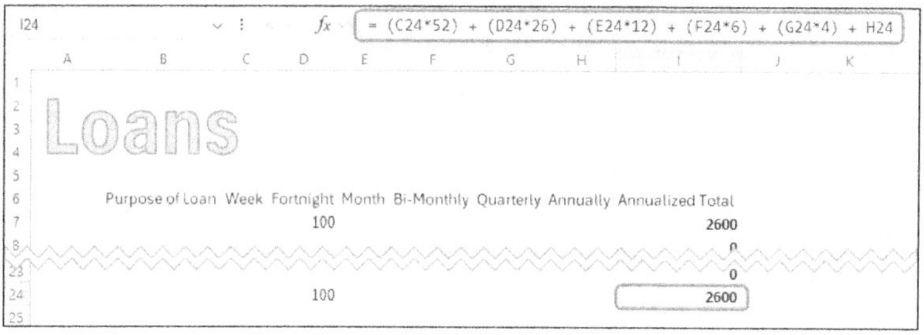

You can test by adding values into other rows, the total for column I should change.

- You are finished with Column **I**.

Totals Row

The totals row, as with the other work sheets, is simply a sum of the values in the column, letting us do all the totals in one move.

- Add the label **Totals** in **B25**
- Add a numeric value in each cell from **C7:CH**
- Select the entire range from **C7:I25**, yes, include the totals row
- Now click the **AutoSum** option in the ribbons **Home/Editing**

- Excel will set the formula to sum the row values in row 25 for all the columns selected

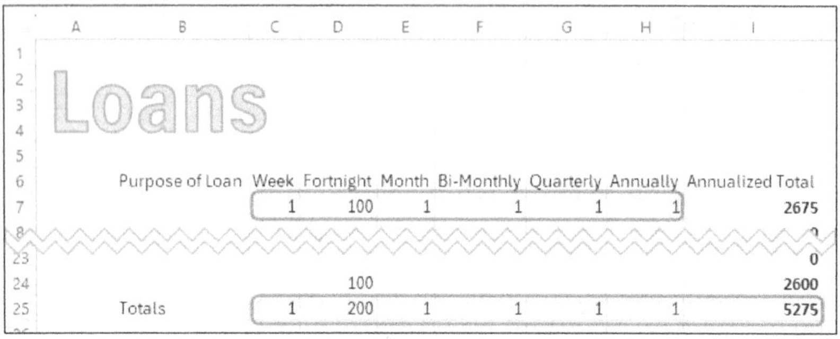

Evaluating the worksheet

Enter some values into the input cells of the Loans worksheet and check the formulas are working correctly, remember, values such as 1, 10, 100, etc. are easier to do the math in your head.

When you are happy all the formula and totals are working, we can now link the Loans worksheet to the budget. We will be linking cell **I25** to the budget, I25 is the total annual repayments for all Loans, and we need this value in the budget, let us do it.

Link to another worksheet

We will format it soon, for now, the ability to link to cells from other worksheets is a powerful tool for both laying out the worksheets in a neat and logical manner and for bringing many pieces of information together. The linked values can be used for display or within formula, in this exercise we will be linking cell I25 from the Loans worksheet into a formula in the **Expenses - Budget** worksheet. Let us do this.

- Click on the **Expenses - Budget** worksheet tab to activate the worksheet.
- Click in cell **E34**, this is the weekly value for the Loans line. We could use any of the period cells, however weekly is a good base period. If you do

prefer to use another, i.e., Month for example, use it and adjust the formula appropriately.

- Type = in the cell to indicate we are starting a formula
- While E34 has focus and you are now in *formula editing mode* because you entered the =, you can now, using the mouse, click on the **Loans** tab Look in the formula bar after Loans becomes visible, you will see the formula reads **=Loans!** This is referring to the cell we are editing in the budget sheet.
- Click cell **I25**, notice the formula above now reads **=Loans!I25** or **=$Loans.I25**
- Press **Enter**; you will be taken back to the Budget worksheet. Notice
    - the value of cell **E34** is the same as I25 on Loans.
    - The annual amount in column J is exceptionally large at this point because we just put an annual amount in a weekly column, the Pie chart also changed and shows a large loan. These will be adjusted in the next step.
- Now we need to change the value to a weekly value, double click cell E34 and edit the formula by putting **/52** after it (or other value if you select another period), the formula will now be **=Loans!I25/52** or **=$Loans.I25/52**

- This will reduce the amount to the weekly value, the total and the Pie Chart will also adjust.

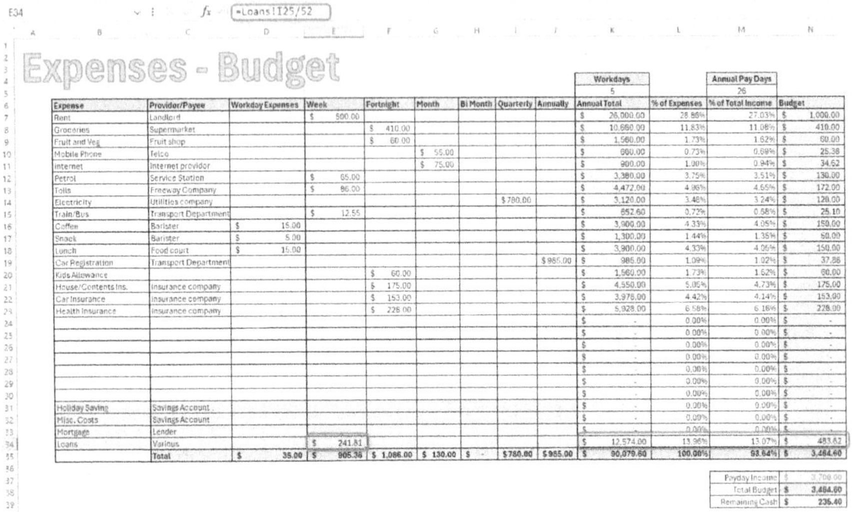

E34 fx =Loans!I25/52

Expenses - Budget

									Workdays		Annual Pay Days	
									5		26	
Expense	Provider/Payee	Workday Expenses	Week	Fortnight	Month	Bi Month	Quarterly	Annually	Annual Total	% of Expenses	% of Total Income	Budget
Rent	Landlord		$ 500.00						$ 26,000.00	28.86%	27.03%	$ 1,000.00
Groceries	Supermarket			$ 410.00					$ 10,660.00	11.83%	11.08%	$ 410.00
Fruit and Veg	Fruit shop			$ 60.00					$ 1,560.00	1.73%	1.62%	$ 60.00
Mobile Phone	Telco				$ 55.00				$ 660.00	0.73%	0.69%	$ 25.38
internet	Internet providor				$ 75.00				$ 900.00	1.00%	0.94%	$ 34.62
Petrol	Service Station		$ 65.00						$ 3,380.00	3.75%	3.51%	$ 130.00
Tolls	Freeway Company		$ 86.00						$ 4,472.00	4.96%	4.65%	$ 172.00
Electricity	Utilities company						$ 780.00		$ 3,120.00	3.46%	3.24%	$ 120.00
Train/Bus	Transport Department		$ 12.55						$ 652.60	0.72%	0.68%	$ 25.10
Coffee	Barister	$ 15.00							$ 3,900.00	4.33%	4.05%	$ 150.00
Snack	Barister	$ 5.00							$ 1,300.00	1.44%	1.35%	$ 50.00
Lunch	Food court	$ 15.00							$ 3,900.00	4.33%	4.05%	$ 150.00
Car Registration	Transport Department							$ 985.00	$ 985.00	1.09%	1.02%	$ 37.88
Kids Allowance				$ 60.00					$ 1,560.00	1.73%	1.62%	$ 60.00
House/Contents Ins.	Insurance company			$ 175.00					$ 4,550.00	5.05%	4.73%	$ 175.00
Car Insurance	Insurance company			$ 153.00					$ 3,978.00	4.42%	4.14%	$ 153.00
Health Insurance	Insurance company			$ 228.00					$ 5,928.00	6.58%	6.16%	$ 228.00
									$ -	0.00%	0.00%	$ -
									$ -	0.00%	0.00%	$ -
									$ -	0.00%	0.00%	$ -
									$ -	0.00%	0.00%	$ -
									$ -	0.00%	0.00%	$ -
									$ -	0.00%	0.00%	$ -
									$ -	0.00%	0.00%	$ -
Holiday Saving	Savings Account								$ -	0.00%	0.00%	$ -
Misc. Costs	Savings Account								$ -	0.00%	0.00%	$ -
Mortgage	Lender								$ -	0.00%	0.00%	$ -
Loans	Various		$ 241.81						$ 12,574.00	13.96%	13.07%	$ 483.62
	Total	$ 35.00	$ 905.36	$ 1,086.00	$ 130.00	$ -	$780.00	$985.00	$ 90,079.60	100.00%	93.64%	$ 3,464.60

Payday Income	$ 3,700.00
Total Budget	$ 3,464.60
Remaining Cash	$ 235.40

Congratulations, you just linked loans to your budget, any changes to the Loan information affecting the total will now come through to the budget, change the test values and make sure the loans value changed in the Budget worksheet.

Formatting the cells

The Loans worksheet now needs to be formatted. You have done a lot of formatting so you can go ahead and format the sheet, without instructions.

It should look like this, just stay with the yellow for input cells.

Loans

Purpose of Loan	Week	Fortnight	Month	Bi-Monthly	Quarterly	Annually	Annualized Total
Car Loan		$275.00					**$7,150.00**
Boat Loan			$452.00				**$5,424.00**
							$0.00
							$0.00
							$0.00
							$0.00
							$0.00
							$0.00
							$0.00
							$0.00
							$0.00
							$0.00
							$0.00
							$0.00
							$0.00
							$0.00
							$0.00
							$0.00
Totals	**$0.00**	**$275.00**	**$452.00**	**$0.00**	**$0.00**	**$0.00**	**$12,574.00**

Setting Input cell protection

You can also go ahead an unlock all the input cells now.

Conclusion

In this chapter, you created the **Loans** worksheet to track loan payments and integrate these amounts into your overall budget. By calculating annualized totals for each loan repayment frequency, you gained a clear view of how loan payments impact your financial standing over the year. Additionally, you linked the Loans worksheet to the Budget worksheet, ensuring loan repayments are included in your budgeting calculations. This integrated approach provides a holistic view of expenses and helps in making informed financial decisions.

Quiz:

1. **What is the purpose of the formula in cell I7 on the Loans worksheet?**
   - a) To add up all loan repayment amounts.
   - b) To display the loan balance.
   - c) To calculate the annualized total for loan repayments.
   - d) To show the amount left to pay off the loan.

2. **When linking cell I25 from the Loans worksheet to cell E34 in the Budget worksheet, what additional step is needed to show weekly values?**
   - a) Subtract the amount by 12.
   - b) Divide the value by 52.
   - c) Multiply by 4.
   - d) Leave it as is since it's already weekly.

3. **What is the purpose of linking the Loans worksheet to the Budget worksheet?**
   - a) To add more columns to the Loans worksheet.
   - b) To include loan repayments in the overall budget.
   - c) To create a separate worksheet for each loan.
   - d) To calculate the loan interest rate.

4. **Why is it important to unlock only the input cells on the Loans worksheet?**
   - a) To prevent accidental changes to formulas and structured data.
   - b) To make the worksheet easier to read.
   - c) To apply conditional formatting.
   - d) To increase processing speed.

Quiz Answers

1. c) To calculate the annualized total for loan repayments.
2. b) Divide the value by 52.
3. b) To include loan repayments in the overall budget.
4. a) To prevent accidental changes to formulas and structured data.

Self-Assessment

1. **Main Learning Points:**

    - You set up a **Loans worksheet** to track loan repayments, using columns to specify payment frequencies.
    - You calculated **annualized totals** for loan repayments, giving a clear yearly view of loan expenses.
    - You **linked data between worksheets** to integrate loan repayments into your overall budget, making your financial overview more accurate.
    - You practiced **cell protection** by unlocking only the input cells, ensuring data integrity.

2. **Self-Check Questions:**

    - How does linking loan repayment data from the Loans worksheet to the Budget worksheet help in financial planning?
    - Can you explain the formula used in cell I7 to calculate the annualized total for loan repayments?
    - Why is it necessary to adjust the linked loan amount to a weekly value in the Budget worksheet?

WS 6 – Mortgage

In this chapter, we will be creating the Mortgage worksheet. This worksheet is designed to store details related to any mortgage you may have, enabling you to incorporate these financial details into your overall budget. It is structured to handle multiple mortgages, ensuring you can track all relevant information efficiently. Additionally, the worksheet includes a helper mortgage calculator to assist with various calculations and some text-based information to provide context and guidance.

The Mortgage worksheet serves as a vital tool for managing one of the most significant financial commitments in a budget. By organizing your mortgage details in a structured table, you can easily monitor payments, interest rates, and other essential aspects. This clarity will help you make informed financial decisions and ensure that your budget accurately reflects your mortgage obligations.

Throughout this chapter, we will focus on setting up the layout and structure of the Mortgage worksheet. This will include creating a table for storing mortgage details and incorporating the helper mortgage calculator. As with the previous worksheets, we will start with the layout and add detailed formatting and formulas later in the course.

By the end of this chapter, you will have a comprehensive Mortgage worksheet that seamlessly integrates with your budget, providing a clear and organized way to manage your mortgage-related finances.

Worksheet and Heading

If you have not already created the **Mortgage** worksheet and heading, please create them now.

Column Headings

- **B6**, *Mortgage for*
  Property name, address or another name you want to reference a specific mortgage
- **C6**, *Original Loan Date*
  The original date the loan was taken out

- **D6**, *Original Term (years)*
  The original term of the loan In years
- **E6**, *Remaining Term (years)*
  Calculated, how long is remaining of the mortgage
- Payment frequencies, enter the loan repayment in the specific period
  - **F6**, *Week*
  - **G6**, *Fortnight*
  - **H6**, *Month*
  - **I6**, *Bi-Month*
  - **J6**, *Quarterly*
  - **K6**, *Annually*
- **L6**, *Totals*
  The total annual repayments you will pay

Totals Row

Just one heading in here

- **E25**, *Totals*

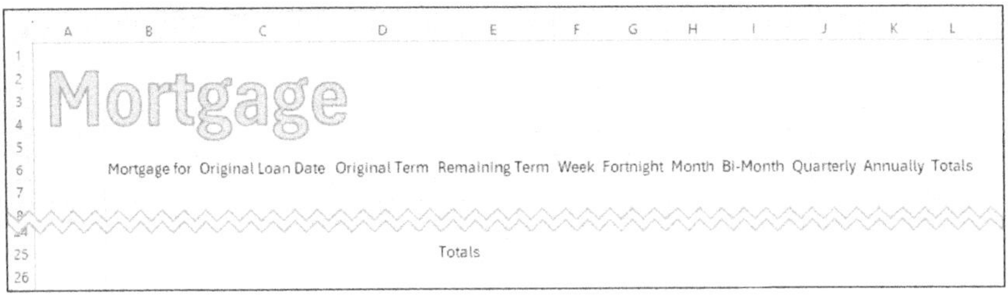

Formula

There are not many formulas in the table, enter them by doing the following

- **C7:C24** will hold dates, because we will be referencing them in formula, we need to ensure that the dates are correctly formatted as dates now otherwise you may get an error with the formula. Format C7:C24 as **Date** now, short date is good ***10/01/2009*** or ***Jan 10, 2009,*** if you prefer, your choice
- **E7**, =MAX(0, D7 - YEARFRAC(C7, TODAY(), 1))

> **Note:** This formula calculates the remaining years on a mortgage. It subtracts the fraction of the year from the current date to the start date (D7 - YEARFRAC(C7, TODAY(), 1)) and ensures the result is not negative by using MAX(0, ...).

- **E8:E24**, drag formula in E7 down to E24

- **L7**, =(F7*52) + (G7*26) + (H7*12) + (I7*6) + (J7*4) + K7

> **Note:** This formula calculates the total annual repayments by multiplying various periodic repayments: weekly (F7) by 52, bi-weekly (G7) by 26, monthly (H7) by 12, bi-monthly (I7) by 6, quarterly (J7) by 4, and annual (K7), then summing them all together.

- **L8:L24**, drag formula in L7 down to L24

- **F25**, =SUM(F7:F24)
- **G25:L25**, drag formula in F25 across to L25

Enter some values in the table and check the total in L25 is correct, see image below for a sample.

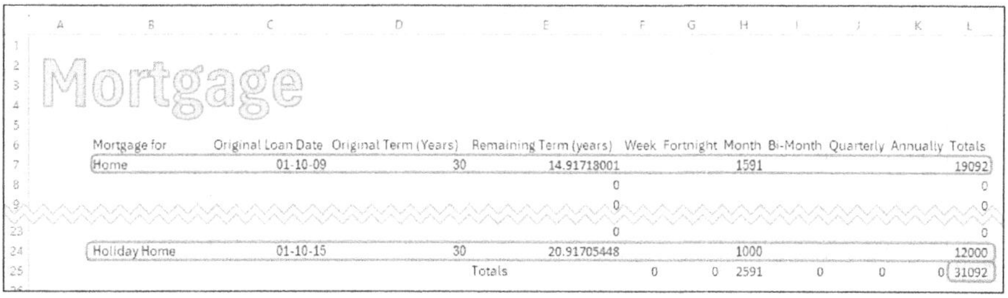

Now you have confirmed the formula are correct, let us move on to formatting.

Formatting

Standard formatting

Format the various ranges within the table by doing the following

- **B6:L6**, Bold, Center, light gray back fill
- **B7:B24**, Text, light yellow back fill (input cells)
- **C7:C24**, Date, light yellow back fill (input cells)

- **D7:E24**, Number, two decimal places, light yellow back fill (input cells)
- **E7:E24**, Number (2 decimal places), no color
- **F7:K24**, Accounting, light yellow back fill (input cells)
- **L7:L24**, Accounting, Light green
- **E25**, Text, no back color, Bold, Centre
- **F25:K25**, Accounting, Light green
- **L25**, Accounting, Bold, any color to make it stand out, size 12 font

Set the borders as shown below and adjust your column widths as appropriate

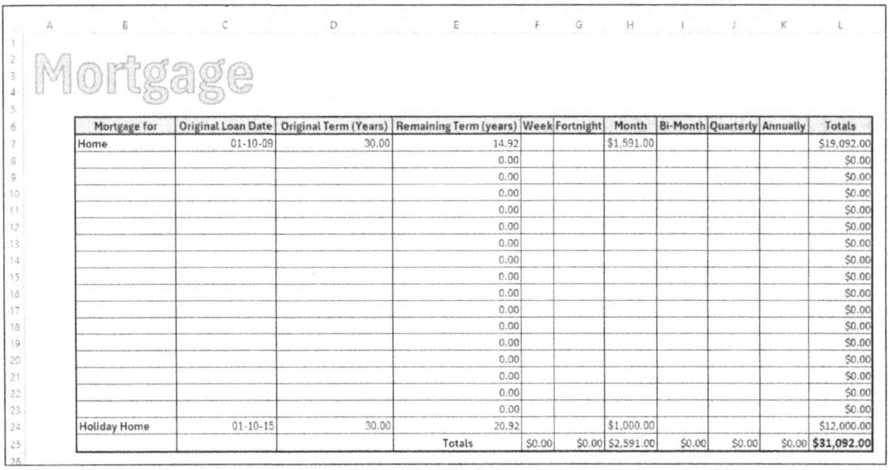

Mortgage for	Original Loan Date	Original Term (Years)	Remaining Term (years)	Week	Fortnight	Month	Bi-Month	Quarterly	Annually	Totals
Home	01-10-09	30.00	14.92			$1,591.00				$19,092.00
			0.00							$0.00
			0.00							$0.00
			0.00							$0.00
			0.00							$0.00
			0.00							$0.00
			0.00							$0.00
			0.00							$0.00
			0.00							$0.00
			0.00							$0.00
			0.00							$0.00
			0.00							$0.00
			0.00							$0.00
			0.00							$0.00
			0.00							$0.00
			0.00							$0.00
			0.00							$0.00
Holiday Home	01-10-15	30.00	20.92			$1,000.00				$12,000.00
			Totals	$0.00	$0.00	$2,591.00	$0.00	$0.00	$0.00	**$31,092.00**

Linking to Budget

Earlier we put a Mortgage line in the Expenses-Budget worksheet on row 33, now we can link it to the mortgage. Enter the following formula

- **E33**, **=Mortgage!L25/52** for Excel or **=$Mortgage.L25/52** for LibreOffice Calc
- This calculates the annual mortgage repayments down to a weekly value. You might need to adjust the formatting for E33.

Helpers

Mortgage Calculator

The Mortgage Calculator is a powerful tool designed to help you understand and manage your mortgage payments effectively. By inputting key details such as the loan amount, annual interest rate, and term (in months), the calculator provides comprehensive insights into your mortgage. It calculates the total number of payments, monthly interest rate, monthly payment, total payment, and total interest over the life of the loan. Additionally, it breaks down your mortgage repayments into weekly, fortnightly, and monthly frequencies, allowing you to plan your budget with precision. This tool is essential for anyone looking to gain a clear picture of their mortgage commitments and financial planning.

> **Disclaimer**: Please note that the calculations provided by this Mortgage Calculator are intended for general informational purposes only and should be accurate within a few dollars of your financial institution who use precise dates and may include additional fees, which could affect the actual repayment amounts. For exact figures and advice tailored to your specific situation, please consult with your financial institution.

	M	N	O	
5				
6		Mortgage Calculator		
7		Loan Amount	$	231,000.00
8		Interest Rate (annual)		7.84%
9		Term (months)		360
10				
11		Total Payments		360
12		Monthly Interest		0.6533%
13		Monthly Payment	$	1,669.30
14		Total Payments	$	600,948.70
15		Total Interest	$	369,948.70
16				
17		Mortgage Repayment - Frequency		
18		Week	$	417.33
19		Fortnight	$	834.65
20		Month	$	1,669.30
21				

To create the Mortgage Calculator, do the following

Labels

Start by entering the labels

- **N6**, *Mortgage calculator*
    - Merge and Centre **N6:O6** and adjust column widths

- **N7**, *Loan Amount*
- **N8**, *Interest Rate (annual)*
- **N9**, *Term (months)*
- **N10,** leave blank
- **N11**, *Total Payments*
- **N12**, *Monthly Interest*
- **N13**, *Monthly Payment*
- **N14**, *Total Payments*
- **N15**, *Total Interest*
- **N16,** leave blank
- **N17**, *Mortgage Repayment - Frequency*
    - Merge and Centre **N17:O17**
- **N18**, *Week*
- **N19**, *Fortnight*
- **N20**, *Month*

Formula

Now enter the formula

- **O11**, =O9

  This is the term in months, if you prefer to use years, change the label in N9 to *Term (Years)* and change this formula to be **=O9*12** to calculate the months and total payments
- **O12**, =(O8/12) the PMT function requires the interest to be monthly.

  This breaks the annual interest rate down to a monthly rate

- **O13**, =IFERROR(PMT(O12, O11, -O7),0)

  This amortization formula calculates the monthly mortgage payment. Here is a breakdown of how it works:

  - **PMT(O12, O11, -O7)**: This is the PMT function, which calculates the payment for a loan based on constant payments and a constant interest rate.
    - **O12**: The monthly interest rate.
    - **O11**: The total number of payments (loan term in months).
    - **-O7**: The loan amount (entered as a negative value to indicate an outflow of money).

- **IFERROR(..., 0)**: This function handles errors in the PMT calculation. If an error occurs, it returns 0 instead of an error message.

So, the formula =IFERROR(PMT(O12, O11, -O7), 0) calculates the monthly mortgage payment based on the provided interest rate, number of payments, and loan amount. If there is an error in the calculation, it returns 0.

- **O14**, =O13*O11
  Multiplies the repayment amount by the number of payments to calculate the total repayments
- **O15**, =O14-O7
  Subtracts the loan amount from total repayments to find the total interest that will be paid
- **O18**, =O13/4
  Calculates the weekly repayment amount, divides monthly by 4 to get weekly, this way you will fully meet the monthly repayment and over the course of a year, you will make one extra month payment.
- **O19**, =O13/2
  Calculates the fortnightly repayment amount, divided monthly by 2 to get fortnightly, this way you will fully meet the monthly repayment and over the course of a year, you will make one extra month payment.
- **O20**, =O13
  The monthly repayment

Formatting

Formatting is basic, do the following

- Accounting
  - **O7**
  - **O13:O15**
  - **O18:O20**
- Percentage
  - **O8**, set to 2 decimal places
  - **O12**, set to 4 decimal places
- Number
  - **O9**, no decimals places
  - **O11**, no decimals places
- Input Cells

    - **O7:O9**, set to light yellow back fill to indicate input, remove cell protection
- Borders
    - **N6:O20**, Set all border
- Headings
    - **N6:O6** and **N17:O17**, Bold, light gray background

Informational text

There are two informational texts on this worksheet, they are there for your information only.

You can leave them out, but they may help you remember these details later. You can place them anywhere you like and format them how you like. Below are the images of these texts.

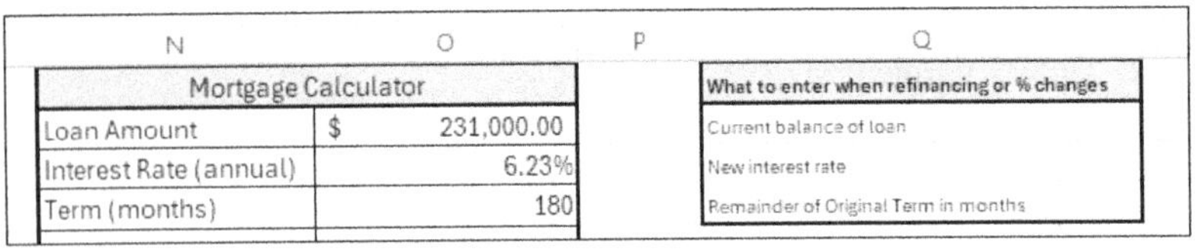

N	O	P	Q
Mortgage Calculator			What to enter when refinancing or % changes
Loan Amount	$ 231,000.00		Current balance of loan
Interest Rate (annual)	6.23%		New interest rate
Term (months)	180		Remainder of Original Term in months

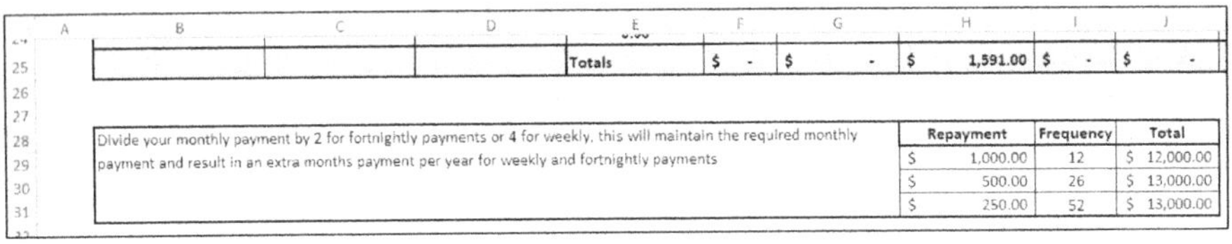

	A	B	C	D	E	F	G	H	I	J
25					Totals	$ -	$ -	$ 1,591.00	$ -	$ -
26										
27										
28		Divide your monthly payment by 2 for fortnightly payments or 4 for weekly, this will maintain the required monthly payment and result in an extra months payment per year for weekly and fortnightly payments						Repayment	Frequency	Total
29								$ 1,000.00	12	$ 12,000.00
30								$ 500.00	26	$ 13,000.00
31								$ 250.00	52	$ 13,000.00

Security

As with other sheets, set the security for all input cells to **unlocked**

Conclusion

In this chapter, you created the **Mortgage** worksheet, an essential tool for managing mortgage payments within your budget. By organizing your mortgage details—including payment amounts, remaining terms, and repayment frequency—you can keep track of one of the most significant financial commitments in your budget. You also created a **mortgage calculator** to help with understanding monthly, weekly, and fortnightly mortgage payments and how they fit into your budget. Finally, you linked the Mortgage worksheet to the Budget worksheet, allowing for a seamless integration of your mortgage into your overall financial overview.

Quiz

1. **What is the purpose of the formula in cell E7 on the Mortgage worksheet?**
   - a) To show the monthly payment amount.
   - b) To calculate the remaining term on the mortgage in years.
   - c) To add up all mortgage payments.
   - d) To display the interest rate.

2. **Which formula calculates the total annual mortgage payments in cell L7?**
   - a) =SUM(F7:K7)
   - b) =(F7*52) + (G7*26) + (H7*12) + (I7*6) + (J7*4) + K7
   - c) =PMT(O12, O11, -O7)
   - d) =O13/12

3. **What does the formula =PMT(O12, O11, -O7) in the mortgage calculator accomplish?**
   - a) It calculates the total interest over the loan term.
   - b) It calculates the monthly mortgage payment.
   - c) It calculates the annual mortgage repayment.
   - d) It determines the total number of payments.

4. **Why did you link cell L25 on the Mortgage worksheet to the Budget worksheet?**
   - a) To add more details to the Mortgage worksheet.
   - b) To integrate mortgage payments into the overall budget.
   - c) To display loan repayment terms in the budget.
   - d) To calculate the mortgage interest rate.

Quiz Answers

1. b) To calculate the remaining term on the mortgage in years.
2. b) =(F7*52) + (G7*26) + (H7*12) + (I7*6) + (J7*4) + K7
3. b) It calculates the monthly mortgage payment.
4. b) To integrate mortgage payments into the overall budget.

Self-Assessment

1. **Main Learning Points:**
    - Created a **Mortgage worksheet** to track mortgage payments and remaining loan terms.
    - Used the **Mortgage Calculator** to calculate monthly and annual mortgage payments based on loan amount, term, and interest rate.
    - Linked the Mortgage worksheet with the Budget worksheet to reflect mortgage payments in the overall budget.
    - Practiced protecting the input cells and setting up calculations for different repayment frequencies.
2. **Self-Check Questions:**
    - How does linking the Mortgage worksheet with the Budget worksheet support your budgeting process?
    - Can you explain how the Mortgage Calculator determines the monthly and total interest payments?
    - Why is it essential to set the input cells to unlocked for ease of use in financial tracking?

Something Extra

Before we finish with the Mortgage worksheet, you may find you need to compare several mortgages, loans or interest rates. You can easily set up several copies of the mortgage calculator by copying and pasting it, as many times as you like in another worksheet, Excel will adjust formulas on each copy.

Then you just change the values as required, below I have copied the Mortgage Calculator to a new worksheet 3 times to compare different loans.

	A	B	C	D	E	F	G	H
1								
2								
3	Loan 1			Loan 2			Loan 3	
4	Mortgage Calculator			Mortgage Calculator			Mortgage Calculator	
5	Loan Amount	$ 100,000.00		Loan Amount	$ 200,000.00		Loan Amount	$ 300,000.00
6	Interest Rate (annual)	7.84%		Interest Rate (annual)	7.84%		Interest Rate (annual)	7.84%
7	Term (months)	360		Term (months)	360		Term (months)	360
8								
9	Total Payments	360		Total Payments	360		Total Payments	360
10	Monthly Interest	0.6533%		Monthly Interest	0.6533%		Monthly Interest	0.6533%
11	Monthly Payment	$ 722.64		Monthly Payment	$ 1,445.28		Monthly Payment	$ 2,167.92
12	Total Payments	$ 260,150.95		Total Payments	$ 520,301.90		Total Payments	$ 780,452.85
13	Total Interest	$ 160,150.95		Total Interest	$ 320,301.90		Total Interest	$ 480,452.85
14								
15	Mortgage Repayment - Frequency			Mortgage Repayment - Frequency			Mortgage Repayment - Frequency	
16	Week	$ 180.66		Week	$ 361.32		Week	$ 541.98
17	Fortnight	$ 361.32		Fortnight	$ 722.64		Fortnight	$ 1,083.96
18	Month	$ 722.64		Month	$ 1,445.28		Month	$ 2,167.92
19								

WS 7 - Holiday Planning

Everyone loves a holiday, seeing unfamiliar places, meeting people and cultures, wonderful...but it costs, and most of us need to save for it. This worksheet will allow you to enter details of your trip and expected expenses and get this into your budget so you can save money for your holiday.

Let's get started.

Worksheet and Heading

If you have not already created the **Holiday Planning** worksheet please create it now.

Column Headings

We have two distinct sections in this worksheet, the first for destination and dates, the second for expense items to save for, let us get started on the first section.

First Headings – Destination and Relevant Dates

The first block contains one row of headings, **B6**:**G6** and one row of data **B7**:**G7**, we will start with the heading.

Column Heading

Enter the following Column Headings into the indicated cells.

- B6, **Destination**
  Where you intend to go.
- C6, **Start Saving Date**
  The date you want to start saving, you will want to start this as early as possible to ensure you can save a manageable amount.
- D6, **Depart Date**
  The day you intend to leave, your total savings should be complete before this date. This date along with the Start Saving Date are used to calculate the **Saving Weeks** you have.
- E6, **Return Date**
  When you are coming back.

- F6, **Total Days**
  How long you will be away, informational purposes only.
- G6, **Saving Weeks**
  The number of weeks between **Start Saving Date** and 1 week before **Depart Date**. Adjust the dates when it is possible to reduce the weekly savings amount to be as low as possible, start as early as possible, depart as late as possible.

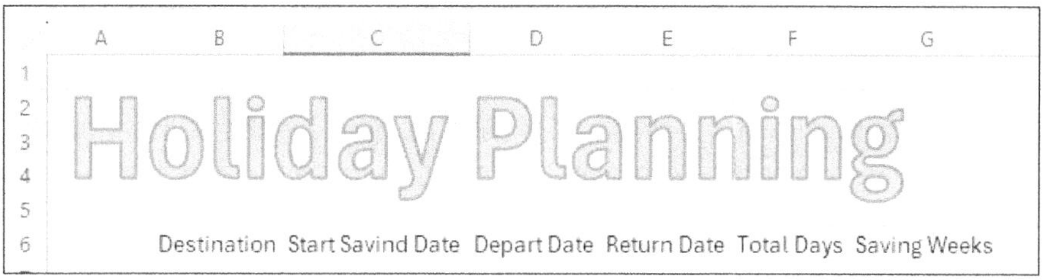

Formatting

- Set the Fill Color for the labels, a light gray background perhaps?
- Format them Bold
- The input cells range from **B7:E7**, set them light yellow
  - o unlock the protection on these cells.
- Set the borders
- **B7**, bold, text
- **C7:E7** format as **Short Date**, centered
- **F7:G7**, number, no decimals, centered

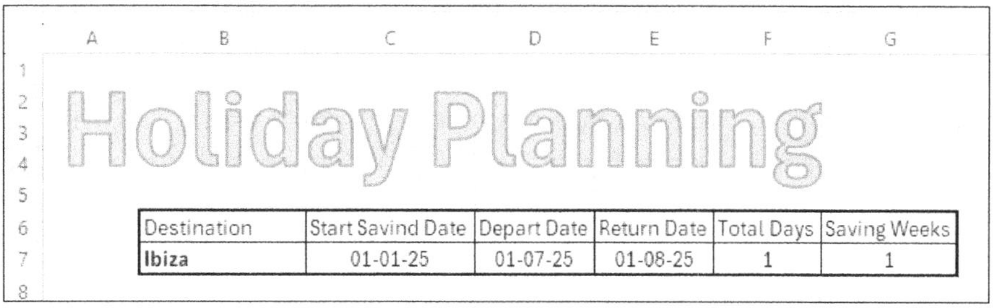

Formula

There are only two simple formulae in this block, cells **F7** and **G7**, set them as shown below.

- **F7**
  The formula is **=E7-D7**, go ahead and type it in. This formula subtracts the **Depart Date** from the **Return Date** to give the total days you will be away. Note that when you subtract one date from another, the result is in days

- **G7**
  The formula is **=((D7-7)-C7)/7** and is used to calculate the number of weeks between two dates, with a specific adjustment to the end date. Here is a step-by-step explanation of what the formula does:
  - **Subtraction of 7 from D7:**
    - D7 contains the Depart Date.
    - By subtracting 7 (D7-7), the formula adjusts the end date back by one week. This ensures the amount will be saved before the depart date. You can adjust this if required, i.e. (D7-28) will give an end saving date 4 weeks before Depart Date.
  - **Subtraction of C7 from the Adjusted D7:**
    - C7 contains the start date.
    - The formula then subtracts the start date (C7) from the adjusted end date (D7-7). This gives the total number of days between the start date and the adjusted end date.
  - **Division by 7:**
    - The result from the previous step (total number of days) is divided by 7 to convert the days into weeks.

So, the formula =((D7-7)-C7)/7 calculates the number of weeks between the start date in C7 and the adjusted end date in D7 (which is shifted back by one week).

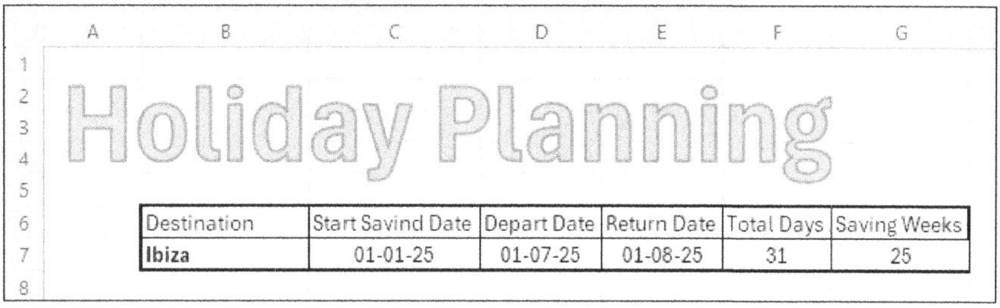

Destination	Start Savind Date	Depart Date	Return Date	Total Days	Saving Weeks
Ibiza	01-01-25	01-07-25	01-08-25	31	25

That finishes the top section, if you have not already done so, enter a destination and some dates so you can evaluate everything is working.

Let's move to the next block.

Second Headings – Saving Targets and Amount

This is even simpler with only three columns and two formulae.

Column Headings

Start by entering the column headings.

- B9, **Expense**, this is an item you are saving that you will need, accommodation, air tickets, food, etc.
- C9, **Cost**, how much you will need for the item for the entire holiday.
- D9, **Notes**, just somewhere you can enter notes about the item.
- Set the Fill Color for the labels, a light gray background.
- Set the font **bold**

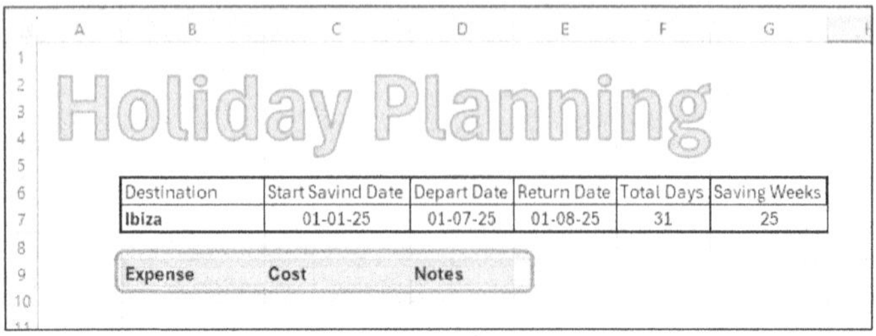

Input Cells

We will be assigning 16 rows to the expenses input section; these will be in the range of **B10:D25**.

If you need more rows later you can insert them, more of that in another chapter, for now, stay with the range values provided.

Fill Color and Protection

Set the following.

- set the fill color, yellow, on cells **B10:D25**
- also unlock the protection on these cells.

Column Formatting

Columns B and D in the second block are text and do not require formatting, Column C, however, is a money column, so it needs to be an accounting format. There are a couple of other cells that also need a currency style format, let us do them all in one go.

- Click cell **C10** to select it.
- Holding down the **Shift key,** click **C26**, this will select all the cells in between
- Let go of the Shift key and hold down the **Ctrl** key and click cell **D26** to select it as well.
- Right Click on any of the selected cells and select **Format Cells**
- Select **Accounting** and click **OK**, this will put the $ sign hard left in the column with the values to the right, enter a numeric value in any of the

cells just formatted to test it.

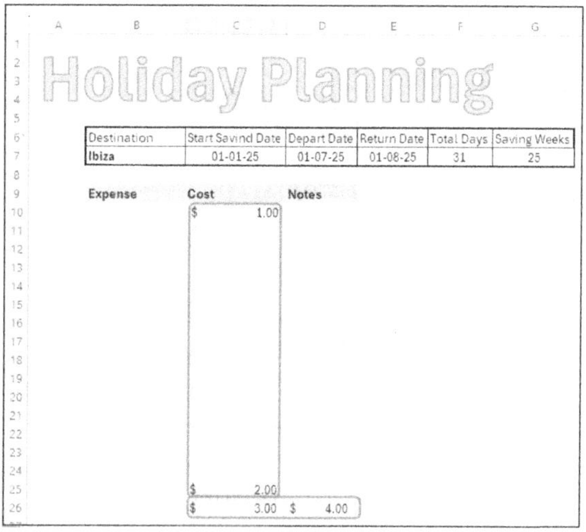

That completes the main block input area, let us prepare the totals row.

Totals Label

Enter the following label on row 26.

- **B26**, **Total Cost.** Make it **Bold** and aligned to the right.

Totals and Weekly Amount Formulae

Three formulas here, type them in as shown below.

- **C26**, the formula is **=SUM(C10:C25)**
  go ahead and type it in. This sums the values in the column.
- **D26**, the formula is **=C26/G7**
  This formula divides the Total Costs in cell C26 with the number of weeks in cell G7 to determine how much you need to save each week to reach the goal.
    - **E26**, Type the following, it will extend into the next column, which is OK here
        - *Save each week to reach goal*

- **D27**, the formula is **=IF(AND(TODAY() >= $C7,TODAY()<=$D7),D26,0)** The formula checks if today's date falls within a range defined by the dates in cells C7 and D7.
    - **E27**, Type the following, it will extend into the next column, which is OK here
        - *Current Budget Amount*

Here is how it works step-by-step:

Condition Check:

- **AND(TODAY() >= $C7, TODAY() <= $D7)**:
    - *TODAY() >= $C7*: Checks if today's date is greater than or equal to the date in cell C7.
    - *TODAY() <= $D7*: Checks if today's date is less than or equal to the date in cell D7.
    - The AND function ensures both conditions must be true.

IF Statement:

- If both conditions are true (today's date is within the range from C7 to D7), the IF function returns the value in cell D26.
- If either condition is false (today's date is not within the range), the IF function returns 0.

Note: If the result is 0, this is perfectly normal — it simply means TODAY's date is not within your planned holiday dates yet. Once the start date arrives, the value will update automatically and be used in the budget when linked.

Evaluate the form by entering data, dates, and check that everything is calculating as you would expect. Now you can

- Determine what you need to save for your holiday by entering the items and estimates of the costs, remember, be generous with estimates, better to save too much than not enough.
- Adjust the Start and Finish saving dates to arrive at a weekly saving amount you can afford.

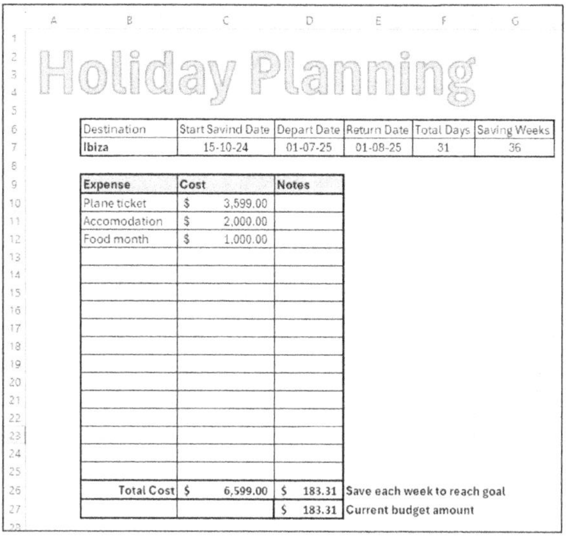

Holiday Planning

Destination	Start Saving Date	Depart Date	Return Date	Total Days	Saving Weeks
Ibiza	15-10-24	01-07-25	01-08-25	31	36

Expense	Cost	Notes	
Plane ticket	$ 3,599.00		
Accomodation	$ 2,000.00		
Food month	$ 1,000.00		
Total Cost	$ 6,599.00	$ 183.31	Save each week to reach goal
		$ 183.31	Current budget amount

Linking to Budget

Linking to the worksheet will allow the savings to be budgeted for. Cell **D27** will be linked to the budget because the formula in **D27** is a date-based formula, the value will only show in the budget when the current date is between the **Start Saving Date** and **Depart Date,** let us get them linked.

- Before we start, some of the cells we will be entering formula into already have the formulas we entered earlier, these will be overwritten.
- Click on the **Expenses – Budget** tab to activate the worksheet.
- Click cell **E31** to select it.
  - Enter the formula =**'Holiday Planning'!D27** or =**$'Holiday Planning'.D27**

    This will enter the value in the date range formula, so the amount shows only when the current date is between the Start and Finish Savings dates

- Click cell **K31** to select it.

    - Note, we will be replacing the existing formula in cell K31
    - Enter the formula **='Holiday Planning'!C26** or **=$'Holiday Planning'.C26**
    - This puts the **Total Costs** in the Annual Total column so it can be included in the Annual Total. This ensures the old formula does not calculate it over 12 months, this is a fixed amount.

- Click cell **N31** to select it.
    - Note, we will be replacing the existing formula in cell N31
    - Enter the formula **=(E31*52)/M5**
      This formula multiplies the weekly amount by 52 to get the annual amount and then divides that by the Annual Pay Days to arrive at the amount that needs to be saved each pay day to reach the target amount by the Depart Date.

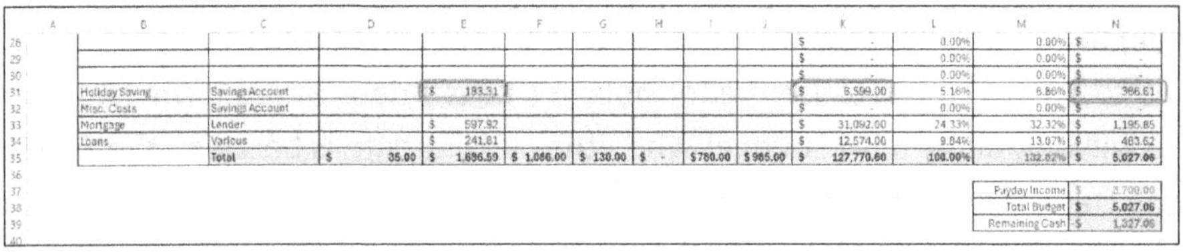

	A	B	C	D	E	F	G	H	I	J	K	L	M	N
28											$ -	0.00%	0.00%	$ -
29											$ -	0.00%	0.00%	$ -
30											$ -	0.00%	0.00%	$ -
31		Holiday Saving	Savings Account		$ 183.31						$ 6,599.00	5.16%	6.86%	$ 386.61
32		Misc. Costs	Savings Account								$ -	0.00%	0.00%	$ -
33		Mortgage	Lender		$ 597.92						$ 31,092.00	24.33%	32.32%	$ 1,195.85
34		Loans	Various		$ 241.81						$ 12,574.00	9.84%	13.07%	$ 483.62
35			Total	$ 35.00	$ 1,696.59	$ 1,086.00	$ 130.00	$ -	$780.00	$985.00	$ 127,770.60	100.00%	132.02%	$ 5,027.06
36														
37													Payday Income	$ 3,700.00
38													Total Budget	$ 5,027.06
39													Remaining Cash	-$ 1,327.06

Conclusion

In this chapter, you developed the **Holiday Planning** worksheet, a tool for budgeting and planning for a holiday. You structured it to include essential information such as destination, travel dates, and expected expenses. By setting a start and end date for savings, you were able to calculate the total amount needed and the weekly savings required between the start/end saving dates. Additionally, you linked the worksheet to the Budget worksheet, allowing holiday savings to be incorporated directly into your overall budget plan. This approach provides a clear path to saving for a holiday without impacting other financial obligations.

Quiz

1. **What does cell G7 in the Holiday Planning worksheet represent?**
    - a) Total number of days for the holiday
    - b) Weeks remaining until the start of the holiday
    - c) Number of weeks to save for the holiday
    - d) Total savings required for the holiday

2. **In which cell do you enter the start date for saving towards the holiday?**
    - a) D6
    - b) C7
    - c) B7
    - d) C6

3. **How is the formula in cell D27 structured to work?**
    - a) It calculates the total number of days between two dates.
    - b) It sets the budget amount only if today's date is within the specified savings period.
    - c) It subtracts the total expenses from the savings amount.
    - d) It calculates the total savings required for the holiday.

4. **What is the purpose of linking cell D27 from the Holiday Planning worksheet to the Budget worksheet?**
    - a) To display the total holiday cost
    - b) To add holiday expenses to the total monthly budget
    - c) To include weekly holiday savings in the budget only during the specified date range
    - d) To calculate total savings for the next holiday

Quiz Answers

1. c) Number of weeks to save for the holiday
2. b) C7
3. b) It sets the budget amount only if today's date is within the specified savings period.
4. c) To include weekly holiday savings in the budget only during the specified date range

Self-Assessment

1. **Key Takeaways:**
    - Created a **Holiday Planning worksheet** to manage and plan for holiday-related expenses.
    - Entered essential details like destination, dates, and savings period to determine the weekly savings amount required.
    - Linked the worksheet to the **Budget worksheet** to automatically incorporate holiday savings into the budget based on the specified date range.
    - Practiced date-based formulas and linking worksheets to align budget planning with savings goals.
2. **Reflective Questions:**
    - How does linking the Holiday Planning worksheet to the Budget worksheet support your overall financial planning?
    - Why is it beneficial to use date-based formulas when planning savings for future events?
    - How would you adjust the worksheet if the holiday dates or budget changed?

WS 8 - Misc. Costs

Miscellaneous costs always seem to arise, sometimes we can plan for them and include them in the budget i.e., new car tires, home appliance replacement (e.g., washing machine, refrigerator), laptop or smartphone replacement.

These costs are not usually part of monthly budgeting but can be planned for in a yearly or periodic budget allocation.

The Misc. Costs work sheet will allow you to enter these items, costs and notes. It will calculate how much to put away each pay period to save for them over the next 12 months.

Worksheet and Heading

If you have not yet created the *Misc. Costs* worksheet and heading, please do so now.

Click on the **Misc. Costs** tab to activate it

Column Headings

We will be using 3 headings for columns **B6**:**D6**, let us start by getting them in place, add the following to the Misc. Costs worksheet.

- B6, **Expense**
  This is a label where you enter that for which you are saving.
- C6, **Cost**
  This is the target amount you are saving for.
- D6, **Note**
  Somewhere for you to enter notes about the expense. You may want to widen this column.
- Format the headings **Light Grey** back, **Bold** and **Centered** in the columns.

Input cells

The input cells are **B7:D22** let's get them setup.

- Set the back color to Light Yellow for cell range **B7:D22**
- **B7:C22**, set the cells **Number Format** to **Accounting**

- Unlock them in **Format Cells, Protection**

Totals Row

As with the other sheets, Totals are simply a summing of the column's values, only **C23** requires totals.

- **B23**, *Total*
- Format it **Bold**, right aligned

Well not much there, as we enter further details in the sheet later, we will want to see the totals, so we will do the formula now.

Totals Formula

During this course, we have been demonstrating different and simple ways to copy similar formulas between cells. We will continue with this method and for now concentrating ONLY on cell **C23**, please do the following.

- In cell **C23** only
    - Enter the formula **=SUM(C7:C22)**, as you know from previous sheets, this formula will SUM the cells from **C7:C22** and put the result in C23
    - To make the Total value stand out, apply the following formatting.
        - Set the cells **Number Format** to **Accounting**
        - Set the **Font Weight** to **Bold**
        - Set **Font Size** to **14**
        - Set Fill Color to any color of your choice.
    - Enter some random values in cells between C6 and C21 and ensure **C2** sums them up correctly.

Finishing up

- Set the borders as you have been for other worksheets.
- Add some data and check the calculation in C23

Misc. Costs

Expense	Cost	Note
Car tires	$ 980.00	Due in 12 months
Clothes Dryer	$ 455.00	Will need replacing in 2 to 3 years
Total	**$ 1,435.00**	

Linking to Budget sheet

The cell we want to link back to the budget is **C23**

Previously, we linked to another sheet by clicking in the target cell and then navigating to and clicking on the source cell, this time we will just type it. We have two links to make here.

- Click the **Expenses - Budget** tab to activate the budget worksheet
- Type the following formula directly into cell **E32**
  ='Misc. Costs'!C23/52 and press **Enter** you will now see the value displayed.
  This is the weekly amount you need to save for the costs.

	A	B	C	D	E	F	G	H	I	J	K	L	M	N
31		Holiday Saving	Savings Account		$ 183.31						$ 6,599.00	5.11%	6.86%	$ 366.61
32		Misc. Costs	Savings Account		$ 27.60						$ 1,435.00	1.11%	1.49%	$ 55.19
33		Mortgage	Lender		$ 597.92						$ 31,092.00	24.06%	32.32%	$ 1,195.85
34		Loans	Various		$ 241.81						$ 12,574.00	9.73%	13.07%	$ 483.62

This is a simple worksheet and could be expanded on, perhaps add date ranges as we did for the Holiday Planner to better control when the saving for these items come into play in your budget. Perhaps you can set that as task to undertake for yourself, try out all these new skills you have been learning.

Congratulations, you have now completed the Misc. Costs worksheet and linked it back to the budget.

Conclusion

The Miscellaneous Costs worksheet allows you to plan for occasional expenses that aren't typically part of monthly budgeting, like replacing appliances, new tires, or phone upgrades. By listing each anticipated expense, setting a target amount, and calculating the amount needed per pay period, you can incorporate these irregular costs into your budget, reducing financial strain when they arise. Linking this worksheet to your main budget ensures that all expected expenditures are accounted for, contributing to a comprehensive financial plan.

Quiz

1. **What is the purpose of the Miscellaneous Costs worksheet?**
   a) Track monthly expenses
   b) Track unexpected, non-recurring expenses
   c) Track savings contributions
   d) Track daily spending

2. **Which column in the worksheet allows you to add specific details about each expense item?**
   a) Expense
   b) Cost
   c) Noted) Total

3. **What formula should be entered in cell C23 to calculate the total Miscellaneous Costs?**
   a) =AVERAGE(C7:C22)
   b) =C7+C22
   c) =SUM(C7:C22)
   d) =PRODUCT(C7:C22)

4. **How is the Miscellaneous Costs worksheet linked to the main budget?**
   a) Through a cell formula in the main budget
   b) By exporting data
   c) By printing the worksheet
   d) Through a separate financial application

Quiz Answers

1. b) Track unexpected, non-recurring expenses
2. c) Note
3. c) =SUM(C7:C22)
4. a) Through a cell formula in the main budget

Self-Assessment

1. **Key Takeaways**

- **Planning for Miscellaneous Expenses:** In this worksheet, you learned how to anticipate irregular or unplanned costs that can arise over the course of a year. By budgeting for these expenses ahead of time, you gain a more realistic and resilient financial plan that can accommodate unexpected costs without derailing your budget.

- **Using Totals and Summing Formulas:** You gained experience of summing a range of costs into a total annual value, which gives you a clear view of the extra amount to set aside to cover these miscellaneous expenses.

- **Linking to the Budget Worksheet:** This worksheet reinforced how to link cells across worksheets, bringing your miscellaneous costs back into your overall budget. This skill allows for centralized budget tracking and easier updates whenever adjustments are needed.

- **Practical Application of Custom Formatting:** By applying unique formatting options to highlight input areas, totals, and notes, you created a worksheet that is easy to update, read, and use regularly.

Reflective Questions

1. **Miscellaneous Planning:** Did you identify which expenses are truly unpredictable versus those that can be planned for? How does separating these costs affect your confidence in your overall budget?

2. **Cost Categorization:** Are there any expenses you would consider adding to the Misc. Costs worksheet of which you hadn't initially thought? How did brainstorming potential expenses change your perspective on budget flexibility?

3. **Linking and Updating Worksheets:** How comfortable are you now with linking data between worksheets? Is there anything you could do to make future updates easier, such as adding more details or notes within cells?

4. **Worksheet Usability:** Do the formatting choices make the Misc. Costs worksheet easy to use over time? Are there any adjustments you would make to improve usability or readability?

5. **Setting a Realistic Savings Goal:** Do the annual totals and linked budget amounts align well with your income? How confident are you that these additional costs won't impact your financial goals, and do you plan to adjust any other areas of your budget to accommodate them?

By addressing these questions, you can ensure your Misc. Costs worksheet remains a valuable part of your budgeting process, helping you prepare for the unpredictable expenses that often arise.

WS 9 - Dashboard

You have come a long way since starting this Excel journey. Now, it is time to bring everything you have learned into one cohesive overview.

In "WS 9 - Dashboard," we will guide you through the steps to construct this handy summary tool.

Dashboard centralizes your data, giving you a quick snapshot of the most vital information. Think of it as your data's "home page".

Before we start creating the Dashboard page, put your real data in each of the worksheets we have completed.

Worksheet and Heading

If you have not yet created the *Dashboard* worksheet and heading, please add them now.

Column Headings

There are four column headings for this worksheet, they begin in column B as we need to reserve column A for some row headings coming up next.

Please create the column headings as described below.

- C8, **Year**
  This is the annual amounts and the values for rows 10 to 14 are linked from other worksheets.
- D8, **Week**
  C8 calculated to a weekly value.
- E8, **Month**
  C8 calculated to a monthly value.

You can format the column headings as you like.

Row Headings

We have put in the heading, so we know the period the values refer to, now we need to know what they are. We will put in a series of labels to identify the data.

Please enter the labels as shown below.

- B9, **Take Home Income**
- B10, **Living Expenses**
- B11, **Debt**
- B12, **Mortgage**
- leave some blank to separate the values from the totals.
- B18, **Total Expenses**
- B19, **Remaining Income**

You can format the labels as you like. Adjust the column widths

Formula and Linking

Column C (year)

To get the data in place, we need to link to the data sources from the other worksheets. The links will be in the cell range of C9:C12, the remaining will be formulas.

Let us link the data by entering the following formula.

- First, format range C9:E19 as **Accounting**
  - C9, **=Income!$Q$22 or =$Income.Q22**
    The **Total Take Home** income from all income sources in the Income worksheet

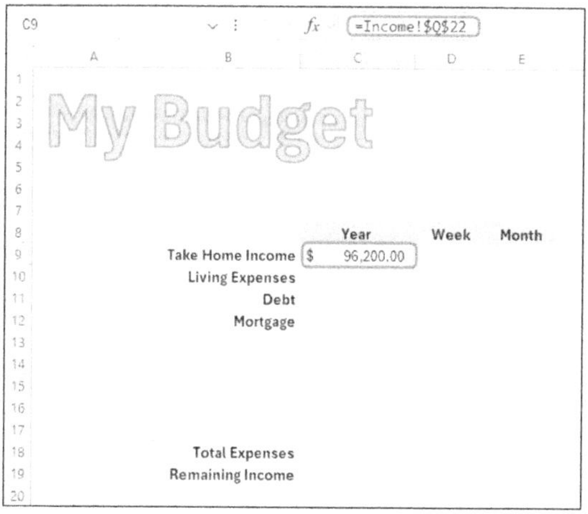

Continue entering the remaining formulae below. If you get a **#REF!** when entering the formula as written below, check the worksheet name matches the formula's worksheet name. If they are different you will need to change the worksheet's name in the formula.

- C10, **=SUM('Expenses - Budget'!K7:K32)** or **=SUM($'Expenses - Budget'.K7:K32)**
  This is summing the living expense items only from K7:K32. Debt and Mortgage are shown separately.

- C11, =**Loans!I25** or =**$Loans.I25**
  This is your total Loan payments for the year.
- C12, =**Mortgage!L25** or =**$Mortgage.L25**
  Your total mortgage repayments for the year
- C18, =**SUM(C10:C12)**
  This is the total of all the above expense values, your total expenses.
- C19, =**C9-C18**
  Subtracts the total expense from total income to calculate the remaining income for the year.

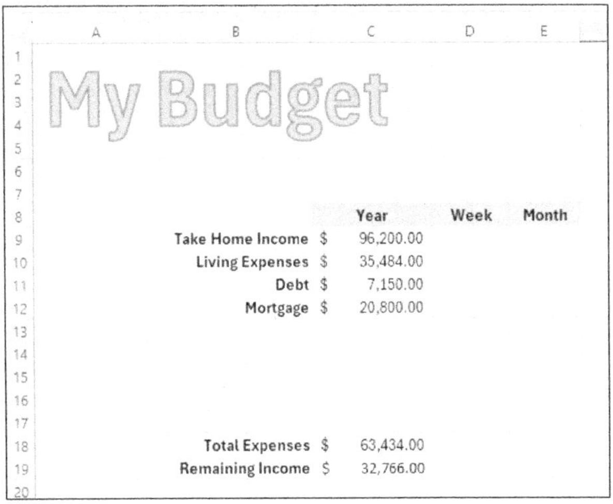

Double check your results are correct.

With column C data now in place, we can calculate the remaining cells in the grid. As with other worksheets, you will only need to enter the formula on in each of the columns and copy it down the grid.

Let us get the formula in

Column D (week)

This will calculate the weekly amount for each of the expense types and totals, please enter them as shown below.

- D9, =**C9/52**
- Click in **D9** to select it and use the drag and copy the cell down to **D19**
- Select cell **D13:D17** and press **Delete** to clear them.

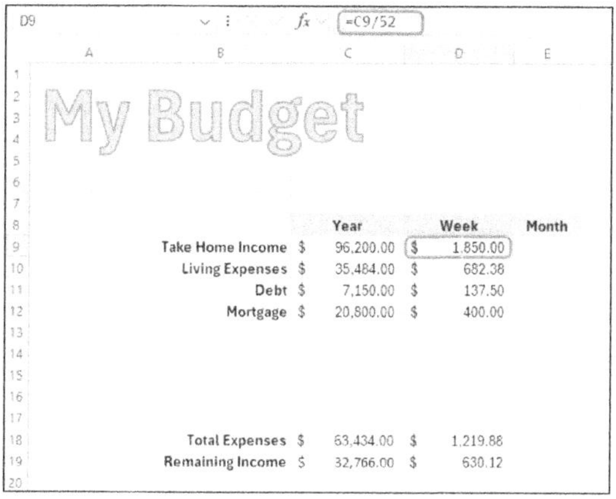

Column E (month)

This will calculate the monthly amount for each of the expense types and totals, please enter them as shown below.

- E9, =**C9/12**
- Click in **E9** to select it using the drag and copy the cell down to **E19**

- Select in cell **E13:E17** and press **Delete** to clear them.

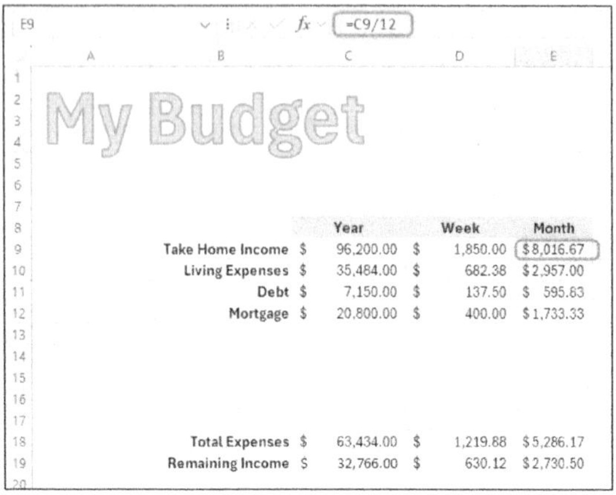

Wait until the chart is in so you can match the colors with the chart.

Let's get the chart in.

Pie Chart

Nothing shows the relationship between data like a nice chart, we will now put in a pie chart to provide an overview of where your annual income is being disbursed.

Pie Chart Data

The chart needs to have the data in a nice little block to display properly. Whilst the Year data in column B is what we are after to feed the chart, rows 13 to 18 are not part of the data we want. To get around this problem, we will simply duplicate the labels and data into a neat little block and point the chart to it. Let us prepare the data first.

- First, the column headings so we know what the data is about, enter the following headings.
  - G8, **Label**
  - H8, **Annual**
  - Format the text and fill color as desired. These will be hidden behind the chart.

- Now the label names, we are referencing the labels in column B, enter the following formulae.
    - G9, =**B10**
    - G10, =**B11**
    - G11, =**B19**
    - G12, =**B12**
- Now the annual values, we are referencing the values in column C, entering the following formula.
    - H9, =**C10**
    - H10, =**C11**
    - H11, =**C19**
    - H12, =**C12**

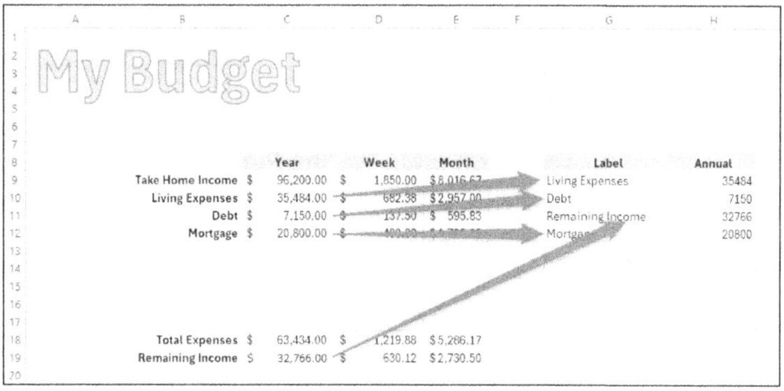

The data for the pie chart is now ready.

> **Note:** As you change data in the individual worksheets, their totals will recalculate automatically. The relevant cells in column C in the Dashboard Worksheet will be updated to show the new total values. This will, in turn, cause the pie chart data to change, and the chart we are about to create will dynamically display the new values graphically. This process is seamless and ensures that your data visualization is always current.

Pie Chart

Now the data is prepared, we can create the chart itself. Please do the following.

Creating the pie chart – Excel

Follow these steps

- Select the chart data in columns **G9:H12**, once selected

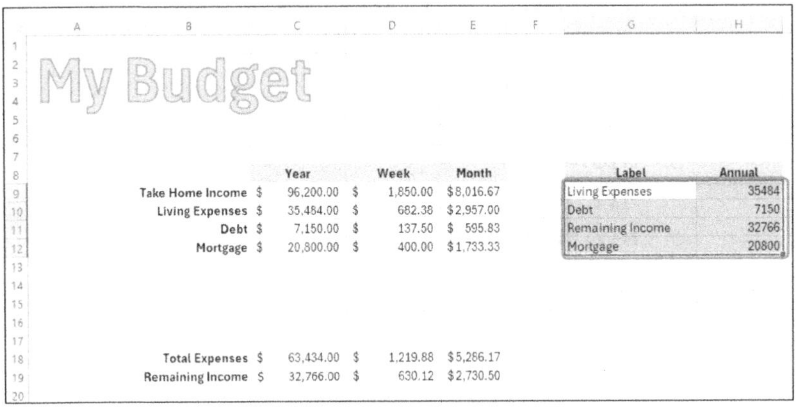

- Click **Insert** menu on ribbon and click the **Pie Chart** icon in the **Charts** group.

- Select the 3D Pie Chart and click it, the chart will be created for you.

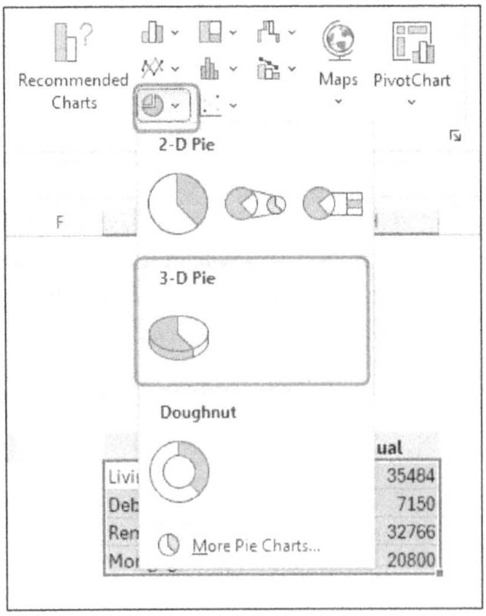

- Move the chart to the right, away from the data for now

    - clicking on the chart.
    - Click and hold the outside line of the box surrounding the entire chart and drag it to where you want it.
- Resize the chart by using the resize controls on each corner and line of the chart frame.
- Rename the chart title by **Double Click** the **CHART LABEL** and enter a new name, such as **Income Disbursement**.

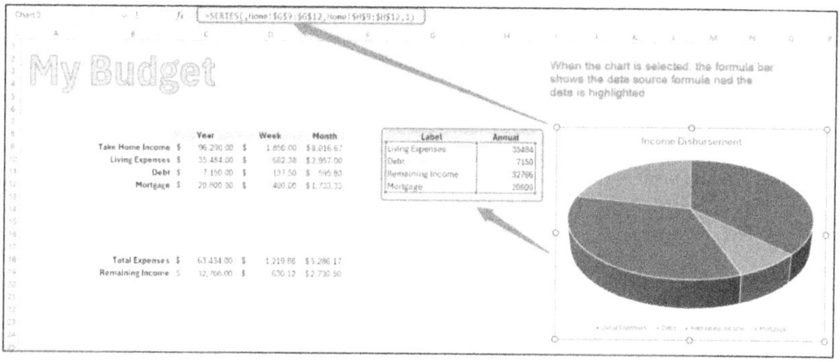

- When the chart is selected, a new group appears in the ribbon, **Chart Design,** with chart options, **Chart Style** are preformatted chart styling you can select from, hover over them and your chart style will change, find one you like and click it. There is also an option in here to change the colors, play with it.

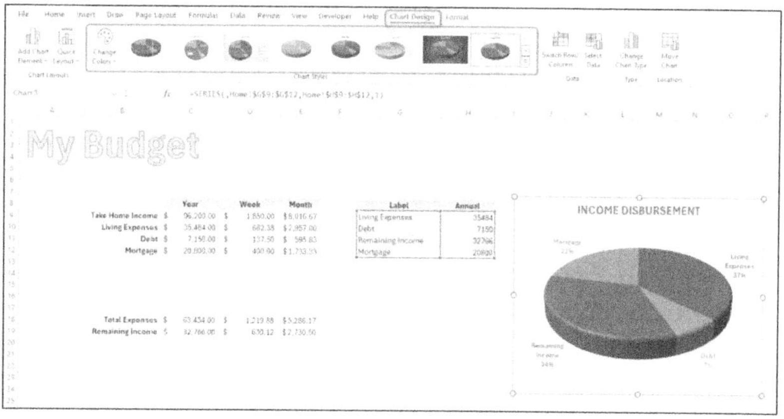

- Make any final adjustments to the chart size, both outer frame and inner chart frame until you have everything looking good.

- Make any final formatting changes to the worksheet
- Move the chart to cover the chart data

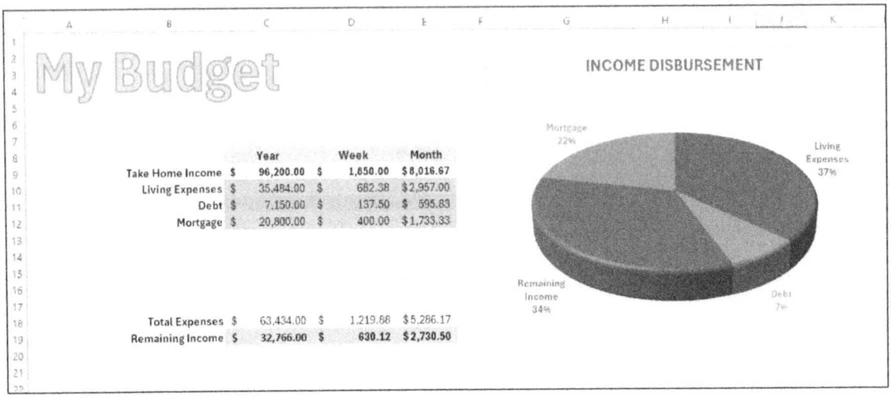

Creating the pie chart - LibreOffice Calc

Follow these steps.

- Resize your screen so you can see the data area as well as a good space to the right to add your chart, use the magnification tool in the bottom/right of the screen
- Select all cells from **G9** to **H12**
- Open Chart Wizard **Insert -> Chart**
  The Chart Wizard will open on step 1. Chart Type. Select **Pie** and leave it on the first option
- Select **2. Data Range**, if you had selected K7:K34 then this range will be in the *Data range* box Data series in Columns will be selected, if so, move to next step. If not enter the following in the **Data range** box and select **Data series in columns**

$Dashboard.$G$9:$H$12

- Select **3. Data Series**, You should see **$Dashboard.$G$9:$G$12** in the Categories box. If it is not there, put it in.
- Select **4. Chart Elements**, Enter the title **Income Disbursement** you can enter a subtitle **Annual**, if you want but not necessary, Clear the **Display Legend** tick box.
- Click **Finish.** Then chart will be displayed, move it to where you want it, resize it.
- *Right Click* on the chart, select the option **Insert Data Labels**, immediately the chart will display $ value as labels.
- *Right Click* on the chart again, this time select **Format Data Labels**, the format window will open.
- *Click* on the **Data Labels** tab, select **Value as percentage** and **Category.** This will display the Expense and Value as the labels.
- In *Placement*, select ***Outside*** to put the label outside the chart pieces

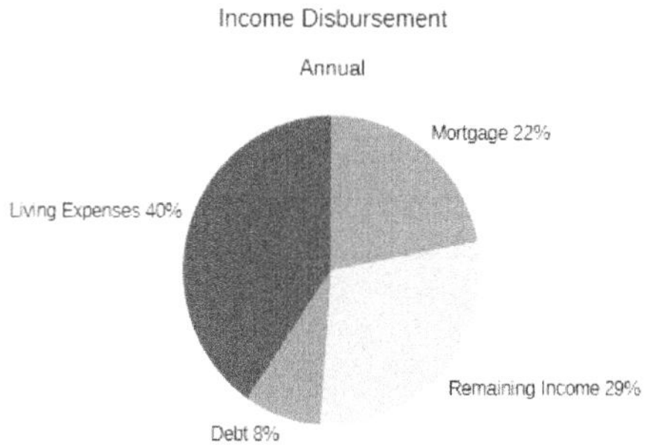

There are many options to format your chart, way too many to get into here. Save your work and play around with the various formatting options until you have it just how you want it.

You do not need to see the data block feeding the chart, you can move the chart over top to cover it up.

Conclusion

In WS 9 - Home, you have created a central dashboard that brings together all essential financial data from your budgeting worksheets. This summary page provides a quick snapshot of your take-home income, total expenses, and remaining income, displayed in a clear and concise layout. By linking data from various worksheets, you ensure that this dashboard remains up-to-date, dynamically reflecting changes made in the underlying sheets. Additionally, the pie chart provides a visual overview of income allocation, making it easier to understand spending distribution at a glance. With this dashboard, you have a comprehensive tool that enhances your budgeting insights and supports informed financial planning.

Thank you for being a resolute learner. Take pride in what you have accomplished and look forward to the many possibilities your new Excel prowess unlocks.

Your journey does not end here. You have successfully completed the Home Budget main application, a significant achievement in itself. Up next, we will delve into creating a worksheet that will help you evaluate job offers. This new tool will empower you to make informed decisions about potential job opportunities, considering various financial factors. Get ready to expand your Excel skills even further and add another powerful tool to your repertoire.

Quiz

1. **What is the primary purpose of the Home worksheet?**
    A) To display detailed monthly expenses
    B) To summarize key financial data from all worksheets
    C) To calculate mortgage payments
    D) To record miscellaneous expenses

2. **Which column on the Home worksheet displays annual amounts linked from other worksheets?**
    A) Column A
    B) Column B
    C) Column C
    D) Column D

3. **How does the pie chart in WS 9 - Home help with budgeting?**
    A) It categorizes expenses into different months
    B) It provides a visual breakdown of income allocation
    C) It calculates weekly expenses
    D) It replaces the need for individual expense entries

4. **If you need to see the weekly equivalent of an annual amount in Column C, which formula would you use in Column D?**
    A) =C9*12
    B) =C9/52
    C) =C9+12
    D) =C9/4

Quiz Answers

1. B) To summarize key financial data from all worksheets
2. C) Column C
3. B) It provides a visual breakdown of income allocation
4. B) =C9/52

Self Assessment

Reflect on the following to assess your understanding and skill with the Home worksheet:

- Are you able to link data from other worksheets accurately into the Home worksheet to display key totals?
- Can you adjust and format the Home worksheet to display information clearly, including setting up annual, weekly, and monthly calculations?
- Do you understand how the pie chart visually represents income distribution, and can you update it dynamically as data changes?
- Are you confident in making any required adjustments to the Home worksheet as new budgeting needs arise?

This worksheet completes the foundational structure for your budgeting application, ensuring that all critical financial insights are easily accessible from one central location.

WS 10 – New Job Pay Comparison

In this chapter, we introduce the New Job Pay Comparison worksheet, a crucial tool for evaluating the financial implications of changing jobs. This worksheet is designed to help you compare your current job income with a potential new job offer, providing a clear view of how the change will affect your monthly finances. By taking all calculations to a monthly value, you can easily assess the impact on your overall budget.

The worksheet includes sections for both your current job income and the new job income, breaking down earnings on a weekly, fortnightly, and monthly basis. It calculates the gross and net monthly income for both jobs, considering taxes and other deductions. Additionally, there are sections for estimating monthly expenses such as transport, fuel, food, and coffee, allowing you to see the net income after expenses for both scenarios.

For those receiving unemployment benefits, the worksheet also includes a detailed section to calculate how your benefits might be affected by the new job. This section helps you understand the sliding scale reduction of benefits based on your new earnings, ensuring you have a comprehensive view of your total income, including both job earnings and adjusted benefit payments.

By the end of this chapter, you will have a clear understanding of how to use this worksheet to make informed decisions about job offers, ensuring that you can confidently evaluate whether a new job will improve your financial situation.

> **NOTE**: You have already learned and used all the skills required for this section, Instruction will be quite simple with little explanation.

Preparing the layout

Note that in this part, we are focusing solely on the layout. The formatting and formulas will be added later as we progress through the course.

Follow the steps to establish a structured and organized worksheet that will serve as a valuable tool in your budgeting application.

Create the Worksheet

If you have not already created the worksheet and heading, do so now.

Creating the Job Comparison Section

Enter the Main Headings

> **Note**, starting on row 4 is a little higher on the sheet than others were, and the heading may cause issues selecting the cell, increase the row height of row 1 a little or alternatively, adjust the heading font size.

- **B4**, "All calculations taken to MONTHLY value"
    - Merge and center cells **B4:C4**
- **C5**, "Current Job Income"
    - Merge and center cells **C5:D5**
- **F5**, "New Job Income"
    - Merge and center cells **F5:G5**
- **H8**, "Difference (Month)"

Creating the Income Section

- **B6**, type "Income"
- Current job side
    - **C6**, "Week"
    - **C7**, "Fortnight"
    - **C8**, "Month"
- New job side
    - **F6**, "Hours per week"
    - **F7**, "Rate per hour"

Create the Income Totals Section

- **B9**, "Income Totals"
- Current job side
    - **C9**, "Month Gross"
    - **C10**, "Tax (Month)"
    - **C11**, "Month Net"
- New job side
    - **F9**, "Month Gross"

- **F10**, "Tax (Month)"
- **F11**, "Month Net"

Create the Expenses Section

- **C12**, "Monthly Estimate values for these values"
  - Merge and center cells **C12:G12**
- **B13,** "Expenses"
- Current job side
  - **C13**, "Transport or Tolls"
  - **C14**, "Fuel"
  - **C15**, "Food"
  - **C16**, "Coffee"
  - **C17**, "Total"
- New job side
  - **F13**, "Transport or Tolls"
  - **F14**, "Fuel"
  - **F15**, "Food"
  - **F16**, "Coffee"
  - **F17**, "Total"

Create the Total row

- **B18,** "Income after expenses"

Create the Unemployment Benefit Calculation Section

- **B20,** "Unemployment Benefit with job calculated over a month -- Only relevant if the above Current Income is from a benefit payment"
- Merge cells **B20:H20** and apply a suitable font and size to make it stand out, preferably in a distinct color (e.g., red) to highlight its importance
- **Enter the headings**:

  - **B21**, "Calculate sliding scale to reduce current benefit payments, these calculations are done pre-tax"
  - **B22**, "Non affected amount (week)"
  - **B23**, "Non affected amount (month)"
  - **B24**, "Amount reduced per $"
  - **B26**, "Income less free earnings"
  - **B28**, "Benefit amount reduced by"
  - **B30**, "Benefit amount retained"
  - **B31**, "Job Earnings after tax"
  - **B32**, "Total Income"
  - **B34**, "Difference"
- **Enter the descriptions:**
  - **D22**, "The weekly amount you can earn before your benefit payments are affected"
  - **D24**, "How much is your benefit payment reduced per $1.00 earned"
  - **D26**, "This amount will be subject to sliding reduction scale on earnings"
  - **D28**, "This amount will be deducted from the benefit payment"
  - **D31,** "What you take home after tax and after paying your estimated monthly expenses."
  - **D32**, "Total take home pay from job plus adjusted benefit payment"
  - **D34**, "This is how much you will be in front/behind after all calculations are taken into consideration"
  - Adjust column widths

The worksheet should look like this.

	A	B	C	D	E	F	G	H
1								
2	Comparison - Current income with new job							
3								
4		All calculations taken to MONTHLY value						
5			Current Job Income			New Job Income		
6		Income	Week			Hours per week		
7			Fortnight			Rate per Hour		
8			Month					Difference (Month)
9		Income Totals	Month Gross			Month Gross		
10			Tax Month			Tax Month		
11			Month Net			Month Net		
12				Monthly Estimate values for these values				
13		Expenses	Transport or Tolls			Transport or Tolls		
14			Fuel			Fuel		
15			Food			Food		
16			Coffee			Coffee		
17			Total			Total		
18		Income after Expense						
19								
20		Unemployment Benefit with job calculated over a month -- Only relevant if the above Current Income is from a benefit payment						
21		Calculate sliding scale to reduce current benefit payments, these calculations are done pre-tax						
22		Non affected amount (week)		The weekly amount you can earn before your benefit payments are affected				
23		Non affected amount (month)						
24		Amount reduced per $		How much is your benefit payment reduced per $1.00 earned				
25								
26		Income less free earnings		This amount will be subject to sliding reduction scale on earnings				
27								
28		Benefit amount reduced by		This amount will be deducted from the benefit payment				
29								
30		Benefit amount retained						
31		Job Earnings after tax						
32		Total Income		Total take home pay from job plus adjusted benefit payment				
33								
34		Difference		This is how much you will be in front/behind after all calulations are taken into consideration				
35								

Put in the formulas

Add the formula to the following cells

- **D9**, *Current Month Gross*, **=(D6*52/12) + (D7*26/12)+D8**
- **D11,** *Current Month Net*, **=D9-D10**
- **G9**, *Month Gross*, **=(G6*G7) * 52/12**
- **D10 and G10**, *Tax (Month)*, nothing yet
    - we will come back to this in the VBA Modules lessons, for now enter the values directly
- **G11**, *Month Net*, **=G9-G10**
- **D17**, Current *Expenses Total*, **=SUM(D13:D16)**
- **G17**, Current *Expenses Total*, **=SUM(G13:G16)**
- **D18**, *Total Current*, **=D11-D17**
- **G18**, *Total New*, **=G11-G17**
- **H9**, *Difference Month Gross*, **=G9-D9**
    - Select and drag this down to **H18** to set the formula on the range
    - Select and Delete **H12**, no formula is required in H12.

- **C23**, *Non affected amount (month)*, **=C22*52/12**
- **C26**, *Income less free earnings*, **=IF((G9-C23)<C23,0,G9-C23)**
- **C28**, *benefit amount reduced by*, **=IF((C26*C24)>D9,D9,C26*C24)**
- **C30**, *benefit amount retained*, **=IF(D9-C28<0,0,D9-C28)**
- **C31**, *Job Earnings after tax*, **=G18**
- **C32**, *Total Income*, **=C30+G18**
- **C34**, *Difference*, **=C32-D18**

All formula will have a zero in them at this stage

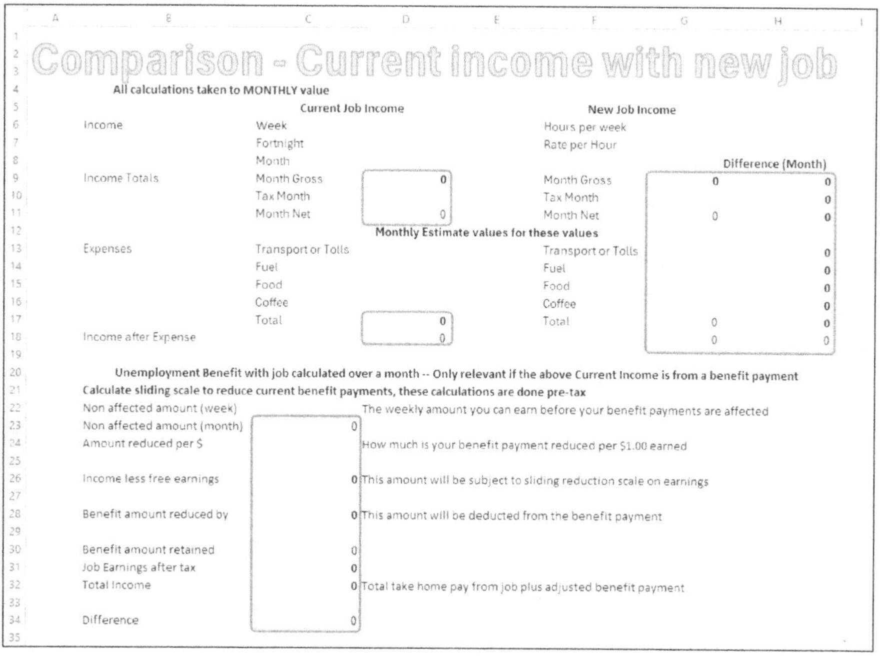

Standard formatting

Set the following formatting to the cells and ranges.

- **Number –** decimal places not required
  - G6
- **Accounting** – 2 decimal places
  - D6:D11
  - D13:D18
  - G7

- G9:G11
- G13:G18
- H9:H11
- H13:H18
- C22:C24
- C26
- C28
- C30:C32
- C34

- **Input Cells** – Yellow Fill Color
  - D6:D8
  - D13:D16
  - G6:G7
  - G13:G16
  - C22
  - C24

Apply Borders and Shading

- **Apply borders** to all the tables to clearly define sections
- **Shade cells** with different colors to visually differentiate between various sections, your choice for colors except the input cells (e.g., yellow for input cells, green for totals)

Set Cell Protection

Set cell protection OFF for all yellow input cells.

Conditional formatting

There is one cell requiring Conditional Formatting, it will require 2 rules

- H18, if value >= 0 then back fill color = green (Libre, select **Good**)
- H18, if value < 0 then back fill color = red (Libre, select **Bad**)

Testing the worksheet

Enter values in the worksheet, keep them simple, i.e., use 10, 100, etc. so you can manually calculate the results easily. Check the results match, below is how the final worksheet should look with values entered and the expected results.

Below is the final formatted sheet with test data in the input cells. Enter the same values in the input cells to check you have the same results. Be sure to reduce the Hours per Week value in G6 to test the conditional formatting in H18, it should turn red when below zero.

	A	B	C	D	E	F	G	H
1	Comparison - Current income with new job							
2								
3								
4		All calculations taken to MONTHLY value						
5			Current Job Income			New Job Income		
6		Income	Week	$ 1,000.00		Hours per week	$ 40.00	
7			Fortnight	$ 1.00		Rate per Hour	$ 27.00	
8			Month	$ 2.00				Difference (Month)
9		Income Totals	Month Gross	$ **4,337.50**		Month Gross	$ **4,680.00**	$ **342.50**
10			Tax Month	$ 500.00		Tax Month	$ 600.00	$ **100.00**
11			Month Net	$ 3,837.50		Month Net	$ 4,080.00	$ **242.50**
12				Monthly Estimate values for these values				
13		Expenses	Transport or Tolls	$ 10.00		Transport or Tolls	$ 10.00	$ -
14			Fuel	$ 11.00		Fuel	$ 11.00	$ -
15			Food	$ 12.00		Food	$ 12.00	$ -
16			Coffee	$ 14.00		Coffee	$ 14.00	$ -
17			Total	$ **47.00**		Total	$ 47.00	$ -
18		Income after Expense		$ 3,790.50			$ 4,033.00	$ 242.50
19								
20		Unemployment Benefit with job calculated over a month -- Only relevant if the above Current Income is from a benefit payment						
21		**Calculate sliding scale to reduce current benefit payments, these calculations are done pre-tax**						
22		Non affected amount (week)	$ 20.00	The weekly amount you can earn before your benefit payments are affected				
23		Non affected amount (month)						
24		Amount reduced per $	$ 0.50	How much is your benefit payment reduced per $1.00 earned				
25								
26		Income less free earnings	$ **4,680.00**	This amount will be subject to sliding reduction scale on earnings				
27								
28		Benefit amount reduced by	$ **2,340.00**	This amount will be deducted from the benefit payment				
29								
30		Benefit amount retained	$ 1,997.50					
31		Job Earnings after tax	$ **4,033.00**					
32		Total Income	$ **6,030.50**	Total take home pay from job plus adjusted benefit payment				
33								
34		Difference	$ 2,240.00	This is how much you will be in front/behind after all calulations are taken into consideration				
35								

Using the New Job Pay Comparison Worksheet

Follow these steps to use the worksheet effectively:

1. Enter your **current job income** in the Current Job Income section.
2. Enter your **new job income** details in the New Job Income section.

3. Enter estimated **monthly expenses** for both jobs (transport, fuel, food, coffee).
4. If applicable, enter your **unemployment benefit details** in the Benefit Calculation section.
5. Review the calculated **net income after expenses** for both jobs.
6. Check the **Difference (Month)** column to see whether the new job will improve your monthly finances.
7. Adjust your inputs as needed to compare different job options or scenarios.

Conclusion

In this chapter, you developed the New Job Pay Comparison worksheet, a valuable tool to assess the financial impact of a potential job change. By setting up sections for both current and new job income, estimated expenses, and net monthly values, this worksheet provides a clear comparison of take-home pay after expenses. Additionally, the inclusion of unemployment benefits calculations allows for a comprehensive view, ensuring you have all the financial insights needed to make informed decisions. This worksheet consolidates the skills you've developed, including linking cells, applying conditional formatting, and using structured calculations to simplify decision-making.

Summary of the Worksheets Section

This chapter wraps up your work on the key worksheets. You've now completed the foundation of your home budgeting system by building and configuring a series of important tools.

Each worksheet serves a specific purpose — from recording income and expenses to planning holidays and evaluating job opportunities.

By mastering the layout, formulas, formatting, and protections across these sheets, you now have a powerful, flexible framework for managing your personal finances with confidence.

As you move forward, you'll see how these worksheets come together in the overall budget summary and reporting features.

Quiz

1. **What is the primary purpose of the New Job Pay Comparison worksheet?**
   a) To track daily expenses
   b) To evaluate the financial impact of a potential job change
   c) To list monthly bills
   d) To calculate income taxes

2. **Which calculation is used to convert weekly income to monthly income?**
   a) weekly income * 12
   b) weekly income * 4
   c) weekly income * 52/12
   d) weekly income / 4

3. **What is the function of the cell H18 in the worksheet?**
   a) To display the total annual income
   b) To show the net difference between the current and new job monthly income after expenses
   c) To calculate the tax on income
   d) To display the amount needed for monthly expenses

4. **Which tool allows you to see how benefits might be reduced based on new income?**
   a) Income section
   b) Expense section
   c) Unemployment Benefit Calculation section
   d) Monthly Summary

Quiz Answers

1. b) To evaluate the financial impact of a potential job change
2. c) weekly income * 52/12
3. b) To show the net difference between the current and new job monthly income after expenses
4. c) Unemployment Benefit Calculation section

Self-Assessment

Key Takeaways

- **Income Comparison**: Understanding how to calculate and compare net income for different jobs provides insight into job changes' financial implications.
- **Expense and Benefit Analysis**: Factoring in both expenses and potential reductions in benefits allows for a comprehensive evaluation of your financial position.
- **Practical Calculation Skills**: Converting income and expenses to monthly amounts ensures that financial impacts are presented in a format aligned with monthly budgeting.

Reflective Questions

1. **Job Income and Expense Changes**: Are there additional income sources or expenses to consider when assessing the impact of a new job?
2. **Unemployment Benefits**: If your benefit payments are affected, do you have a clear understanding of how the reduction scale will impact your net income?
3. **Worksheet Accuracy**: Is the worksheet layout clear, and are the conditional formatting rules (e.g., for positive or negative differences) effective in providing a quick, accurate summary?

This self-assessment encourages you to reflect on how well the worksheet meets its purpose and helps in accurately assessing job changes.

Chapter 7: VBA Macros

Introduction to VBA, creating and using macros for automation.

> **Reminder: Save Your Workbook Correctly**
>
> If you are using Microsoft Excel, make sure you save your workbook as a Macro-Enabled Workbook (.xlsm) before adding any macros.
>
> If you are using LibreOffice Calc, continue saving your file as an Open Document Spreadsheet (.ods).
>
> Saving in the correct format ensures your macros are kept and will work correctly after closing and reopening the workbook.
>
> This ensures you can continue working with macros without unexpected issues later.

VBA Macros

Excel uses *VBA Macros*, while LibreOffice Calc uses *LibreOffice BASIC Macros*. Throughout this book, any reference to "VBA Macros" also applies to LibreOffice BASIC Macros unless otherwise noted. Where there are differences, specific guidance will be provided for each platform.

VBA (Visual Basic for Applications) Macros are scripts written in the VBA programming language that automate tasks in Microsoft Office applications, such as Excel. Macros can perform repetitive actions quickly, streamline complex workflows, and enhance the functionality of Excel worksheets by allowing users to create custom commands and functions.

> **Please note** that this is not meant to be a comprehensive course in macro development. As rich as Excel is in functions, you may need specialized functions that Excel does not provide. You can create these functions yourself using macros to meet your specific needs. This makes VBA a powerful tool as it allows the creation of bespoke functionality in the workbook, we will only be concentrating on our specific needs for our budget application to demonstrate this powerful feature.

Tip for LibreOffice Users

Macros in this book are written using VBA (Visual Basic for Applications) for Microsoft Excel.
LibreOffice Calc uses a different macro language called LibreOffice BASIC.

Adapted LibreOffice versions of the macros (such as for tax calculations) are available from the book's support GitHub page.

Click or scan the QRCode

You can also learn more about LibreOffice macros by visiting the official help page:

Developer Options

Developer Options in Excel provide access to tools for creating, editing, and managing VBA macros. This includes the Visual Basic for Applications (VBA) editor, where you can write and modify VBA code, and the ability to add form controls like buttons and text boxes to your worksheets. Enabling the Developer tab in Excel unlocks these powerful features, allowing you to customize your Excel environment and automate tasks. We will enable them shortly.

Tip for LibreOffice Users

LibreOffice Calc does not use a Developer tab like Excel.
To access macro-related tools in LibreOffice, go to **Tools → Macros** on the top menu.
From there, you can manage, create, and edit macros without needing to customize the toolbar.

What is a Function

A **Function** in VBA is a block of code that performs a specific task and returns a value. Functions are used to execute calculations, manipulate data, or perform operations that can be reused throughout your VBA code. They can accept inputs, known as arguments, and use these inputs to generate and return a result.

What is a SUB

A **SUB** (short for Subroutine) in VBA is a block of code that performs a specific task but does not return a value. Subroutines are used to execute actions, such as modifying worksheet data, displaying messages, or interacting with other Excel features. Unlike functions, subroutines cannot be used in worksheet formulas, but they can be called from functions.

What is a Macro

A **Macro** in VBA is a recorded or written sequence of commands and actions that automate tasks in Excel. Macros can include both functions and subroutines, allowing for complex workflows and repetitive processes to be executed with a single command. Macros can be triggered manually by the user, assigned to a button, or set to run automatically based on certain events in the workbook.

> **Note**: When a cell or named range is referenced directly in a VBA macro, it is not automatically adjusted in the VBA code if the cell or range is moved or renamed. This can lead to errors or unexpected results in your macro if the referenced cells or ranges are modified. Unlike Excel formulas, which update automatically when cell references change, VBA code requires manual updates to reflect any changes in cell coordinates or named ranges. Therefore, it is essential to keep your VBA code in sync with any structural changes in your worksheets to ensure your macros continue to function correctly. We will cover how to identify when this has happened and how to fix it at the end of this chapter.

Enough of the intro, let us get started on Macro development.

Activating Developer tools (Excel Only)

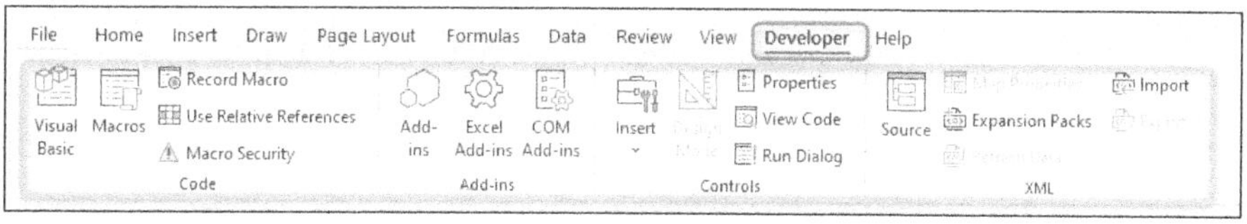

Developer tools are found in the **Developer** tab on the Excel ribbon, it is not activated by default in Excel, if you cannot see the tab, activate by doing the following

- Select **File** from the ribbon menu
- Select **Options** at the bottom of the left panel. The *Excel Options* window will pop up.

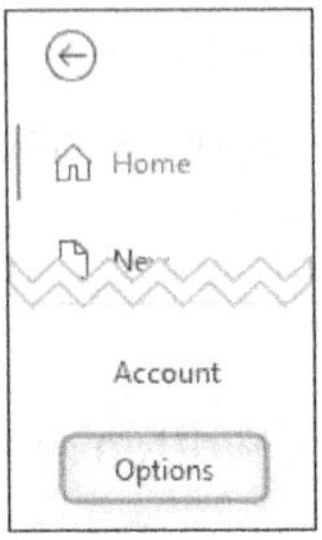

- Select **Customize Ribbon**, the display will present two panels
- Look in the right side panel, scroll down until you find the option **Developer**, it is unticked, tick it.
- Click **OK**, the **Developer** tab will appear in the ribbon

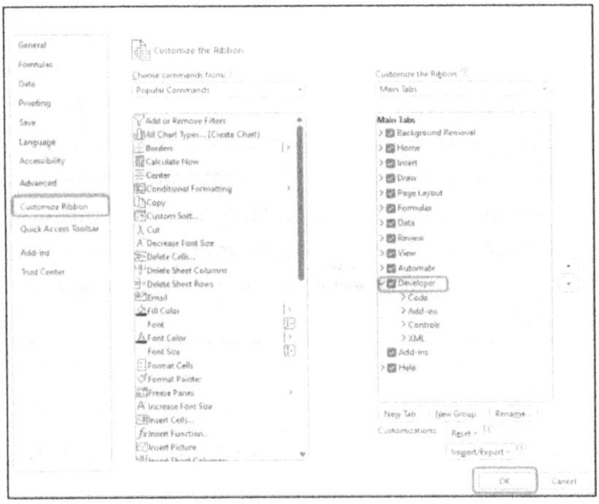

Congratulations, you have now activated the Developer tools, and you are ready to delve into the magic of Macros, Functions and VBA.

Bespoke functions in Excel

In Excel, standard functions like SUM, VLOOKUP, and IF cover a wide range of calculations and operations. However, there are situations where these standard functions may not meet specific needs. In such cases, bespoke functions can be created to perform customized tasks, enabling Excel to handle unique or complex calculations that would otherwise require manual work.

Bespoke functions are custom-made functions developed using **VBA (Visual Basic for Applications)** or **Office Scripts**. These functions add specialized functionality, allowing users to automate tasks, perform unique calculations, or integrate Excel with other systems. By using bespoke functions, you can tailor Excel precisely to your needs, making it a powerful, flexible tool for specialized tasks.

Examples of When to Use Bespoke Functions

- **Converting User Selections**: You can create functions to accept user selections from a dropdown and convert it to a numeric value Excel can use in formula.
- **Advanced Tax Calculations**: A bespoke function can calculate tax payments based on multiple parameters and varying tax brackets, handling details beyond the reach of standard functions.
- **Archiving large chunks of data**: Bespoke functions can be used to prepare and archive data for future reference and maintain the historical record in a fraction of the time it would take to do it manually.

These bespoke functions transform Excel from a standard tool into a highly customized solution, providing functionality that meets precise business or personal requirements.

In the previous chapters we included several inputs that would serve us better if they were functions.

They are

- Pay Periods
  Used in the **Expenses – Budget** worksheet to match the budget with the pay frequency.
  An ideal candidate for a bespoke function is to use the *Pay Periods* table in the **Lookup Tables** worksheet and convert it to meaningful value for the

workbook to use, i.e., 52, 26, etc.

- Tax Week
  The amount of tax to pay in the **Tax Week** column in the *Income* worksheet, currently the value is entered after using an external tax calculator. Tax calculations are complex and cannot be achieved with cell formula alone, at least not in an easy to read format.
  An ideal candidate for a bespoke function to calculate the tax and return the amount.

We will start with **Pay Periods** where you will also be introduced to dropdowns.

Pay Periods

Here you will learn to

- Prepare the worksheet for setting up a dropdown
  - We need to add new value in N5 to store the selected value of the dropdown item selected
- Create a Combo Box (dropdown) to select the pay period
  - This will be a list of options, remember we setup and named the **Pay Periods** range in ***WS1 – Lookup Tables*** back at the start, now we get to use them; each will be assigned a value we will use by placing in M5

> **Note**: If you did not set up the Pay Periods range earlier, please go back to *WS1 – Lookup Tables* and ensure the tables and ranges are set up, you will be needing them now.

- Create a VBA Macro function to process the selection and set the Pay Period value in **M5**.

You will see how it ties together as we work through it. To start, we want to put in a Combo Box for you to select the pay periods. A Combo Box needs a list, which we will get to soon, however, it outputs an integer value representing the user's selection, i.e., 1,2,3,4.... This value needs to be put in a cell somewhere so it can be referenced by other cells or code to convert it to something useful.

In the next step, we will prepare a place to receive this selection value.

Prepare the worksheet for the dropdown

Some small changes are required to fit the dropdown in, we do not want to place it in column L because that is too close to the WorkDays, now we get to learn how to move stuff around, do the following

- **Make a backup of your workbook** — we're about to rearrange a few things, and it's always best to be safe.
- Activate worksheet **Expenses – Budget**
- Move **Annual Pay Days**, cells **M4:M5** to **N4:N5**
    - Select the **Annual Pay Days** cells **M4:M5**
        - When selected, hover over the border and the cursor will change to the drag cursor
        - Hold down the left mouse button and drag it to the right, keep on same rows, to column **N** and let go, the two cells will now be in column **N**
            - Note that nothing else changed, Excel automatically changed any formula referencing **M5** to **N5,** so you don't have find and change them, nice. Check one of the formulas in column N.

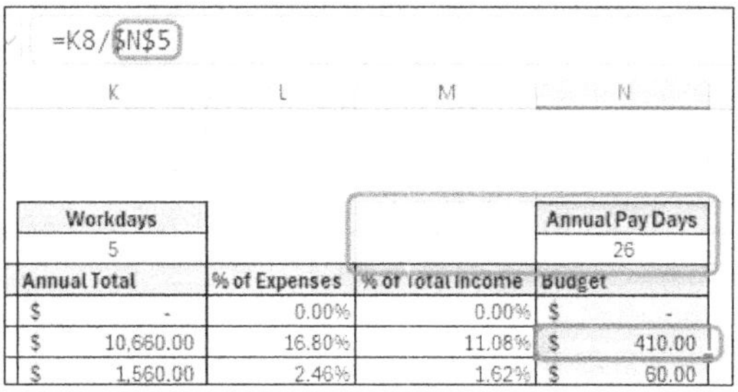

Now to set up a place for the dropdown

- **M3**, Type **Set your pay period**
- **M3:N3**, Merge and Centre, **Bold** and set a back fill color of your choice
- **M4**, Type - **Pay Period**
- **M5**, format as **general**
- **M5:M6** should have no back color, they are no longer input cells
- Format as you wish

	L	M	N
1			
2			
3		Set your Pay Period	
4		Pay Period	Annual Pay Days
5			26
6	% of Expenses	% of Total Income	Budget

That is now done, you have prepared a place to put the selection in cell **M5**, now we create the dropdown to allow the user to select their pay period.

Create a Combo Box to select the pay period

> **Note**: The steps to create a Combo Box differ slightly between Excel and LibreOffice Calc.
> We will cover both methods so you can follow along regardless of which program you are using.

For Excel

- Put Combo Box on screen
    - Click worksheet tab ***Expenses – Budget*** to activate the worksheet
    - Click the new ***Developer*** tab on the ribbon to open the Developer Tools
    - In the ***Controls*** section, click on ***Insert*** to open the available Controls window, these are separated by *Form Controls* and *Active-X Controls*. We will be using **Form Control**
    - In the **Form Controls**, find and select the **Combo Box**.

> **Tip**: Hovering the mouse over the top of each one will display the controls name, try second control on top row.

    - Click on the Combo Box when you find it, the window will disappear and when you move down to the main form, your mouse pointer will be a cross. Click anywhere to place the dropdown, you can resize and move it later.
- Assign its list, linked cell and protection
    - If you have lost focus on the Combo Box, **right click** on it and select **Format Control** to open the *Format Control* window
    - Click the **Control** tab
    - Type the following in each of the input boxes
        - Input range: **Pay_Periods**
          This is the name of the range you created earlier, if there is a problem, check the range and name spelling
        - Cell link: **M5**
        - Drop down lines: **4**

Check 3-D shading if you like, might be fun

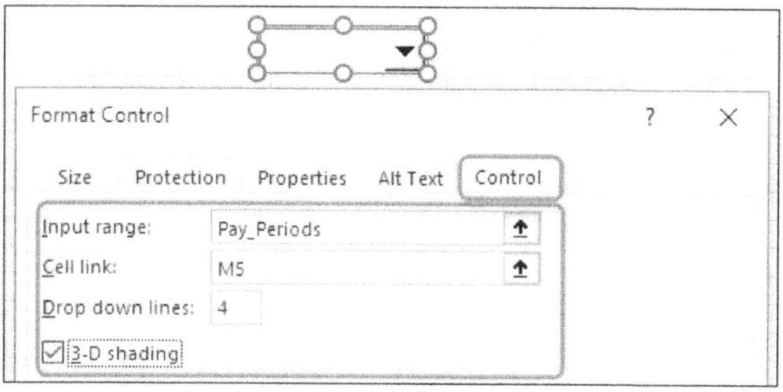

    - Click the **Protection** tab
    - Uncheck **Locked**, the Combo Box will function when worksheet is locked
    - Click **OK**

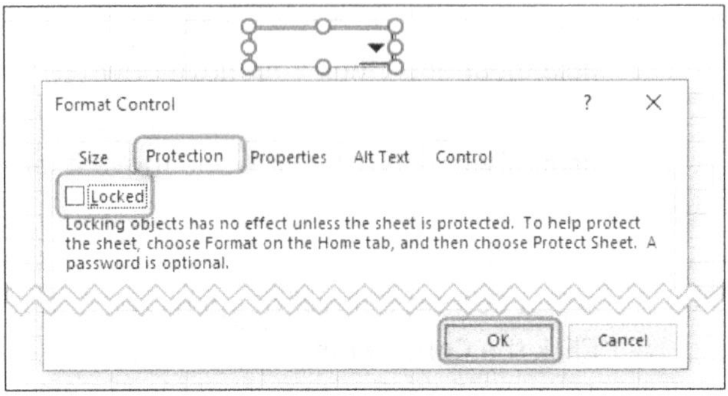

- Test the **Combo Box**
    - Make selection changes in the Combo Box, ensure the following values appear in cell M5 when selections are made, if your values are not as below, check the order of the Pay Periods in the lookup table. These are assigned by Excel based on their order of appearance in the lookup table.

Option	**Value**
Year	1
Month	2
Fortnight	3
Week	4

- Set the display order
    - Right Click the Combo Box
    - Select **Order**
    - Select the top option, **Bring to Front**
      This ensures the Combo Box will stay on top if you put other controls on the form
- Resize and Move
    - Right click on the Combo Box
    - Resize using the **resize handles**, make it the same size as cell **M5**

- Right click and hold the mouse button on the Combo Box again and you can drag it where you want, place it right over the top of cell **M5**
- Make any final size adjustments so it fits perfectly

For LibreOffice

LibreOffice Calc Combo Boxes work a little differently than in Excel:
they cannot use Named Ranges directly and require you to manually enter the list of options.

You can still easily set up a ComboBox dropdown in LibreOffice Calc for selecting your Pay Period.
Follow these steps:

1. Activate Design Mode

- Go to **View → Toolbars → Form Controls** to open the Form Controls toolbar.
- Click **Toggle Design Mode** (pencil icon) to enter design mode.

2. Insert the ComboBox

- Click the **Combo Box** button in the Form Controls toolbar.
- Draw the Combo Box on the worksheet near or over cell **M5**.

3. Set ComboBox Properties

In **Control Properties** (Right-click → Control Properties):

- **General Tab:** Find the following properties and set them as shown
    - **Name**: cmbPayPeriod
    - **Dropdown**: Yes
    - **Font**:
        - Size: 12
        - Style: Bold
    - **Line count**: 4
    - **List entries**: Enter each item on its own line:

      Year
      Month
      Fortnight
      Week
- **Data Tab:**

- **Linked Cell**: Type M5

Leave Source Type and Bound Field blank — no need to adjust them.

4. Final Steps

- Close Properties popup
- Exit design mode: Click **Toggle Design Mode** again to turn it off.

Now when a user selects a Pay Period from the dropdown, the macro will automatically update the corresponding value in M5 for calculations, Excel it will be a numeric value, LibreOffice Calc it will be a text string.

- Test the dropdown works by making selections and ensure M5 changes.
- When happy everything works, go back into Design Mode and move the ComboBox to cover **M5**
- Save your workbook.

You've now created a Combo Box dropdown, linked it to cell M5, and confirmed it's working correctly. Great job!

Now for the final step: we'll create a LibreOffice BASIC macro that ties everything together. When you select a pay period from the dropdown, LibreOffice Calc will update cell M5. Our macro will then:

1. Read the selected value from M5,
2. Determine the number of pay periods per year (e.g., 12 for monthly, 52 for weekly), and
3. Write the result into cell N5 — which will automatically update your budget calculations.

It's a simple bit of automation that makes a big impact — and yes, **you've got this!** 😊

Getting the code

To use the macros needed for your budgeting system:

- Download the ready-to-use macro files from GitHub — scan or click the QR code provided.
- Both Microsoft Excel VBA and LibreOffice BASIC versions are available in the GitHub Macros folder.

This ensures you are using the correct, tested code without needing to type anything manually.

Inserting the Macro Code

Once you download the ready-to-use macro file from GitHub:

- **If you are using Microsoft Excel**:
    1. Open your budgeting .xlsm workbook.
    2. Press **Alt+F11** to open the VBA Editor.
    3. Right-click **Modules**, choose **Import File**, and select the cmbPayPeriods_Change_Excel.bas file.
    4. Save your workbook as a Macro-Enabled Workbook (.xlsm).
- **If you are using LibreOffice Calc**:
    1. Open your budgeting .ods workbook.
    2. Adjust macro security settings if needed under **Tools → Options → LibreOffice → Security**

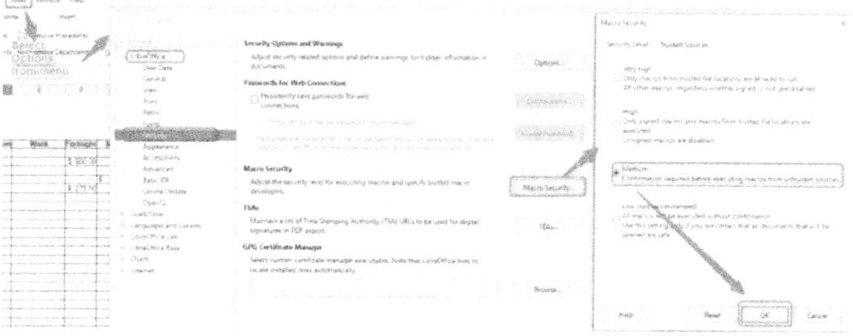

    3. **Tools -> Macros -> Edit Macros**, this will open the **LibreBasic** window

4. Locate your workbook in the list, open the levels down to Module1, there will be a sub in there named **Main**, LibreOffice Calc created this when you created the file, Dbl-Click it to open the code window. You should see the REMark (comment) and the **Sub Main** ass shown below.

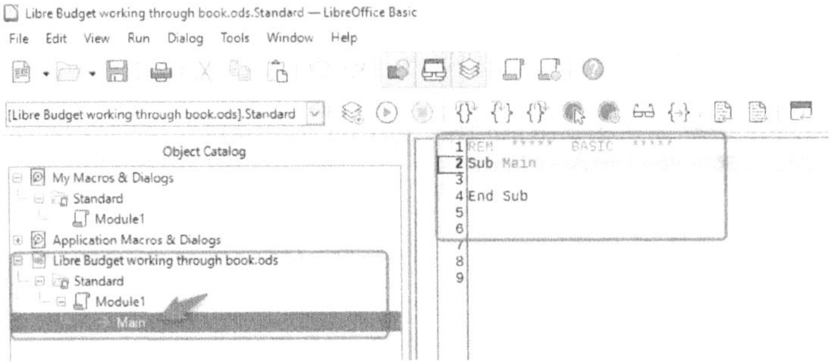

5. Put your cursor in front of *Sub Main* and insert 3 blank lines, to make room for the new code. Then put your cursor on line 3, this will be the insert point.

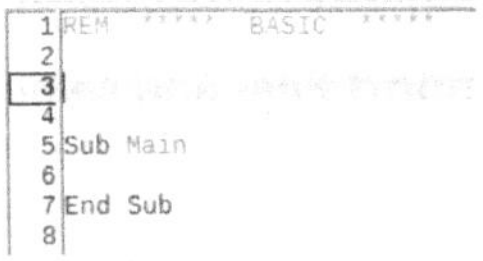

6. Select the **Import BASIC** as shown below, a file browser will open.

7. Navigate to and Select the **cmbPayPeriods_Change_Libre.bas** file you downloaded.

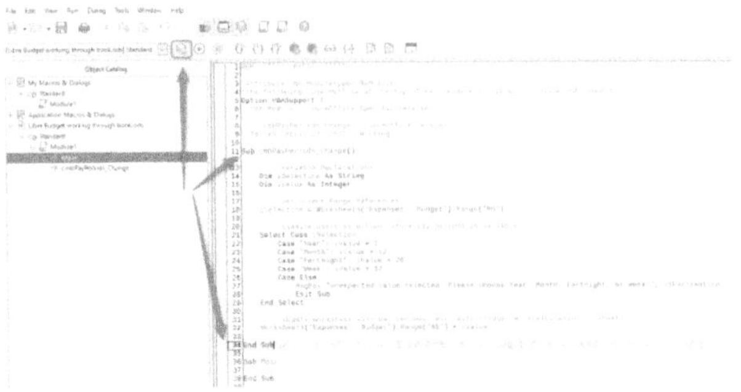

You can also click the **Compile** button to compile the code. LibreOffice Calc will check if the code is syntactically correct and nothing is out of place. If everything is OK, nothing will happen, silence...but if there is a problem then you will be notified. In this case, silence is good.

You can close the LibreBASIC window if you like.

How the cmbPayPeriods_Change Macro Works

The cmbPayPeriods_Change macro reads the user's selection from the dropdown, calculates the correct annual pay periods, and updates the linked cell.

Important Behavior Differences:

- In **Microsoft Excel VBA**, the dropdown stores **numbers** (1, 2, 3, 4) — so the code checks numeric values.
- In **LibreOffice BASIC**, the dropdown stores **text labels** ("Year", "Month", "Fortnight", "Week") — so the code checks the selection text.

In both cases, the correct number of pay periods is set automatically by the code when linked for further calculations.

Linking the VBA Sub to the Dropdown (Excel)

Now that your Combo Box is placed on the worksheet, you need to connect it to the macro you imported earlier.

Follow these steps in **Microsoft Excel**:

1. Right-click the Combo Box to select it, then right-click again to open the context menu.
2. Click **Assign Macro**.
    - The Assign Macro window will open.
3. From the list of available macros, select **cmbPayPeriods_Change**.
    - (If you don't see it, make sure you have imported the macro correctly.)
4. In the "Macros In" dropdown, make sure you select **This Workbook**.
5. Click **OK** to complete the link.

Your Combo Box is now connected. Whenever you make a selection, the VBA macro will automatically run to update your pay period calculations.

Linking the Macro to the Dropdown (LibreOffice)

In **LibreOffice Calc**, linking a macro to a Combo Box is slightly different.

Here's what to do:

1. Make sure you are still in **Design Mode** (View → Toolbars → Form Controls → Toggle Design Mode ON).
2. Right-click the Combo Box and select **Control Properties**.
3. In the Control Properties window:
    - Go to the **Events** tab.
    - Next to **Item Status Changed**, click the small ... button.
4. Click **Assign -> Macro** The **Assign Action** window will open:
    - Select your budgeting workbook (e.g., BudgetWorkbook.ods).
    - Expand the Modules list and find the module with our macros.
    - Select **cmbPayPeriods_Change**.
    - Click **OK**.
5. Exit Design Mode (View → Toolbars → Form Controls → Toggle Design Mode OFF).

Your Combo Box is now fully functional in LibreOffice — changing a selection will automatically update your calculations!

Testing Your Dropdown

Now that your Combo Box is linked to the macro, test that it works correctly:

1. Make a selection from the dropdown list.
2. Confirm that:
    - Cell **M5** updates to show the selected pay period value.
    - Cell **N5** updates automatically with the correct number of pay periods.
    - Budget values that depend on pay periods recalculate as expected.

How the Process Works Behind the Scenes

Whenever you change the dropdown selection:

1. **User Selection**: You select a new pay period from the Combo Box.
2. **Value Stored**: The linked cell (M5) is updated with the selected text or number.
3. **Macro Triggered**: The linked macro (cmbPayPeriods_Change) runs automatically.

4. **Macro Actions**:
    - It reads the value from M5 into a variable.
    - It uses a Select Case structure to determine the correct number of pay periods for that selection.
    - It writes the calculated value into **N5**.
5. **Workbook Updates**: Formulas throughout the workbook recalculate based on the new value in N5.

After completing these steps, your pay period selection and budget calculations are now fully dynamic!

Troubleshooting Tip: If Your Dropdown Isn't Working

If you select a value but nothing happens:

- **Check that macros are enabled** in your program settings (both Excel and LibreOffice require this).
- **Make sure Design Mode is turned off** (especially in LibreOffice).
    - In LibreOffice: Go to View → Toolbars → Form Controls and click Toggle Design Mode to deactivate it.
- **Confirm the correct macro is assigned** to your Combo Box or button.
- **Ensure the Combo Box is linked to the correct cell (M5)** and that your macro is looking at the right location.

Small missteps are common — a quick check of these settings usually fixes the problem!

Self-Assessment

Key Takeaways

- **Automation Basics**: VBA allows you to automate repetitive or complex tasks in Excel, saving time and reducing error.
- **Custom Functions and Subroutines**: By creating subroutines and functions, you can extend Excel's capabilities beyond standard formulas.
- **Linking Controls with Code**: Using Combo Boxes and other controls in combination with VBA code opens new ways to interact with data.

- **Best Practices with References**: It's essential to keep VBA code updated when modifying worksheet names or cell references to avoid issues.

Reflective Questions

1. How might macros benefit your existing budgeting tasks in this workbook?
2. What other Excel tasks could be automated through VBA to improve efficiency?
3. Did linking the Combo Box to VBA code provide new insights into connecting user actions with automated functions?

Calculate Tax

Automating Tax Calculation (CalculateTax Macro)

To streamline your budgeting workbook, we use a macro called **CalculateTax**. This macro automatically calculates income tax, deductions, and net income based on your weekly income, pay period, and lookup tables.

Important:
Rather than typing this macro manually, you can download the ready-to-use files from GitHub.
Both Microsoft Excel VBA and LibreOffice BASIC versions are available.

To access the macro files:

- Scan the QR code provided in the book, or
- Visit the GitHub repository under the Macros section.

This ensures you are using the latest, tested version without typing errors — especially important for LibreOffice users, where macro syntax differs slightly.

Adapting the Budget System for Other Countries

Important Note:
This budgeting system was originally developed based on Australian income tax rules. However, it is fully customizable to suit other countries and tax systems.

How it works:

All tax rates, thresholds, and levy settings are stored in the Lookup Tables worksheet — not hardcoded into macros.
If you live outside Australia, you can simply edit the lookup tables to match your country's current tax laws.
No VBA code changes are needed — the CalculateTax macro will automatically use the updated figures.

What you need to do:

- Update the tax bracket ranges, rates, and any applicable deductions in the **Lookup Tables** worksheet.
- Refer to your local government's tax website or a qualified professional to obtain the correct figures.
- After updating the tables, verify your settings by checking a few examples — such as:
    - Comparing the results against a recent payslip, or
    - Using your country's official online tax calculator to confirm the tax amounts.

Example:
If you are located in the United States, United Kingdom, Canada, or elsewhere, you can adjust the lookup tables to reflect your federal, state, or provincial tax rates as needed.

⚠ Important Disclaimer – Please Read Before Continuing

> **Disclaimer** – Tax Accuracy and Regional Differences
> This tax calculator is provided as an educational example only.
> The sample logic and tax tables are based on Australian PAYG tax rates (2023–24).
> These may not reflect current Australian laws and will not apply to users in other countries.
>
> Tax laws and thresholds change regularly, and rules vary widely between countries.
> Always check that the values in your workbook match the latest data from your local government, employer, or tax authority.
>
> If you're not comfortable setting up or maintaining the automated tax calculator, it's perfectly fine to leave the Tax field as a manual entry.
> This approach is often more accurate and easier to maintain, especially when tax amounts are shown on your pay slip or can be verified using an official tax calculator.
>
> As your skills grow, you may choose to adapt the code and lookup tables to suit your own country's tax rules or build a custom solution tailored to your needs.

Accessing the CalculateTax Macro

If you've read the above disclaimer and feel confident proceeding with the tax calculator setup, continue with the steps below.

If you prefer to keep tax as a manual entry, simply skip this section and jump ahead to '**Archive Worksheet**'.

⚠ **Please back up your workbook before proceeding with this section. This ensures you can revert to a clean copy if anything doesn't work as expected.**

You have two options to access the CalculateTax macro:

Copy and Paste:
You can copy and paste the macro directly from the GitHub repository into your workbook. Locate the relevant CalculateTax file, open it and copy/paste the contents into your existing Module...the one with the dropdown code you just put it. This ensures accuracy and saves time, or

Download and Import:
You can download the ready-to-use macro files from GitHub as you did with the dropdown code. Scan or click the QR code provided.

Both **Microsoft Excel VBA** and **LibreOffice BASIC** versions are available.

Once the code is in place, you will still need to test it.

If you want to learn more about VBA programming, you can get started with this VBA programming tutorial after you have completed this course.

Now that the code is in place, it's time to test it. Test it in the development environment through the **Immediate Window**, a window that allows developers, you, to execute commands, including running functions and viewing the results.

Let's get started!

Testing the Code

To thoroughly test the CalculateTax function, we will use both a single test and the following logic table to ensure the function behaves correctly under various scenarios. When we are happy the results are accurate, we can then be confident to put it to work in the worksheet.

Testing the Code in Excel (Immediate Window)

You will use this method during development of the function as it is a quick and simple way to run the function and look at the result, we will use the Immediate Window in the development environment.

1. If you are not already in the VBA Development view, enter it by pressing **Alt+F11**, a shortcut to the VBA window
2. Somewhere in the window, usually at the bottom, there should be a panel named **Immediate**. If you cannot see it, press **Ctrl+G**, the window will open, and the cursor will be flashing.
3. Type the following **? CalculateTax(1000,"Y","Y")** and press **Enter**
    a. **?** tells Excel to print the result of the function onscreen
    b. The remainder is the function name and the parameters we want to pass in
4. The result should be **161.66**
5. Adjust the parameters and call it again, compare the results to the logic table below.

Testing the Code in LibreOffice (Test Subroutine)

LibreOffice BASIC does not have an Immediate Window like Excel VBA.

To test your CalculateTax macro during development, follow these steps:

1. Open the Macro Editor (press Alt+F11).
2. Create a **new module** (Right-click → Insert → Module) and rename it TestCode.
3. Inside the TestCode module, type the following simple code:

```
Sub TestCode
  MsgBox CalculateTax(1000, "Y", "Y")
End Sub
```

4. Click the green **Run** button (or press F5) to run the TestCode subroutine.
5. A message box should appear showing the result, **161.66**.

This method allows you to quickly test your macros while developing them — just like using the Immediate Window in Excel.

This method of testing is repetitive but is ideal while developing the function. However, when there are numerous combinations, use a logic table to plan out the testing as below.

Now that we've tested the basic function, let's take it a step further and plan smarter testing with a logic table.

Logic Table

A logic table is a structured tool used to systematically test the behavior of a function or algorithm by listing all combinations of input values and their expected outcomes, expected outcomes would be manually calculated in most cases. It helps ensure that the function handles different scenarios correctly and consistently. By detailing the inputs and expected results, a logic table provides a clear and organized way to validate the functionality and identify any errors or edge cases that need to be addressed.

This logic table includes different combinations of Weekly Income, ClaimingTFT, and Taxable values to ensure the function behaves correctly under various scenarios. We are using three income groups resulting in four combinations for each group.

Weekly Income	ClaimingTFT	Taxable	Expected Result	Actual Result
340	Y	Y	0	
340	Y	N	0	
340	N	Y	64.6	
340	N	N	0	
1000	Y	Y	161.66	
1000	Y	N	0	
1000	N	Y	228.16	
1000	N	N	0	
10000	Y	Y	1799.34	
10000	Y	N	0	
10000	N	Y	1865.84	
10000	N	N	0	

Testing Instructions

To test the CalculateTax function, follow these steps:

1. **Prepare the Function**: Ensure the CalculateTax function is correctly implemented in your VBA module and works by using a single test as described earlier.
2. **Set Up Test Data**: Click on **Test Worksheet** tab to move focus to the test sheet.
    a. Click in cell **A1,** be sure to put it in A1 only so the following coordinates will match
    b. **Enter the data** from the logic table above by either.
        i. Input the Weekly Income, ClaimingTFT, and Taxable values in separate columns or
        ii. Copy/Paste from book if you are using an electronic version
        iii. Download or open from Github and copy/paste the table into the Work Sheet.

Open the sample file in GitHub using QR Code so you can copy/paste the table into your worksheet.

- Copy using Raw Copy

- Paste into cell **A1**, format it for readability if required

3. **Apply the Function**: In **E2,** apply the CalculateTax function.
    a. **=CalculateTax(A2, B2, C2)**
    b. A2, B2, and C2 contain the test values, the result of the first row should be zero
4. **Copy formula**: Drag **E2** down to **E13** to copy the formula, at this point the function will be run for each line.

5. **Check Results**: Compare the function's output with the expected results in the logic table. Verify that the function returns the correct tax calculations for each combination of inputs.

E2 fx =CalculateTax(A2, B2, C2)

Weekly Income	ClaimingTFT	Taxable	Expected Result	Actual Result
340	Y	Y	0	0
340	Y	N	0	0
340	N	Y	64.6	64.6
340	N	N	0	0
1000	Y	Y	161.66	161.66
1000	Y	N	0	0
1000	N	Y	228.16	228.16
1000	N	N	0	0
10000	Y	Y	1799.34	1799.34
10000	Y	N	0	0
10000	N	Y	1865.84	1865.84
10000	N	N	0	0

6. **Adjust and Debug**: If any discrepancies are found, review the function code and adjust, as necessary. Use debugging techniques to identify and fix any issues.

By systematically testing the Calculate Tax function with this logic table, you can ensure it handles various scenarios accurately and robustly.

Let us assume everything worked, now we can use the function in the budget.

Calling function from a formula

In testing, you have already put the function in a formula, now you need to put it in the appropriate places in the workbook. There are two places we need to put this

- **Income worksheet**

  This will be a simple call to the function, and we will take the result returned

  - Put the following function call in cell **O7**, you will replace the fixed value currently in the **O7**
  - **=CalculateTax(G7,F7,E7)**
  - Select and Drag **O7** to **O21** to copy the formula to the range **O7:O21**

    - You have now implemented the function call in the Income worksheet and the tax amounts will have changed. Use an online tax calculator to validate the results.
    - Remove the Yellow background from **O7:O21**, also relock them as they are no longer input cells, you may want to make them bold to stand out.
- **New Job Pay Comparison**
  This will be used in two places, and each will perform a calculation on the result to bring the result to a monthly amount
    - **D10**, type the following formula
        - **=(CalculateTax((D9 *12) / 52,"Y","Y") * 52)/12**
    - **G10**, type the following formula
        - **=(CalculateTax(((G9 *12) / 52),"Y", "Y") * 52)/12**

  Again, validate the results with an online tax calculator.

> **Note**:
> Earlier we used a sub to update the worksheet directly, because the sub had cell references in the VBA code, we cannot easily move the two cells it references or change the name of the worksheet without adjusting the VBA.
>
> This Tax Calculator is a function and accepts parameters, the VBA does not directly interact with the worksheet, it does its thing and returns the result to the calling formula. This means the formula will act like any other formula, if you move it around, Excel will adjust the parameters co-ordinates accordingly, as when you copied it.

Conclusion

In this chapter, you have learned how to create and implement a custom VBA function to automate complex tax calculations. Here are the key takeaways from this section:

1. **Writing and Integrating VBA Functions:** We started by discussing the importance of VBA functions in automating tasks that are too complex for standard Excel formulas. You learned to write a VBA

function, specifically the CalculateTax function, and integrate it into your worksheet to streamline the tax calculation process.

2. **Testing the Function:** We emphasized the importance of thorough testing to ensure the function works correctly under various scenarios. You learned how to use the Immediate Window for quick tests and how to create a logic table to systematically test the function with different input combinations.
3. **Using the Function in Worksheets:** Finally, we demonstrated how to call the CalculateTax function from worksheet formulas, ensuring it dynamically calculates the tax based on the data entered in your Income worksheet and the New Job Pay Comparison worksheet.

By following these steps, you have gained valuable skills in automating complex calculations using VBA, testing your functions systematically, and integrating them into your Excel worksheets to enhance functionality and efficiency. This knowledge not only simplifies your current project but also equips you with the tools to tackle similar tasks in the future.

If you'd like to explore VBA programming in more depth and build on the skills you've learned, you can start with the official Microsoft VBA Programming Getting Started Guide.

This resource provides clear explanations, examples, and best practices to help you unlock even more possibilities within Excel and other Office applications.

Keep experimenting, building, and enhancing your knowledge to make the most of what VBA can offer!

Quiz

1. **What does the CalculateTax VBA function return if the Taxable parameter is set to "N"?**
   a) The tax rate
   b) Zero
   c) Weekly income
   d) Medicare levy only

2. **What purpose does the Immediate Window serve when testing a VBA function?**
   a) Editing VBA code
   b) Running functions and viewing results immediately
   c) Displaying cell formulas
   d) Showing Excel's background processes

3. **Why is it advantageous to use a logic table for testing a function?**
   a) It organizes test cases for thorough, systematic verification
   b) It allows you to format cells easily
   c) It enables color-coding of cells based on values
   d) It automatically checks for errors

4. **How does the CalculateTax function handle Medicare Levy calculations?**
   a) Applies a standard rate across all incomes
   b) Calculates based on taxable income over a threshold
   c) Adds Medicare levy to non-taxable income
   d) Ignores Medicare levy

5. **What does setting up a tax function in VBA allow you to do in your workbook?**
   a) Automatically update taxes without manual calculations
   b) Apply Excel's built-in tax formulas
   c) Customize cell backgrounds
   d) Sort data based on tax rates

Quiz Answers

1. **What does the CalculateTax VBA function return if the Taxable parameter is set to "N"?**
   Answer: b) Zero

2. **What purpose does the Immediate Window serve when testing a VBA function?**
   Answer: b) Running functions and viewing results immediately

3. **Why is it advantageous to use a logic table for testing a function?**
   Answer: a) It organizes test cases for thorough, systematic verification

4. **How does the CalculateTax function handle Medicare Levy calculations?**
   Answer: b) Calculates based on taxable income over a threshold

5. **What does setting up a tax function in VBA allow you to do in your workbook?**
   Answer: a) Automatically update taxes without manual calculations

Self-Assessment

Key Takeaways

- **Custom VBA Functions**: Creating a VBA function lets you perform complex calculations directly within worksheet formulas, enhancing Excel's functionality.

- **Logic Table Testing**: Testing your function with a logic table helps ensure it handles a variety of scenarios accurately and consistently.

- **Error Handling in VBA**: By implementing error handling in your VBA function, you can ensure stability and handle unexpected inputs gracefully.

- **Reusable Code**: Integrating the tax function across multiple worksheets demonstrates how to reuse code effectively in different parts of a workbook.

Reflective Questions

1. **How could this tax calculation function simplify other areas of your budgeting tasks?**

2. **Are there other complex calculations or processes in your workbook that would benefit from a similar VBA approach?**

3. **Did testing the function using the Immediate Window and logic table help you understand the value of structured testing for accuracy?**

Archive Worksheet

At the end of your budget period, after you have entered your actual expenses and reviewed your progress, you may want to save the data in the Expense – Actuals worksheet for future reference.

Saving this data allows you to create a historical record of your financial performance, which can be invaluable for several reasons:

- It enables you to analyze trends over time, helping you understand your spending patterns and identify areas for improvement.

- It helps you make more accurate future budgets by comparing actual spending against budgeted amounts.
- It provides a comprehensive view of your financial history, useful for tax preparation, financial planning, or loan applications.

In this section, we will set up an easy-to-use archiving feature that will help you save your Expense – Actuals data efficiently and securely.
You will be able to focus on improving your financial health without worrying about losing valuable information.

How you use this historical data is up to you — our goal for now is to get the archiving system working.

Introduction

The approach we are taking is simple but highly effective:

- We will create a VBA Subroutine that takes a **snapshot** of the Expense – Actuals worksheet and copies it to a **new worksheet**.
- The new worksheet will have the current Month and Year appended to its name.
- It will not have any formulas — only the raw data values.
- A button will trigger the archive routine whenever you are ready.

This makes saving your budget history easy, safe, and quick.

Getting the Code

Copy and Paste:
You can copy and paste the macro directly from the GitHub repository into your workbook. Locate the relevant **ArchiveSheetWithValues** file, open it and copy/paste the contents into your existing Module...the one with the dropdown code you just put it. This ensures accuracy and saves time, or

Download and Import:
You can download the ready-to-use macro files from GitHub as you did with the dropdown code. Scan or click the QR code provided. Import the file as you did with the Pay_Periods macro

Both **Microsoft Excel VBA** and **LibreOffice BASIC** versions are available.

This ensures you are using the correct, tested code without worrying about typos!

Final Notes

After inserting the macro:

- You can create a **Button** (Form Control) on the Expense – Actuals worksheet.
- Assign the macro to the button.
- Clicking the button will instantly archive your worksheet for easy reference later!

We will guide you through creating and assigning buttons shortly.

Important Tip

Worksheet names in Excel and LibreOffice are limited to **31 characters**.
If your original worksheet name is very long, appending a date could exceed this limit.
Always keep worksheet names reasonably short to avoid issues.

How the Macro Works

1. **Function Details:** Provides information about the author, date, and purpose of the subroutine.
2. **Variable Declaration:** Declares variables to reference worksheets and controls.
3. **Get Active Worksheet Name:** Retrieves the name of the currently active worksheet.
4. **Set Reference to Active Worksheet:** Assigns the active worksheet to a variable for easier reference.
5. **Generate New Name Based on Date:** Creates a new name incorporating the current date.
6. **Copy Worksheet and Rename:** Copies the active worksheet, moves the copy to the end, and renames it.
7. **Replace Formulas with Values:** Pastes over all formulas with static values to lock in the data.
8. **Remove Buttons:** Loops through and deletes any buttons copied into the new sheet.
9. **Save Workbook:** Saves the workbook to ensure the archive is preserved.

Calling the Macro with a Button (Microsoft Excel)

You can place a button on any worksheet to run the ArchiveSheetWithValues macro however we specifically want to archive the **Expense – Actuals** worksheet

Action	Steps
Activate Worksheet	Activate the Expense – Actuals worksheet
Add a button	Developer tab → Insert → Form Controls → Button. Draw the button on the screen where you want it. The Assign Macro popup will automatically appear.
Assign the macro	When prompted, select ArchiveSheetWithValues.
Customize the button	Right-click → Edit Text → Change the label to "Archive this worksheet". Click outside of button to save change and deselect button
Format the button	Right-click → Format Control → Adjust protection, font, size, etc. as you require
Final placement	Resize and move the button as needed.

Clicking the button will now automatically archive the active worksheet.

Calling the Macro with a Button (LibreOffice Calc)

In LibreOffice Calc, the process is slightly different but achieves the same result:

Action	Steps
Activate Worksheet	Activate the **Expense – Actuals** worksheet
Enter design mode	**Tools Tab → Toggle Design Mode** The Push Button is in the last group of icons. Hover over the icons to see their names. 
Add a button	Go to Form Controls toolbar → Click **Push Button**.
Draw the button	Click the button icon then draw the button on the worksheet Above the Comment column is good.
Open Properties	Right-click the button → Select **Control Properties**.
Set the Label	In the Control Properties window, under the *General* tab, set the *Label* field to "**Archive this worksheet**". Set *Name* to "**ArchiveWS**"
Assign the macro	Still in Control Properties, under the *Events* tab: next to *Execute Action*, click the small "**...**" button. Choose **Macro**, then select **ArchiveSheetWithValues** from your workbook's available macros. Close the popups.

Action	Steps
Final placement	Adjust the size and position of the button as needed onscreen. Later you may want to go in and adjust font size, colors, etc.
And finally	**Tools Tab → Toggle Design Mode** To turn off Design Mode, you cannot click the button while in design mode

Clicking the button will now automatically archive the active worksheet

Bonus Tip for LibreOffice
Make sure "Design Mode" is turned OFF after creating the button.
Otherwise, clicking the button will just select it instead of running the macro.
You can toggle Design Mode from the Form Controls tab or the Tools tab.

Testing the Archive Macro

After assigning the ArchiveSheetWithValues macro to your new button, it's time to test it to make sure everything is working correctly.:

1. Activate any worksheet — you can create a test worksheet if you like.
2. Click the **Archive** button you created.
3. A new worksheet will appear.
   - The name will include the original name plus the date (e.g., Expenses - Actual_2025_Jul_11).
   - or if archived multiple times: Expenses - Actual_2025_Jul_11_Copy1, Copy2, etc.
   - All formulas will be replaced by **values only** — no live calculations.
4. Review the new worksheet and ensure it archived correctly.

Once verified, your archiving system is ready!

How to Use the Archive System

Each time you finish a budgeting period:

1. Enter your actual expenses into the **Expenses – Actuals** worksheet.
2. Add comments where necessary for future reference.
3. Click the **Archive** button to create a permanent record.
4. Clear the **Actual** and **Comments** columns ready for the next period.

At the end of a financial year:

- Save a copy of the entire workbook as a new file for long-term storage.
- Example filename:
  Home Budget – FY 2024/2025

You are now ready to continue budgeting into the next year!

Conclusion

In this chapter, you took your Excel skills to the next level by exploring VBA macros and learning how to automate repetitive tasks.

From customizing dropdowns to archiving data efficiently, you now have the tools to streamline your budgeting system and reduce manual effort.

Even a few simple macros can make your home budget easier to maintain and less prone to errors.

As you continue building your budgeting application, remember that VBA macros offers almost limitless possibilities for future enhancements.

Quiz

1. **What is the primary purpose of the ArchiveSheetWithValues subroutine?**
    - a) To save the workbook
    - b) To create a new workbook
    - c) To create a snapshot of the Expense - Actuals worksheet with values only
    - d) To archive all worksheets in the workbook

2. **What does the ArchiveSheetWithValues subroutine do with formulas on the copied worksheet?**
    - a) Retains them
    - b) Converts them to values
    - c) Deletes them
    - d) Changes them to comments

3. **Which VBA control allows you to run the ArchiveSheetWithValues subroutine with a single click?**
    - a) Form Control button
    - b) Combo Box
    - c) Scroll Bar
    - d) Option Button

4. **What should you do with the Expense - Actuals worksheet after archiving it?**
    - a) Delete the worksheet
    - b) Save a copy of the worksheet
    - c) Clear the Actual and Comment columns for the next period
    - d) Copy the worksheet to another workbook

5. **Why is it important to archive your Expense - Actuals worksheet periodically?**

- a) To maintain a historical record for analysis and future budgeting
- b) To reset the workbook automatically
- c) To create a backup in case of system failure
- d) To send data to external systems for processing

Quiz Answers

1. c) To create a snapshot of the Expense - Actuals worksheet with values only
2. b) Converts them to values
3. a) Form Control button
4. c) Clear the Actual and Comment columns for the next period
5. a) To maintain a historical record for analysis and future budgeting

Self-Assessment

Key Takeaways

- **Value of Archiving:** Archiving your financial data at the end of each budget period is essential for tracking spending patterns, analyzing trends, and refining future budgets based on actual spending.
- **VBA Automation:** By using VBA to automate the archiving process, you can quickly and easily save a snapshot of your data, ensuring it is secure and accessible for future references.
- **Single-Click Archiving:** Linking the archiving subroutine to a button in the worksheet simplifies the process, making it user-friendly and efficient.
- **Future Budgeting Insights:** Maintaining archived worksheets helps provide historical context for budgeting decisions, offering a resource for planning and financial analysis.

Reflective Questions

- How could maintaining an archive of your expenses help you make better financial decisions in the future?
- What other worksheets or data might benefit from a similar archiving process for record-keeping?
- How could you expand on the archiving function to create a more comprehensive or detailed financial history?

By understanding the value of organized financial records, you're better prepared to create a robust budget management system, and you've also gained valuable VBA skills to make this process efficient.

Chapter 8: Modifying and Enhancing Worksheets

Dynamic worksheet modifications, Inserting, moving, copying, and deleting data

Modifying Work Sheets

Excel workbooks and worksheets are dynamic, often requiring changes to accommodate evolving needs. This budget is no exception. As you use it, you may need to add rows, introduce new features, or make other adjustments. This section will guide you through some basic tasks such as copying cells or worksheets, inserting or deleting rows, and more. We will also highlight important considerations for each task to ensure you make these changes effectively.

What do we mean by dynamic?

Excel's intelligent referencing system is a key feature that ensures calculations remain accurate and up to date when changes are made. This system automatically updates formulas and references whenever cells, rows, or columns are moved, added, or deleted. For instance, if you insert a new row within a range of data, Excel adjusts the cell references in your formulas to account for the new row, maintaining the integrity of your calculations. This dynamic updating capability is essential for keeping your workbook functional and dependable, allowing you to adjust as needed without having to manually modify all related formulas.

While Excel's intelligent referencing system is powerful and will perform flawlessly for you, there are certain limitations to be aware of when modifying your workbook.

- Excel will not automatically update formulas or references embedded within VBA code, so any changes to cell locations or worksheet names embedded in the VBA code or macro must be manually updated in your macros. Additionally
- Excel does not adjust references in text strings or comments, so these must also be revised manually if they contain cell references that have changed.

- Be mindful of named ranges as well; while Excel updates the references for named ranges, it will not notify you of potential conflicts or errors that may arise from these changes.

Understanding these limitations is crucial to maintaining the accuracy and functionality of your workbook as you make modifications, let's get started.

The Golden Rules of modification

Before making any modifications to your Excel workbook, it is essential to understand and adhere to two crucial rules:

1. **Backup Your Workbook:** Always create a backup of your workbook before starting any modifications.
2. **Ensure Rule One is Obeyed:** Verify that you have made a backup.

Take a moment to consider the implications if something were to go wrong during your modifications and your workbook becomes unusable. By following these rules, you can safeguard your work and ensure that any potential issues can be quickly resolved or reversed. With these precautions in place **and a backup made**, let us proceed with the modifications.

Note on Terminology

In the following sections, we will frequently refer to Rows, Columns, Cells, and Ranges. While each of these elements has its specific function within an Excel worksheet, their behavior is quite similar when it comes to operations like inserting, moving, copying, and deleting. Whether you are working with a single cell, a full row, a column, or a defined range of cells, the methods and considerations for modifying them often overlap. Understanding this similarity will help you apply the concepts learned in one context to another, making your work with Excel more efficient and intuitive. As you go through these sections, keep in mind that the principles discussed can be adapted to different parts of your worksheet seamlessly.

Ctrl-Z: Is your friend.

When making modifications to your Excel workbook, mistakes are inevitable. Fortunately, Excel's undo feature, activated by pressing Ctrl-Z, allows you to quickly reverse your most recent actions. This can save you time and frustration by easily correcting errors and experimenting with changes without fear of permanently damaging your work. Always remember that Ctrl-Z is there to help you recover from missteps and maintain the integrity of your workbook. Excel remembers the last 100 changes you have made, and each use of Ctrl-Z will undo them one at a time.

Ctrl-Y: redo
You can use Ctrl + Y (or F4 on some versions) to redo the last undone action in Excel. Similar to undo, the redo command works sequentially, meaning you can redo multiple actions in the order they were undone, as long as you haven't performed a new action since the last undo.

Inserting

Inserting rows is a fundamental task in Excel that allows you to add new data areas to your worksheet. Whether you are expanding your data set or preparing for additional entries, knowing how to insert rows efficiently is essential. This section will guide you through the steps to insert rows, ensuring your data remains well-organized and your formulas are updated automatically.

Activate the **Income** worksheet, we will be inserting both columns and rows in this worksheet.

Columns

For this exercise, we want to insert a new column so we can see income on a bi-annual (6 month) basis, and do the following

First, check if inserting a column is going to mess with other parts of the worksheet, to add a bi-annual column, we need to put it between the current columns J and K, the *Weekly Breakdown Calculator* is in the way, we need to move it

- Select the range **J2:L4** the entire calculator
- Grabbing the selection frame, drag it to the right and let go.

  - Excel, You cannot drop it so any is covering the existing location so you will need to at least move to column **M.**
  - LibreOffice Calc will allow you to move it on column over, but move it to **M** anyway, well out of the way.
  - Both will have changed the cell references automatically so nothing will change as far as the numbers go, test it still works.
- We will cover moving cells and ranges in more detail a little later.

Now we have cleared the way to add a new column

- Click on the header on column K, column K will highlight indicating it is selected.
- Right-Click
- Select **Insert** from the menu, a new column will be inserted

The new column is now column K, old column K and everything to the right of it has moved over one column, Notice the values in the moved cells have not changed, they were dynamically updated by Excel. The new column is blank, so you need to do a few things to finish it.

- **K6,** Type in the new heading, ***Bi-Annual***
- **K7**, type in the new formula to calculate the quarterly value, the new formula is
  - **=(G7*52)/2**
- Select **K7** and drag down to **K21** to copy the formula to the remaining cells in the **K7:K21** range
- **K22**, type in the total formula
  - **=SUM(K7:K21)**
- Examine the *Expenses – Budget* worksheet, specifically cell **N37** which references worksheet, you should see no changes as Excel would have updated the link to the new location of the Income total.

You can now move the Weekly Breakdown Calculator back if you like.

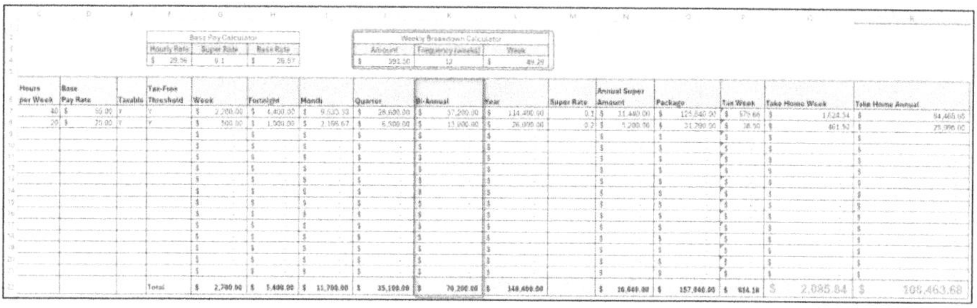

Rows

Inserting rows is similar to columns, let us get started. In this scenario, your YouTube channel is now monetized, you need to add new rows for the income stream, while at it, we will add 5 more for future streams.

- Select rows 17 to 21, this is 5 rows
- Right-Click anywhere in the selection
- Select **Insert** from the menu, 5 new rows will be inserted BEFORE the selection,

Notice the Total row values have not changed, the formula in these cells has been dynamically updated to include the new row. As with the columns, the row is blank so you will need to update the formula, this can be done with one operation

- Select **B16:R16**
- Using the drag box, drag it down to row 20, the new row. All the formula of row 19 will be copied to row 21.
- If you had a zero in cell **M16**, Reset the SuperRate in the new cells to zero if Excel dynamically.
- Add some values to test, check it went through to the Budget sheet

And that is it for inserting rows and columns. You can now include new columns and rows as required, handy for when you get more income streams from side hustles, online media like YouTube, etc., it all counts.

Moving

Moving cells within a worksheet helps in reorganizing your data to improve readability and analysis, it can also be required when inserting rows or columns.

This section will cover the methods for moving cells, ensuring that the integrity of your data and formulas is maintained. Learn how to efficiently reposition data without disrupting the functionality of your workbook.

When moving cells, there are several things you need to be mindful of

- **Make a backup before you do anything**
- **Formula and Reference Integrity**:
  - **Relative and Absolute References**: Understand how the move will affect cell references in formulas. Relative references may change based on their new location (=A1), while absolute references will remain the same (=$A$1).
  - **Dependent Formulas**: Ensure that formulas in other parts of the worksheet that depend on the moved cells are updated correctly.

Hint: From the ribbon, you can use the Formulas/Formula Auditing options to check what is dependent on a cell you wish to move. In LibreOffice Calcthese are in the Tools menu

Trace Precedents will show what cells the current cell depends on for its result, these are displayed with blue borders and arrows, the dots along the arrows are the cells used in the current cells formula.

Trace Dependents will show the cells that are dependent on the current cell. These are the cells you should check after moving to make sure there are no errors.

Show Formulas will display the formula in the cells

Evaluate Formula will run the formula in the cell

Use these tools to assist you when moving cells around.

- **Merged Cells**:
  - Ensure that the range you are moving does not conflict with existing merged cells in the destination area.
- **Data Validation**:
  - Check if the cells being moved contain data validation rules and ensure these rules are still valid in the new location.
- **Conditional Formatting**:
  - Make sure that any conditional formatting rules applied to the range are still appropriate and valid after the move.
- **Cell Formatting**:

  - Be aware of any specific cell formatting (such as borders, shading, or font styles) that might be disrupted or lost during the move.
- **Named Ranges**:
  - If the cells being moved are part of a named range, update the named range definitions accordingly.
  - Verify that any formulas or references that use these named ranges are updated.
- **Hidden Rows/Columns**:
  - Check if the range includes any hidden rows or columns, and how the move will affect the visibility and structure of the worksheet.
- **Protected Sheets**:
  - Ensure that the worksheet or cells you are moving are not protected, this can prevent the move.
- **Data Overwrite**:
  - Be cautious about moving cells to a location where there is existing data, as this will overwrite the existing content.
- **Linked Cells and External References**:
  - Be mindful of any links to other worksheets or external files that might be affected by the move. You may need to update any references in linked cells to the new location.

After you move cells, always check the worksheets that are dependent on the cells, if they are not right, move them back (use **Ctrl-Z,** this will also reverse any dynamic changes).

Earlier we moved the *Weekly Breakdown Calculator* temporarily so we could insert a new column. We mentioned that you cannot drop it anywhere over the current location of the calculator, in the next exercise we will work around that.

You can move a single cell or multiple cells, if there are problems Excel will either tell you or you will see values changing in the formula cells that depend on the moved cell/s, remember to check other worksheets as well.

Let us look at the most common scenario that could be problematic.

- You want to move the calculator one column over to column **K**,

  - you select the range **J2:L4**, drag and drop at column **K** and Excel says "**We cannot do that to a merged cell**, all you can do is click OK, to get around this you can
  - Select the range again
  - Move it to a location away from the new location, for this exercise the bottom of the worksheet, there is a lot of room there, let it go
  - It should still be selected, but if not, reselect it, move it back to the top but let go at column **K**

> **Note**: you can move it anywhere as long as you drop it where no part is within the boundaries of the selection's original location, the destination location is not part of merged cells, and you are not overwriting existing data. If you get existing data warnings but cannot see anything, check the row and column headers to ensure there are no hidden rows or columns where you are trying to drop it.
>
> You may have to move cells around more than once to get them to where you want them.

Copying

Copying data is a crucial skill for creating duplicates, backups, or transferring data across different parts of your workbook. This section will walk you through the steps to copy cells, rows, and even entire sheets, while ensuring that references and formulas remain accurate and functional.

The scenario is that you have a current local holiday in the planning for next summer you are saving for, but you also want to go on holiday to another country in about 18 months and you want to start saving now. You need another holiday planner. Here is how you would do it.

- Activate **Holiday Planning** worksheet
- Select range **B6:G27**, this is the original Holiday Planner
- **Right-Click** and select **Copy**. The selection will have a green, moving, dashed border. This border will stay active until you do any other

operation other than paste, once it is gone, you can no longer paste the selection.

- Click in **J6** and then **Right-Click** in J6, select the first **Paste** option. This will create a duplicate of the planner.
- You will need to adjust the formula in cell **L27** to
  =IF(AND(TODAY() >= $K7,TODAY()<=$L7),L26,0)
  The $'s in the D26 formula locks in the columns so they did not dynamically update when copying
- You will also need to link current budget amount back to the **Expenses – Budget** worksheet to ensure it is included in the budget, you have two options
  1. Adjust the formula in **Expenses – Budget E31** to
     ='Holiday Planning'!D27+'Holiday Planning'!L27
     This will combine both planners into one line OR
  2. You could insert another *Holiday Saving* row in **Expenses – Budget** and link that back to the new planner. If you do this, ensure the formulas across the row are added, remember, they will be blank. You will be able to see both planners individually in the budget.
- You can add as many planners as you want, you could also add them to a new worksheet if you need many planners.

Deleting

Deleting rows or cells is necessary for cleaning up your workbook and removing unnecessary data or gaps.

Deleting data, rows or columns is easy, select what you want to remove, and press delete, quite simple however, deleting data can cause issues for anything dependent on it; here are a few things to consider before pressing **Delete**.

1. **Backup Your Workbook**: Always create a backup of your workbook before making any deletions or major changes to prevent data loss. I say this a lot, be safe.
2. **Impact on Formulas**: Check if the data, rows, or columns you are deleting are referenced in any formulas. Deleting these can break the formulas.

3. **Impact on Named Ranges**: Verify if the data is part of any named ranges. Deleting it may affect other parts of your workbook that rely on these ranges.
4. **Data Dependencies**: Identify dependencies in your workbook. Data used in charts, pivot tables, or linked to other worksheets should be reviewed to avoid disrupting their functionality.
5. **VBA Code References**: Ensure the data is not referenced in any VBA code. Deleting it could cause errors in your macros.
6. **Hidden Data**: Look for any hidden rows or columns that might contain important data before deleting visible ones.
7. **Conditional Formatting**: Consider any conditional formatting rules that might be affected by the deletion.
8. **Worksheet Structure**: Ensure the overall structure and layout of your worksheet will not be compromised by deletion.
9. **Shared Workbooks**: If the workbook is shared, communicate with other users before making significant changes to avoid conflicts and data loss.
10. **Using Ctrl-Z**: Remember, you can always use Ctrl-Z to undo the deletion if something goes wrong. Ctrl-Z does have some limitations and may not always be able to undo actions, so it is better to be cautious and verify before deleting anything **AND have a backup**.

Modifying Dropdowns

In Chapter 7, we set up a dropdown and used a custom VBA function to determine the correct number of pay periods in a year based on the user's selection. We used this approach to give you some hands-on experience using VBA or LibreBASIC code, which is an important part of this workbook—and a valuable skill to have.

That method worked well, and we could leave it at that. However, there are two additional pay periods in the Income work area that weren't included in the original dropdown — and we'd like to add them in.

To make the system more flexible and easier to maintain, we'll now revise the original setup. We'll start by updating the named range used for the dropdown, and then gradually move away from the VBA macro approach. Instead, we'll use a **VLOOKUP-based method** driven by a lookup table — making it easier to modify or expand in the future without needing to touch any code.

- **For Excel users**, we'll begin by adjusting the named range and dropdown setup, then transition to a VLOOKUP-based approach.
- **For LibreOffice users**, since Calc doesn't support using named ranges in dropdowns the same way, we'll take a slightly different route — still using VLOOKUP, but adapted to LibreOffice's capabilities.

Here's how we'll do it.

The changes to the dropdown are minimal. However, we first need to set up the *Pay Periods* table in *Lookup Tables* worksheet first so let's do that.

- Add the two new pay periods as shown below, Quarter and Bi-Annual

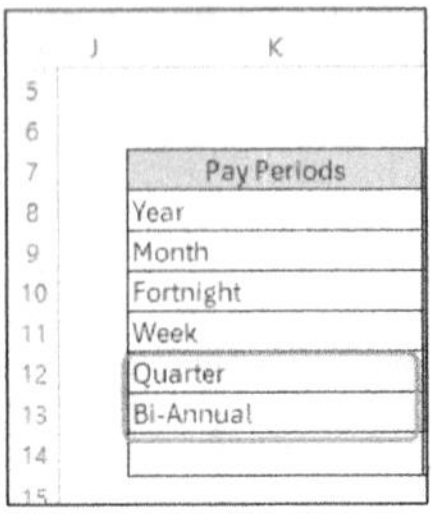

For Excel

- We need to change the range of the defined name to use the two new entries,
  - Select **Formulas/Name Manager** from the top menu, the Name Manager screen will open
  - Click on **Pay_Periods**, the *Refers To* box will display the range coordinates

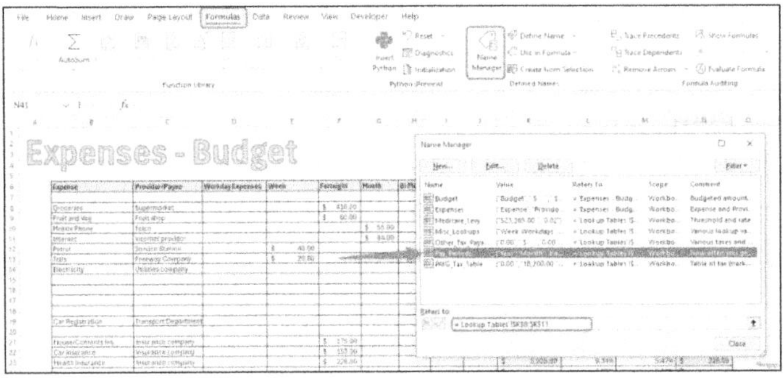

Click on the reference in the **Refers To** box, you will be taken to the range**.**

- The range on the worksheet will have a green broken border around it. Click in the formula and change the last digit to a 3 so it reads as: 'Lookup Tables'!$K$8:$K$13. You'll be immediately taken back to the original screen and the *Name Manager* will close. You have changed the *Pay_Periods* range to include the new periods.

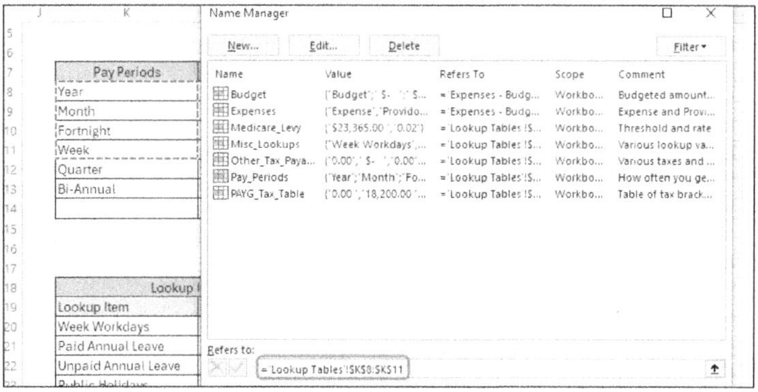

- The dropdown also needs to be updated to show the two new entries
  - **Right click** the dropdown to open the menu
  - Select **Format Control** to open the *Format Control* window
  - Select **Control** tab and change **Drop down lines** from 4 to 6 and click **OK**

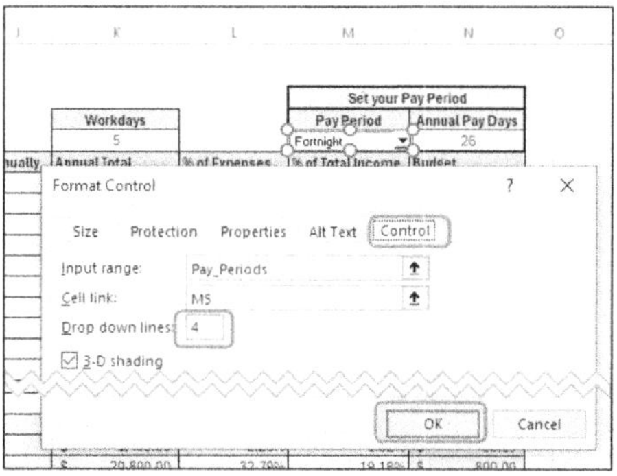

  - Check the dropdown, you will need to click anywhere on the sheet then open the drop down list, you should now see 6 rows.

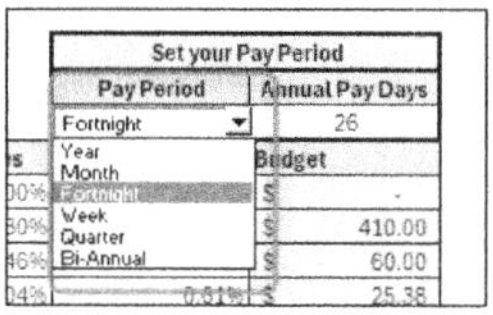

> **Note**: The original VBA macro is still linked to the dropdown. If you select one of the new entries, you'll see a message warning that the number is not 1–4. Let's disconnect that macro next.

- To remove the Macro reference on the dropdown
  - Right Click the dropdown
  - Select Assign Macros, the Assign Macros window will open. The *Macro name* will display the assigned Macro, it will already be selected so press Delete on the key board to clear it and select OK

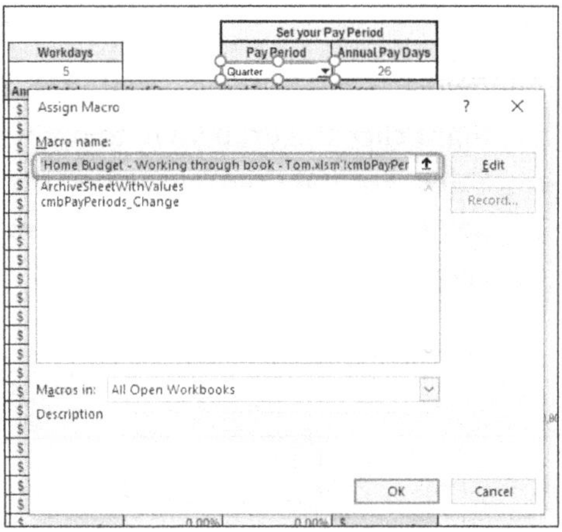

  - Try the dropdown now, you will notice the pay periods value no longer changes. We are now ready to implement the new changes.

For LibreOffice

As you may remember from earlier, LibreOffice Calc Combo Boxes work a little differently than in Excel:
they cannot use Named Ranges directly, and require you to manually enter the list of options.

You can easily add new ComboBox items in LibreOffice Calc for selecting your Pay Period.
Follow these steps:

1. Activate Design Mode

- Go to **View → Toolbars → Form Controls** to open the Form Controls toolbar.
- Click **Toggle Design Mode** (pencil icon) to enter design mode.

2. Select the Pay Periods ComboBox

3. Set ComboBox Properties

In **Control Properties** (Right-click → Control Properties):

- **General Tab:** Find the following properties and set them as shown
    - **Line count**: 6 (to allow for the two new items)
    - **List entries**: Enter new items as shown:

        Year
        BiAnnual
        Quarter
        Month
        Fortnight
        Week

Nothing else needs to be changed

4. Final Steps

- Close Properties popup
- Exit design mode: Click **Toggle Design Mode** again to turn it off.

Test the dropdown by selecting a pay period, everything should work—except when you select one of the new items. In that case, you'll get this message:

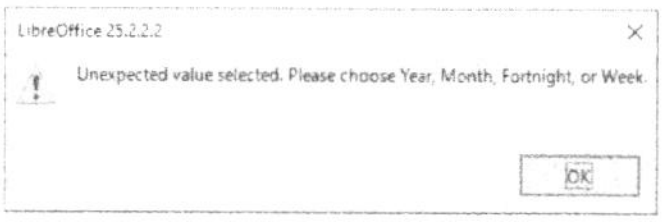

This is because the LibreBASIC code does not recognize the new values.

At this point, you have two choices: modify the LibreBASIC code to recognize the new values, or switch to a VLOOKUP-based approach. In this workbook, we'll use VLOOKUP, both to simplify future changes and to give you practical experience with lookup functions.

5. Set ComboBox Properties

- In **Control Properties** (Right-click → Control Properties):

- Click **Events** tab
- Clear the value in **Item status changed**, this is the Function call. This removes the link between the ComboBox and the old macro that no longer applies now that we're switching to VLOOKUP.
- Close Properties popup
- Exit design mode: Click **Toggle Design Mode** again to turn it off.

At this point, the dropdown selections will no longer change the budget. We can now proceed with hooking in the VLOOKUP

For both Excel and LibreOffice

The following will work for both, there is a little difference in the cell referencing so both methods will be displayed, choose what you need.

Adding the New lookup columns

We now need to set up the Pay Period table in Lookup Tables to use a VLookup

- Click Lookup Tables worksheet to activate it
- Add two new columns and the values as shown below. That is all the setup we need but let's take a moment to explain it.

Pay Periods	Dropdown Value	Pays per Year
Year	1	1
Month	2	12
Fortnight	3	26
Week	4	52
Quarter	5	4
Bi-Annual	6	2

  - **Pay Periods** as you know is the list the dropdown is displaying, as mentioned previously, the values in the dropdown are assigned by Excel, in our case they will be 1 – 6. LibreOffice Calc will still use the **Pay_Periods** text
  - **Dropdown Value** column are the values the dropdown will put in cell M5, just like before. We will use this value for the Excel VLookup to locate what the user selected

- **Pays per Year** are the number of pays per year each selection represents; this is the number our VLookup will return.

Adding the VLOOKUP

- Activate **Expenses – Budget worksheet**
- In cell **N5**, clear the existing formula that references the old macro logic.
- In cell **N5**, add the following formula and press **Enter**

    - Excel

      =VLOOKUP($M$5,'Lookup Tables'!L8:M13,2,FALSE)

    - LibreOffice Calc

      =VLOOKUP(M5, $'Lookup Tables'.K8:M13, 3, FALSE)

Try the dropdown, select a few options and ensure the value in N5 changes along with the column N's calculated budget values.

If it all worked, great, this is now done...only the explanation to go. If there are problems, go back on each step and check the values are correct. Now we'll examine how this works, we will refer to the Excel formula but the LibreOffice Calc formula works exactly the same way.

The formula =VLOOKUP($M$5,'Lookup Tables'!L8:M13,2,FALSE) is using the VLOOKUP function to search for a value in a specified range and return a corresponding value from another column. Here's a breakdown of each part of the formula:

- **VLOOKUP**: This function searches for a value in the leftmost column of a specified range and returns a value in the same row from a specified column.

- **$M$5**: Where the dropdown puts the selection value (1-6), this is the **lookup value**, or the value to search for within the range. The $ signs indicate that the cell reference is **absolute**, meaning it won't change if the formula is copied to another cell.

- **'Lookup Tables'!L8:M13**: This is the **table array** or the range of cells where VLOOKUP will search for the value in $M$5. The range refers to the new columns put in the Pay_Periods table.
  - **Excel** uses columns L:M, the value returned from the dropdown in Excel is numeric so it looks up the L value in the table and return the column M value

  - **LibreOffice Calc** dropdown returns a string into M5 so it range must include the string names to search on so its columns are K:M, the K column has the string value to lookup and column M (3) has the value to return.

- **2 or 3**: This is the **column index number**, which tells VLOOKUP which column in the specified range from which to return the value.

  Why Excel Uses Column 2 and LibreOffice Uses Column 3

  - **Excel**
    - **2** means it will return the value in the **second column** (column M) of the range 'Lookup Tables'!L8:M13
  - **Libre**
    - **3** means it will return the value in the **third column** (column M) of the range 'Lookup Tables'.K8:M13

- **FALSE**: **Understanding the Final Argument in VLOOKUP**
  This is the range lookup argument, which specifies whether you want an exact match (FALSE) or an approximate match (TRUE). Setting it to FALSE means VLOOKUP will look for an exact match of the value in $M$5.

Tip: Always Use Exact Match with VLOOKUP
When using `VLOOKUP`, the final argument controls how matches are found:
- FALSE (or `0`): *Exact Match*
- TRUE (or omitted): Approximate Match, which assumes the list is sorted alphabetically or numerically

This formula searches for the exact value in cell $M$5 within the first column (L) of the range 'Lookup Tables'!L8:M13. When it finds a match, it returns the corresponding value from the second column (M) of that range. If no exact match is found, the formula will return an error (e.g., #N/A).

Conclusion

In this section, we've explored essential Excel tasks for modifying and enhancing worksheets. We covered dynamic features such as inserting, moving, copying, and deleting data, which enable flexibility in organizing and updating information. Understanding Excel's intelligent referencing system allows us to make changes confidently, knowing formulas will often adjust automatically. However, we also highlighted limitations, especially when working with VBA code, named ranges, and conditional formatting. By mastering these skills, you can adapt your Excel workbooks to evolving needs while maintaining accuracy and functionality. Remember, backing up your work before major modifications is essential.

With that, you've completed one of the most hands-on chapters. Let's review.

Quiz

1. **What is Excel's intelligent referencing system?**
   a) A tool that automatically updates formulas when rows or columns are inserted, moved, or deleted
   b) A function that automates data entry
   c) A format painter tool
   d) A feature that protects sheets from editing

2. **When moving cells, which reference type will adjust to the new location?**
   a) Absolute references
   b) Relative references
   c) Fixed references
   d) Dependent references

3. **Which shortcut can be used to undo the last action in Excel?**
   a) Ctrl + Y
   b) F4
   c) Ctrl + Z
   d) Shift + F9

4. **What should you check before deleting data that may be used elsewhere in the workbook?**
   a) Impact on formulas, named ranges, and dependent cells
   b) Workbook font style
   c) Excel's protection mode
   d) Cell colors

Quiz Answers

1. a) A tool that automatically updates formulas when rows or columns are inserted, moved, or deleted
2. b) Relative references
3. c) Ctrl + Z
4. a) Impact on formulas, named ranges, and dependent cells

Self-Assessment

Key Takeaways

- **Intelligent Referencing**: Excel automatically adjusts most formulas when cells are inserted, deleted, or moved, making it adaptable to dynamic changes.
- **Moving and Copying Data**: When moving or copying cells, ensure all references are correct and that dependent formulas are not impacted.
- **Backups**: Always back up your workbook before making substantial changes to avoid data loss.
- **Using Ctrl-Z**: The undo feature is essential for quickly correcting errors and experimenting with adjustments without worry.

Reflective Questions

- How can I apply Excel's intelligent reference to save time when making layout changes in my worksheets?
- Have I developed a habit of backing up my work before making major modifications, and if not, how can I incorporate it into my workflow?
- What steps will I take to ensure data dependencies, such as formulas and named ranges, are not impacted when moving or deleting cells?

By reflecting on these concepts and skills, you can build confidence in making efficient and safe changes to your Excel workbooks, enhancing both productivity and accuracy.

Chapter 9: Security and Protection

Protecting workbooks and worksheets, Managing user input cells

Security

When we have completed the spreadsheet, we will want to protect it for several reasons.

- Protect your sensitive data from prying eyes, this spreadsheet will contain your financial information, your spending habits and your planned holidays.
- Define where you can and cannot enter data to protect the cell formula.
- Protect your intellectual property, formula and code.
- Hiding specific worksheets from view and not allowing access to them

Let us begin protecting the spreadsheet.

Unprotecting User Input cells and ranges

We touched on this subject in previous chapters as a quick rundown to prep for setting cell level security as we worked through the chapters so a little of what is to follow is repeated but is included here to give a holistic view of basic security.

All cells in Excel default to having the cell protection option set to locked. This means that when the worksheet is secured, all cells will become locked by default, and you will not be able to edit or modify them.

This is a good thing for most cells. However, we do want to interact with the spreadsheet by entering values into some cells. To do this, we need to unlock the cells we plan to use to enter data, settings and other values we want to edit during normal use of the budget application.

> **Note**: Setting the protection at the cell level has no effect until the worksheet is secured.

During the creation of the worksheets, we have been setting the input cells to a yellow background to make them stand out and using yellow as a common theme color for all input cells throughout the workbook, we have also been setting the protection. Before we can move on, we need to ensure that the required cells are unprotected. If you are sure you have unlocked all input cells you can jump to **Protecting the Worksheets**, if you are not sure, please double check before proceeding to the next section.

> **Note**: Do not worry if you miss any, you can always unlock the worksheet and go fix it up.

Unprotected cells – Input cells

Here are all the tabs and ranges you need checked, followed by instructions on how to unprotect the cells. All of the following cell coordinates cell are based on if the course was followed exactly as instructed, other changes you will need check coordinates of your final worksheets.

- **Home** tab.
  The Home tab does not have any input cells, all cells should remain at their default, locked.
- **Income** tab.
  The Income tab has the following ranges of cells that should be unlocked.
  - A7:F26
  - M7:M26
  - F4:G4
  - K4:L4

  All other cells should remain locked.

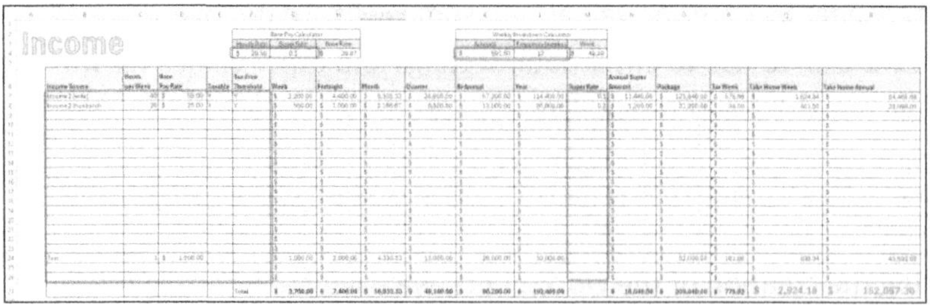

- **Expenses - Budget** tab
  The Expenses - Budget tab has the following ranges of cells that should be unlocked.
    - B7:J30
    - K5

  All other cells should remain locked.

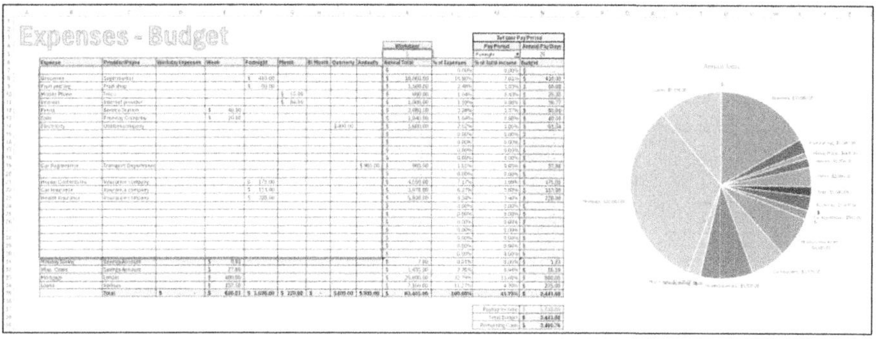

- **Expenses - Actuals** tab
  The Expenses - Actuals tab has the following ranges of cells that should be unlocked.
    - E7:E34

  All other cells should remain locked.

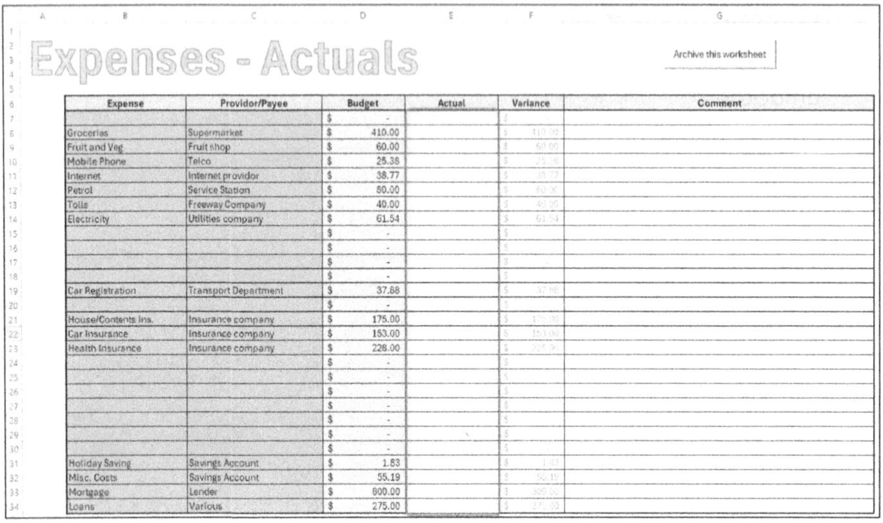

Expenses - Actuals

Archive this worksheet

	Expense	Providor/Payee	Budget	Actual	Variance	Comment
7			$ -		$ -	
8	Groceries	Supermarket	$ 410.00		$ 410.00	
9	Fruit and Veg	Fruit shop	$ 60.00		$ 60.00	
10	Mobile Phone	Telco	$ 25.38		$ 25.38	
11	Internet	Internet providor	$ 38.77		$ 38.77	
12	Petrol	Service Station	$ 80.00		$ 80.00	
13	Tolls	Freeway Company	$ 40.00		$ 40.00	
14	Electricity	Utilities company	$ 61.54		$ 61.54	
15			$ -		$ -	
16			$ -		$ -	
17			$ -		$ -	
18			$ -		$ -	
19	Car Registration	Transport Department	$ 37.88		$ 37.88	
20			$ -		$ -	
21	House/Contents Ins.	Insurance company	$ 175.00		$ 175.00	
22	Car Insurance	Insurance company	$ 153.00		$ 153.00	
23	Health Insurance	Insurance company	$ 228.00		$ 228.00	
24			$ -		$ -	
25			$ -		$ -	
26			$ -		$ -	
27			$ -		$ -	
28			$ -		$ -	
29			$ -		$ -	
30			$ -		$ -	
31	Holiday Saving	Savings Account	$ 1.83		$ 1.83	
32	Misc. Costs	Savings Account	$ 55.19		$ 55.19	
33	Mortgage	Lender	$ 800.00		$ 800.00	
34	Loans	Various	$ 275.00		$ 275.00	

- **Loans** tab
  The Loans tab has the following ranges of cells that should be unlocked.
    - B7:E24

  All other cells should remain locked.

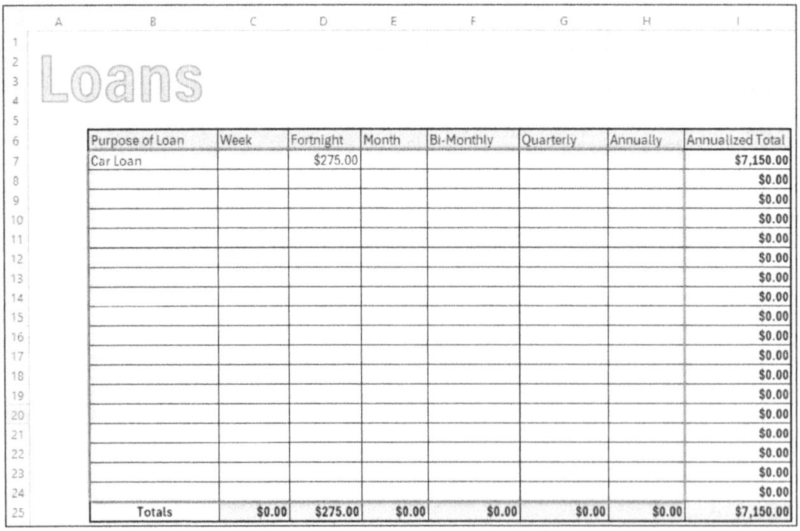

Loans

	Purpose of Loan	Week	Fortnight	Month	Bi-Monthly	Quarterly	Annually	Annualized Total
7	Car Loan		$275.00					$7,150.00
8								$0.00
9								$0.00
10								$0.00
11								$0.00
12								$0.00
13								$0.00
14								$0.00
15								$0.00
16								$0.00
17								$0.00
18								$0.00
19								$0.00
20								$0.00
21								$0.00
22								$0.00
23								$0.00
24								$0.00
25	Totals	$0.00	$275.00	$0.00	$0.00	$0.00	$0.00	$7,150.00

- **Mortgage** tab
  The Mortgage tab has the following ranges of cells that should be unlocked.
  - B7:D24
  - F7:K24
  - O7:O10

  All other cells should remain locked.

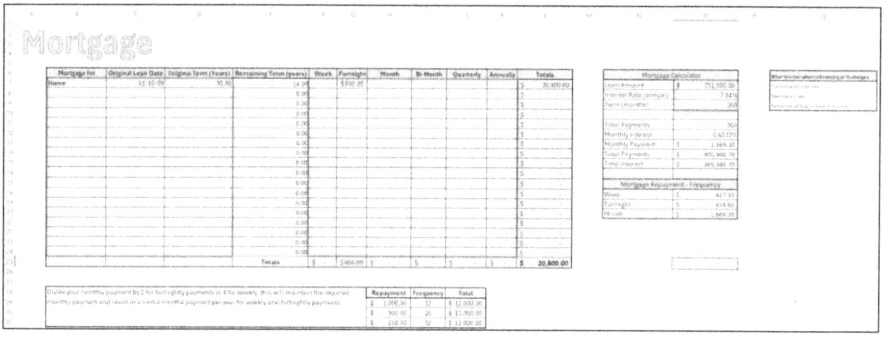

- **Holiday Planning** tab
  The Income tab has the following ranges of cells that should be unlocked.
  - B7:E7
  - B10:D25

  All other cells should remain locked.

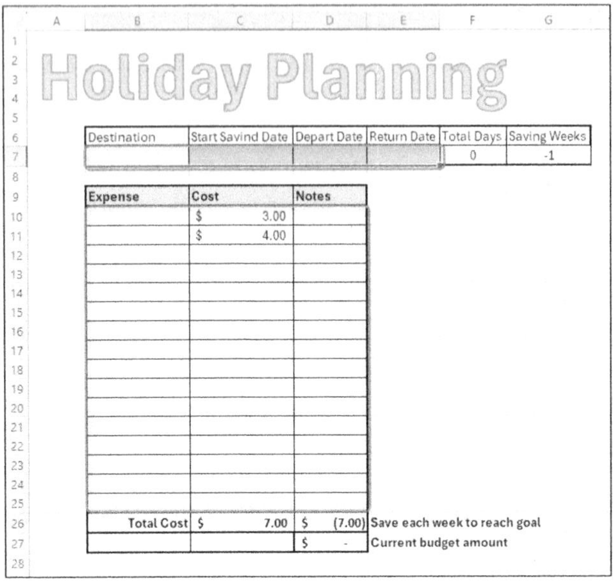

- **Misc. Costs** tab
  The Income tab has the following ranges of cells that should be unlocked.
    - D6:D8
    - D13:16
    - G6:G7
    - G13:G16
    - C22
    - C24

All other cells should remain locked.

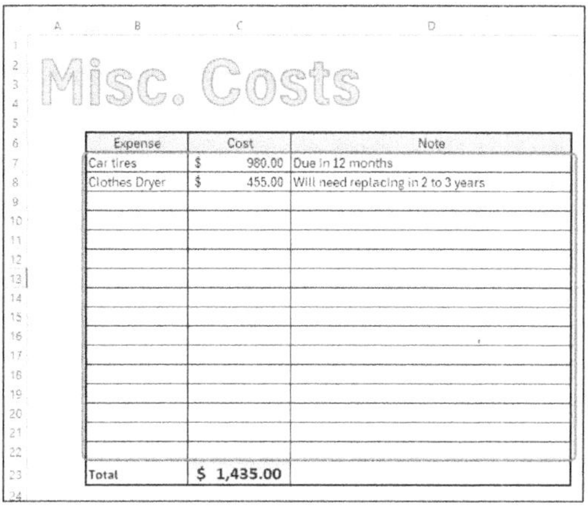

Misc. Costs

Expense	Cost	Note
Car tires	$ 980.00	Due in 12 months
Clothes Dryer	$ 455.00	Will need replacing in 2 to 3 years
Total	$ 1,435.00	

- **New Job Pay Comparison** tab
  The New Job Pay Comparison tab has the following ranges of cells that should be unlocked.
    - B7:D22

All other cells should remain locked.

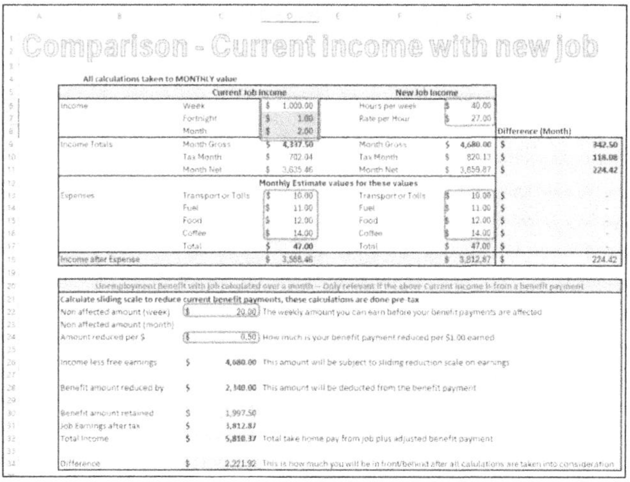

Comparison - Current Income with new job

All calculations taken to MONTHLY value

	Current Job Income			New Job Income		Difference (Month)
Income	Week	$ 1,000.00		Hours per week	$ 40.00	
	Fortnight	$ 1.00		Rate per Hour	$ 27.00	
	Month	$ 2.00				
Income Totals	Month Gross	$ 4,337.50		Month Gross	$ 4,680.00	$ 342.50
	Tax Month	$ 702.04		Tax Month	$ 820.13	$ 118.08
	Month Net	$ 3,635.46		Month Net	$ 3,859.87	$ 224.42
	Monthly Estimate values for these values					
Expenses	Transport or Tolls	$ 10.00		Transport or Tolls	$ 10.00	$ -
	Fuel	$ 11.00		Fuel	$ 11.00	$ -
	Food	$ 12.00		Food	$ 12.00	$ -
	Coffee	$ 14.00		Coffee	$ 14.00	$ -
	Total	$ 47.00		Total	$ 47.00	$ -
Income after Expense		$ 3,588.46			$ 3,812.87	$ 224.42

Unemployment Benefit with job calculated over a month – Only relevant if the above Current income is from a benefit payment

Calculate sliding scale to reduce current benefit payments, these calculations are done pre-tax

Non affected amount (week)	$ 20.00	The weekly amount you can earn before your benefit payments are affected
Non affected amount (month)		
Amount reduced per $	$ 0.50	How much is your benefit payment reduced per $1.00 earned
Income less free earnings	$ 4,680.00	This amount will be subject to sliding reduction scale on earnings
Benefit amount reduced by	$ 2,340.00	This amount will be deducted from the benefit payment
Benefit amount retained	$ 1,997.50	
Job Earnings after tax	$ 3,812.87	
Total Income	$ 5,810.37	Total take home pay from job plus adjusted benefit payment
Difference	$ 2,221.92	This is how much you will be in front/behind after all calulations are taken into consideration

- **Lookup Tables** tab

  The Lookup Tables tab has the following ranges of cells that should be unlocked.

    - B10:C14
    - F10:F14
    - B21:H25
    - B30:C30
    - L20:L26

  All other cells should remain locked.

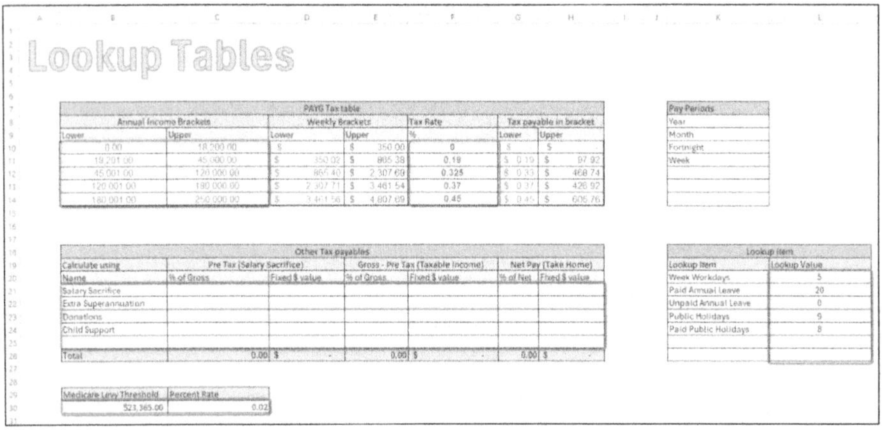

Unlocking cells for data entry

To recap on unprotecting cells, follow these steps.

- Select the range of cells to be unlocked, see lists in previous section. You can select multiple ranges at the same time using Ctrl and Shift keys.

> **Note**: You can select the entire worksheet by clicking in the top/left corner of the worksheet grid.
> Doing this first and locking all cells ensure that only the ranges you unlock later will be editable.

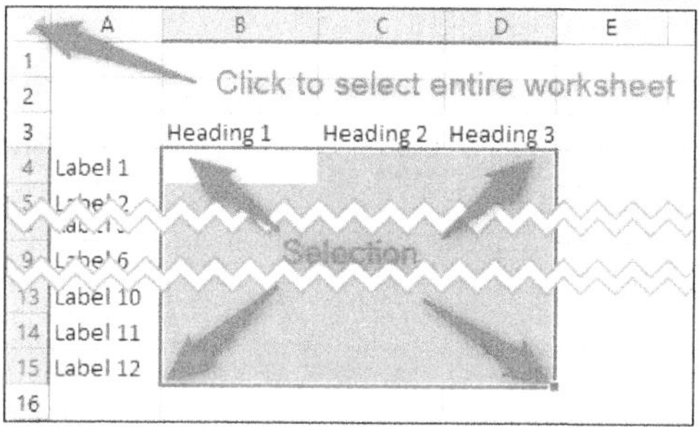

- Right Click anywhere in the selection and choose **Format Cells** from the popup menu.
- In the *Format Cells* window, select the **Protection** tab.
- Clear the **Locked** check box.

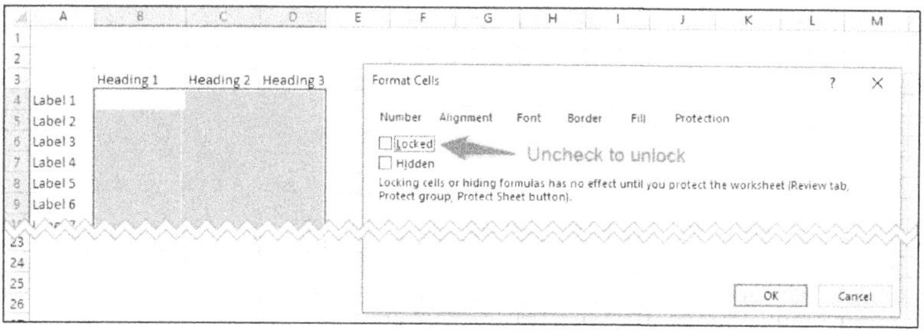

After you have confirmed and unlocked all the cell ranges listed in *Unprotected cells – Input cells,* you can continue to the next stage, Protecting the Worksheets.

Protecting the Worksheets

Protecting the worksheet will activate the locked/unlocked settings of the cells and offer more options to permit or deny your certain functions within the worksheet whilst it is protected.

- Using a password is optional, you can simply lock and unlock at will, using a password offers more security of course.
- Write down the password and store it somewhere safe, away from the computer. If you forget your password, you will not be able to unprotect and modify the worksheet.
- Right Click the tab of the worksheet you want to protect to activate the worksheet and open the menu, select **Protect Sheet**. The Protect Sheet window will open.

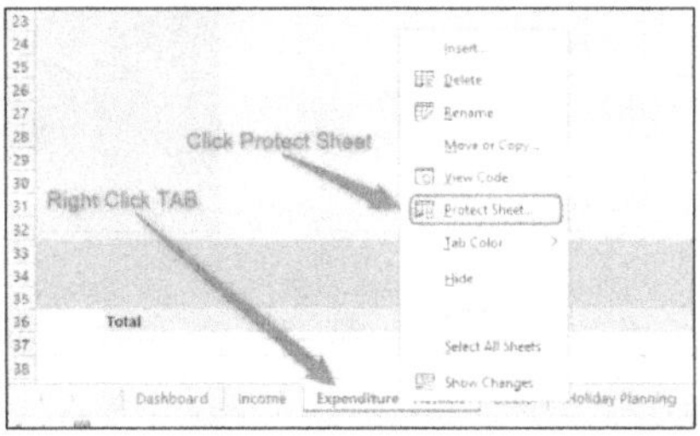

- The option **Protect worksheet and contents of locked cells** are already ticked, leave it ticked, if it is clear, tick it.

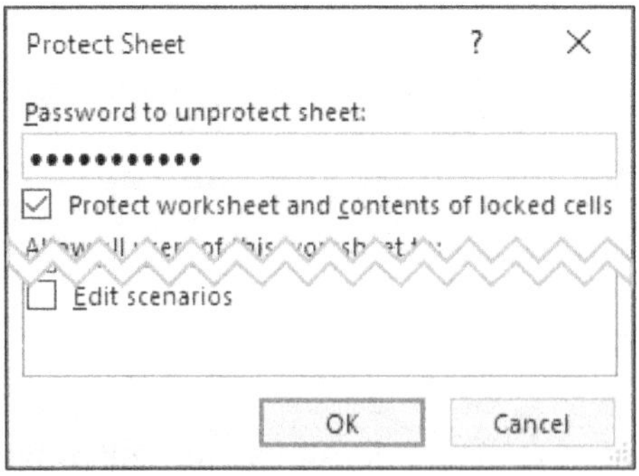

  - Unticking this disables the **OK** button and stops you from setting options for protecting the worksheet.

- The bottom section has 15 options, the first two are already ticked.

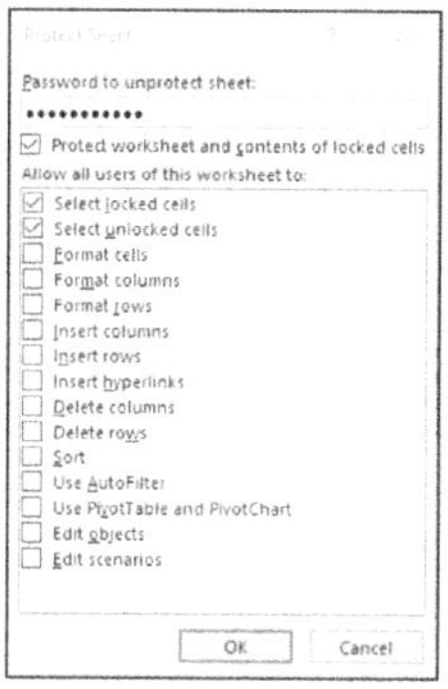

You can tick or clear these options, if ticked it will allow all worksheets to use that option, if cleared, they cannot use it.

- The first two allow you to select cells, you may keep both ticked or.
  - Untick **Select Locked Cells** and
  - Tick **Select Unlocked Cells**

  And you will be restricted to ONLY the unlocked cells.
- All the other options are not needed for this worksheet or workbook, so leave them unticked. In the unlikely event you need to enable any of these options, simply tick the desired option to activate it.
- Enter the password you want in the top **Password to unprotect sheet** box and click **OK.**

  This is the password you will be prompted for if you try to unprotect the worksheet.

- Re-enter the password in the **Confirm Password** window that will open and click **OK.**

The worksheet is now protected, you will only be able to modify cells you have unlocked and will not be able to modify other cells. If a user tries to modify a locked cell, they will get the following message from Excel.

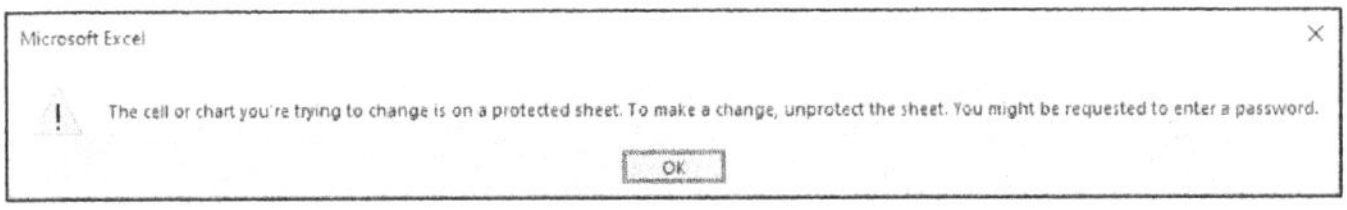

To unprotect the worksheet

- Right Click the tab of the worksheet you want to unprotect to activate the worksheet and open the menu, select **Unprotect Sheet**. The Unprotect Sheet window will open.

> **Note**:
> This is an easy way to check if you have set protection for the worksheet, the menu option will toggle between Protect and Unprotect.

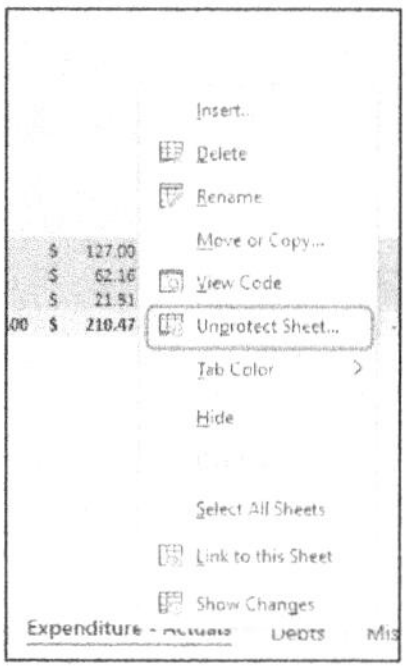

- Enter the password you previously set in the **Password** box and click **OK.** If the password was correct, the password window will close, you will return to the worksheet and the worksheet will be unprotected.

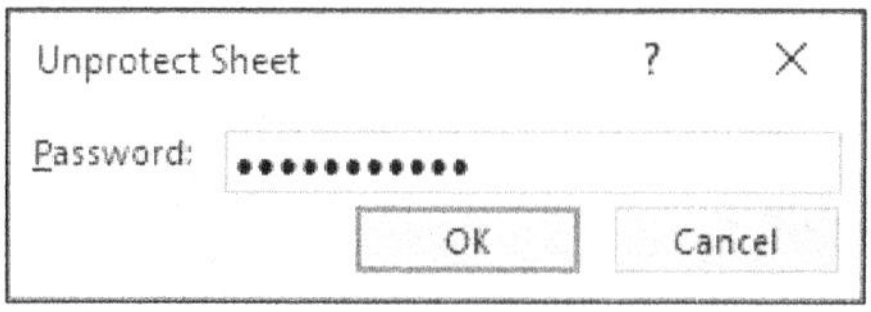

- After unprotecting the worksheet, you can make modifications to the worksheet. You will also need to protect the worksheet again when you have finished making your changes.

Protecting the Workbook

Protecting an Excel workbook is crucial for various reasons, especially when dealing with sensitive, confidential, or critical data. Here are the primary reasons why you should consider protecting your Excel workbook:

- **Data Integrity**: To prevent unintentional changes, deletions, or errors that could distort the data and lead to inaccurate results or conclusions.
- **Confidentiality**: If the workbook contains confidential or proprietary information, it is essential to restrict unauthorized access.
- **Prevent Misuse**: Protecting a workbook can prevent others from exploiting or misusing the information for purposes other than that for which it was intended.

- **Control Access**: You can specify what others can view or edit the workbook, ensuring that only authorized personnel can access or modify the data.
- **Maintain Professionalism**: In a business setting, it is professional to share documents that viewers cannot accidentally alter, ensuring the recipient sees the document as the author intended.
- **Preserve Formulas**: Often, Excel workbooks contain complex formulas that are essential for automated calculations. Protecting these cells ensures these formulas are not accidentally deleted or modified.
- **Protection from Malicious Intent**: Theres always a risk of someone intentionally trying to alter or corrupt the data, especially in shared or networked environments.
- **Structural Consistency**: Prevents others from adding, deleting, hiding, or renaming worksheets, thus maintaining the workbook's structure.
- **Customization**: Excel's protection features allow for a customized level of security, from protecting individual cells to entire worksheets or the workbook structure.
- **Feedback Control**: If you are sending out a workbook for feedback, protection can ensure that reviewers only comment or suggest in designated areas rather than change the original content.
- **Maintain Macros**: If you have embedded macros in your workbook for automation, protection ensures they cannot be viewed or modified, maintaining their functionality.
- **License and Copyright Protection**: For creators who sell Excel templates or tools, protection ensures that intellectual property remains secure, and others cannot easily replicate or distribute the tool without permission.

In summary, protecting an Excel workbook ensures the safety, integrity, and confidentiality of your data. Given the multiple layers and types of protection Excel offers (from basic cell protection to encrypting with a password), you can tailor protection to fit their specific needs.

Let us get started.

- Select **File** and then File Menu will open.

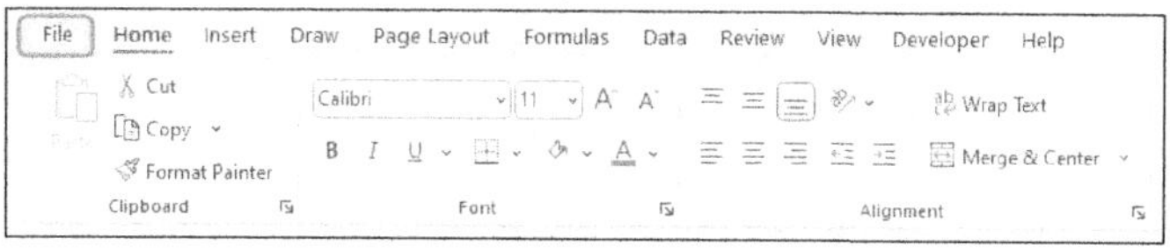

- Click **Info**, the Info screen the **Protect Workbook** box and choose **Encrypt with Password**, the **Encrypt Document** window will open

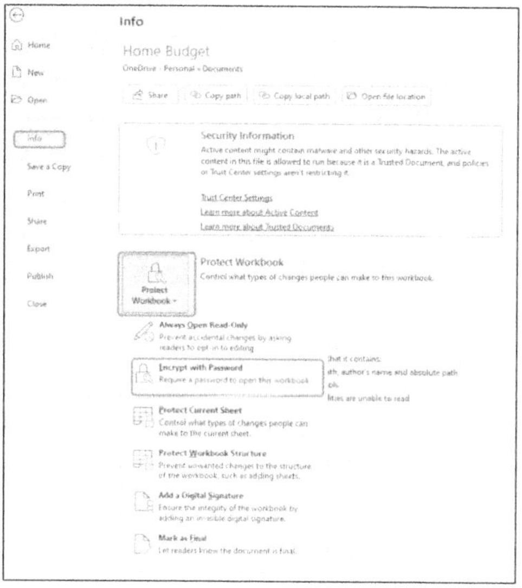

- **Read** the **Caution:** below the input box **BEFORE** proceeding, when you understand the caution, you can proceed.

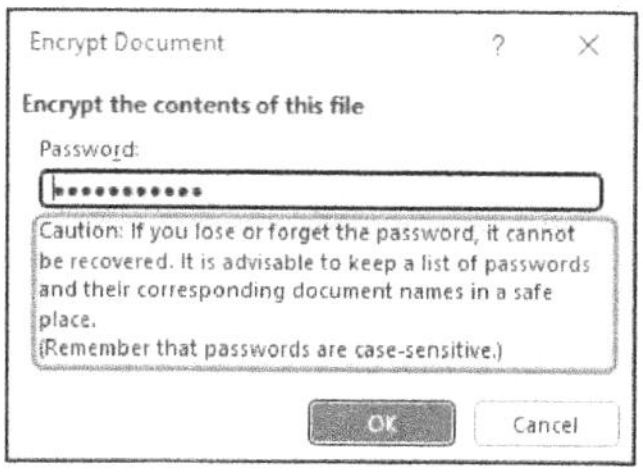

- Enter a password in the **Password** box, and then select **OK**.

- Confirm the password in the **Reenter Password** box, and then select OK.

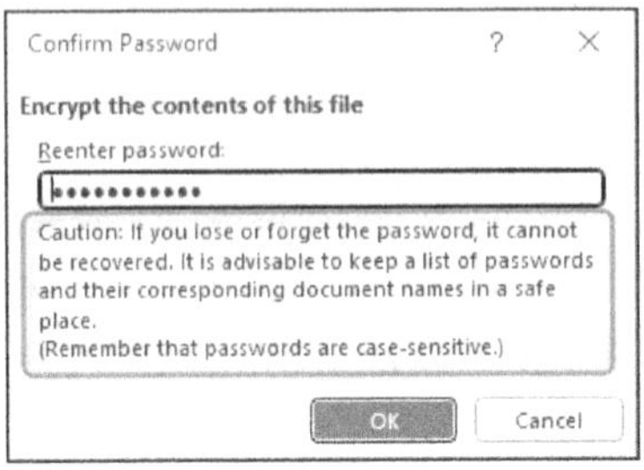

- Write down the password and store it somewhere safe, away from the computer. If you forget your password later, you will not be able to open the file.

Your workbook is now protected, to get access to the contents you will need to enter the password.

If you wish to change or remove the password

- Open the file and enter the password when prompted.
- Click **File, Info, Protect Workbook, Encrypt with Password**
- If you change the password, **enter** and **confirm** the new password when prompted.
- If unprotecting the Workbook, **clear** the password box.
- Press **OK.**

LibreOffice Calc

In LibreOffice Calc, workbook-level protection is more limited than in Excel — it focuses on protecting individual sheets and locking down structure (like preventing adding/removing sheets) rather than full workbook-level encryption or password protection.

To Protect a Worksheet (most common):

- Go to the sheet you want to protect
- Click Tools → Protect Sheet
- (Optional) Enter a password

- Check the boxes for what you still want to allow (e.g., selecting cells, sorting, etc.)
- Click OK

To Protect Workbook Structure (e.g., prevent adding/deleting sheets):

- Click Tools → Protect Spreadsheet Structure
- (Optional) Enter a password
- Click OK
- This prevents users from:
- Inserting or deleting sheets
- Renaming or moving sheets

To Make the Entire Workbook Read-Only (Save-As Lock):

- Go to File → Save As
- In the Save dialog, click Save with password
- When prompted:
- Enter a password
- Uncheck "Open file read-only" if you want to allow viewing
- You can optionally allow editing only with a second password

This encrypts the file and can require a password to open or modify.

Conclusion

In this chapter, we covered essential security and protection techniques for Excel workbooks, particularly valuable when handling sensitive financial data. Protecting a workbook not only prevents unauthorized access but also helps maintain the integrity of formulas and macros, preserving your hard work and intellectual property. By selectively unlocking input cells, we allow necessary data entry while safeguarding other areas. Additionally, workbook-level protection with passwords can ensure that sensitive information remains secure, enhancing professionalism and peace of mind.

Quiz

1. **What is the primary purpose of unlocking specific cells in an Excel worksheet before protecting it?**
   a) To prevent accidental deletion
   b) To allow data entry in designated areas
   c) To add conditional formatting
   d) To improve data visualization

2. **What does workbook-level protection mainly help with?**
   a) Adding formulas
   b) Enhancing data validation
   c) Controlling access and safeguarding the workbook structure
   d) Enabling conditional formatting across worksheets

3. **Which of the following is *not* affected by Excel's protection feature?**
   a) Locked cells
   b) Formulas within locked cells
   c) Cell comments or notes
   d) VBA code references

4. **What should you always do before setting up protection on your workbook?**
   a) Enter a password
   b) Create a backup of your workbook
   c) Merge all cells with formulas
   d) Disable undo functionality

5. **How can you change or remove a password-protected workbook password?**
   a) Re-save the workbook with a new name
   b) Open the workbook and change it under File > Info > Protect Workbook
   c) Select all cells and clear formatting
   d) Passwords cannot be changed once set

Quiz Answers

1. b) To allow data entry in designated areas
2. c) Controlling access and safeguarding the workbook structure
3. d) VBA code references
4. b) Create a backup of your workbook
5. b) Open the workbook and change it under File > Info > Protect Workbook

Self-Assessment

Key Takeaways

Selective Cell Locking: By unlocking only necessary input cells, you ensure data entry areas remain accessible while protecting key formulas and functions.

Worksheet Protection: Worksheet-level protection is highly effective for preventing accidental modification while allowing specific areas for data input.

Password Management: Using passwords is an effective way to secure sensitive data, but it requires careful management as passwords cannot be recovered if forgotten.

Reflective Questions

How can I implement selective locking in other Excel workbooks to enhance security without restricting necessary access?

What steps will I take to manage and store workbook passwords securely?

How might protecting a workbook influence collaboration and data sharing within my organization?

These practices in security and protection ensure your Excel workbooks remain both functional and secure, helping you maintain data integrity while allowing controlled access where needed.

Appendix A: Using LibreOffice Calc with This Book

Welcome LibreOffice Users!

This book has been written primarily for Microsoft Excel users. However, many readers may prefer to use LibreOffice Calc — a free and powerful alternative to Excel.

The good news is that you can complete this budgeting system successfully using LibreOffice Calc, with only minor adjustments along the way.
This appendix provides a quick guide to help you adapt the instructions if you are using LibreOffice.

Key Differences Between Excel and LibreOffice Calc

Feature	Microsoft Excel	LibreOffice Calc
Saving Files	.xlsm (Macro-Enabled Workbook)	.ods (Open Document Spreadsheet) recommended for macro compatibility; .xlsx supported but may lose macro functionality
Named Ranges	Formulas → Name Manager	Sheet → Named Ranges and Expressions → Manage
Formula Separators	Comma (,) between arguments	Usually comma (,) between arguments; sometimes semicolon (;) depending on your regional settings
Creating Charts	Insert → Chart → Wizard	Insert → Chart (Wizard steps look different but offer similar options)

Feature	Microsoft Excel	LibreOffice Calc
Data Validation (Dropdowns)	Data → Data Validation	Data → Validity
Macros	VBA (Visual Basic for Applications)	LibreOffice BASIC (different macro language and syntax)
Print Setup	Page Layout → Print Setup	Format → Page Style

Important Tips for LibreOffice Users

File Saving:

If you are using Microsoft Excel, save your workbooks as .xlsm (Macro-Enabled Workbook) to keep all macro functionality.

If you are using LibreOffice Calc, it is recommended you save your files as .ods (Open Document Spreadsheet).

Saving as a .xlsx is possible but may cause some macros to be disabled or lost when reopening the file.

If an .ods file created in LibreOffice is later opened in Microsoft Excel, the data and formulas will remain intact, but any LibreOffice macros will not function in Excel.

Formulas:

LibreOffice may require semicolons (;) between formula arguments instead of commas (,), depending on your regional settings.

Example:

Excel: =IF(A1>100,"Yes","No")

LibreOffice: =IF(A1>100;"Yes";"No")

Formula Separators: Comma (,) vs Semicolon (;)

LibreOffice Calc sometimes uses different symbols to separate formula arguments based on your computer's **regional settings**.

In many countries (such as Australia, United States, United Kingdom, Canada), formulas separate arguments with a **comma (,)**, just like Microsoft Excel.

In many European countries (such as Germany, France, Italy), a comma is used as the decimal separator in numbers (123,45 instead of 123.45).
To avoid confusion, LibreOffice Calc uses a **semicolon (;)** to separate function arguments instead.

If you encounter formula errors:

Go to **Tools → Options → LibreOffice Calc → Formula → Separators**.

Set the **Function Argument Separator** to a **comma (,)** if you want to match this book's examples.

Being aware of this small difference will save you confusion when writing or copying formulas.

Named Ranges:
In LibreOffice, manage named ranges by selecting **Sheet → Named Ranges and Expressions → Manage...** instead of using Excel's Formulas tab.

Macros:
This book provides VBA macros designed for Microsoft Excel.
LibreOffice uses a different macro language called **LibreOffice BASIC**, and cannot directly run Excel VBA code.

However, adapted versions of the required macros (such as the Tax Calculation macro) are available as LibreOffice BASIC files.

Both the Excel and LibreOffice-compatible macros can be downloaded from the GitHub support page:

Chart Creation:
The chart creation process uses a different wizard layout, but the fundamental steps are the same: select data → insert chart → choose chart type → adjust settings.

Print Setup:
Print scaling, margins, and headers are adjusted through **Format → Page Style** instead of the Page Layout tab.

Tips for a Smooth Experience

💾 Save your files regularly.

🔍 Check that your formulas work correctly after adapting them.

⚙️ Enable macro support appropriately under **Tools → Options → LibreOffice → Security**.

⍰ Reach out to LibreOffice's online community forums if you encounter unexpected behavior or compatibility issues.

Conclusion

LibreOffice Calc is a capable alternative to Microsoft Excel.
While the appearance and some menus differ, the core functionality needed for home budgeting remains the same.
With a little adaptation, you can follow every chapter in this book and build your complete home budgeting system — using free software!

Appendix B: Creating an Accounting-Style Currency Format in LibreOffice Calc (with Locale Codes)

In Microsoft Excel, the **Accounting format** cleanly aligns currency symbols to the left of the cell and values to the right, adding extra padding for a professional, readable layout. LibreOffice Calc does not include this format by default, but you can **manually recreate it using a custom number format**.

Custom Format Code

To apply this layout:

1. Select your cell range (e.g., D7:D21)
2. Right-click → **Format Cells**
3. Go to the **Numbers** tab
4. Choose category: **Number**
5. In the **Format code** box, enter for Australia:

   [$$-C09]* #,##0.00;-[$$-C09]* #,##0.00

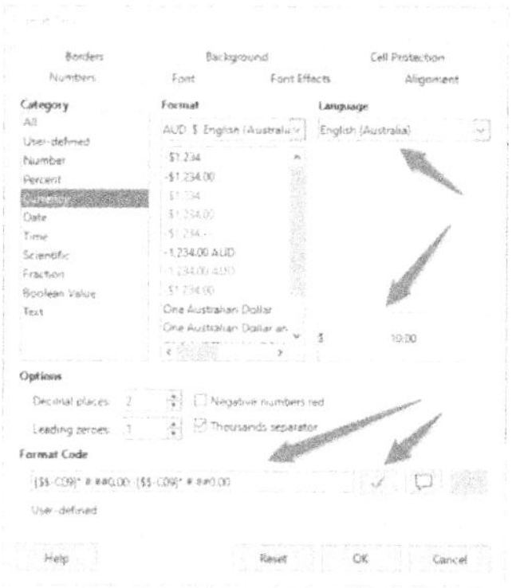

6. Click **Add** to save this style under **User-defined**

7. You can now use this format wherever you need an Accounting style format for currency

Locale Codes and Regional Symbols

The -C09 in the format string is a **locale identifier**. It controls how the number is displayed — including decimal and thousand separators, and sometimes spacing.

You can change the locale code or currency symbol to match your region:

Country	Locale Code	Currency Symbol	Example Format
United States	409	$	[$$-409]* #,##0.00;-[$$-409]* #,##0.00
Australia	C09	$	[$$-C09]* #,##0.00;-[$$-C09]* #,##0.00
United Kingdom	809	£	[$£-809]* #,##0.00;-[$£-809]* #,##0.00
Canada (Eng.)	1009	C$	[C-1009]* #,##0.00;-[C-1009]* #,##0.00
New Zealand	1409	NZ$	[NZ-1409]* #,##0.00;-[NZ-1409]* #,##0.00
Euro (EU)	40C	€	[€-40C]* #,##0.00;-[€-40C]* #,##0.00

If unsure which to use, just leave the locale as the default, **-409**. Most users won't notice — and it still looks clean and balanced.

Notes:

- This format only **visually mimics** the Accounting style. The currency symbol is fixed, so if you change your regional settings, the symbol won't automatically update.

- LibreOffice Calc doesn't support this formatting in the **Currency** category — you must use **Number** and enter the format manually.

Final Words: Your Journey Ahead

Congratulations on completing Mastering Excel for Home Budgeting! By working through this book, you've not only developed essential Excel skills but also crafted a personalized budgeting tool that empowers you to manage your finances effectively.

Learning is a continuous process, and the skills you've gained here are just the beginning. With your newfound knowledge, you can customize and expand your budgeting workbook, explore more advanced Excel features, or even venture into automating tasks with VBA.

Remember, the true power of Excel lies in its adaptability. Your home budgeting application can evolve with your needs—whether you're planning a vacation, tracking investments, or preparing for significant life events.

I encourage you to continue experimenting, practicing, and refining your skills. If you encounter challenges or have feedback, don't hesitate to reach out through the resources provided in this book. Your input helps us improve and ensures that future learners benefit from your insights.

Thank you for embarking on this journey with me. Here's to a future of informed decisions, financial clarity, and the confidence to tackle any spreadsheet challenge that comes your way!

Tom

Appendix C: Completed Worksheets (Examples)

This appendix presents completed examples of the key worksheets from *Mastering Excel for Home Budgeting*. The worksheets are shown in the same order they are built and populated throughout the book.

Some of the worksheets, such as the Home Dashboard, draw their data from other sheets and are shown here in their final, fully populated state for reference.

To assist readers of the printed version, full-color versions of all images are also available for download from the project's GitHub repository:

Note: Some images have been rotated 90° or split into sections to improve readability in the printed format. The original layout is preserved in the digital support materials.

Lookup Tables

PAYG Tax table						
Annual Income Brackets		Weekly Brackets		Tax Rate	Tax payable in bracket	
Lower	Upper	Lower	Upper	%	Lower	Upper
0.00	18,200.00	$ -	$ 350.00	0	$ -	$ -
18,201.00	45,000.00	$ 350.02	$ 865.38	0.16	$ 0.16	$ 82.46
45,001.00	135,000.00	$ 865.40	$ 2,596.15	0.3	$ 0.30	$ 519.23
135,001.00	190,000.00	$ 2,596.17	$ 3,653.85	0.37	$ 0.37	$ 391.34
190,001.00	250,000.00	$ 3,653.87	$ 4,807.69	0.45	$ 0.45	$ 519.22

Other Tax payables						
Calculate using	Pre Tax (Salary Sacrifice)		Gross Pay (Taxable Income)		Net Pay (Take Home)	
Name	% of Gross	Fixed $ value	% of Gross	Fixed $ value	% of Net	Fixed $
Salary Sacrifice						
Extra Superannuation						
Donations						
Child Support						
Total	0	$ -	0	$ -	0	$ -

Medicare Levy Threshold	Percent Rate
$ 23,365.00	0.02

PAYG Tax table						
Annual Income Brackets		Weekly Brackets		Tax Rate	Tax payable in bracket	
Lower	Upper	Lower	Upper	%	Lower	Upper
0.00	18,200.00	$ -	$ 350.00	0	$ -	$ -
18,201.00	45,000.00	$ 350.02	$ 865.38	0.19	$ 0.19	$ 97.92
45,001.00	120,000.00	$ 865.40	$ 2,307.69	0.325	$ 0.33	$ 468.74
120,001.00	180,000.00	$ 2,307.71	$ 3,461.54	0.37	$ 0.37	$ 426.92
180,001.00	250,000.00	$ 3,461.56	$ 4,807.69	0.45	$ 0.45	$ 605.76

Pay Periods
Year
Month
Fortnight
Week

Misc. Lookups	
Lookup Item	Lookup Value
Week Workdays	5
Paid Annual Leave	0
Unpaid Annual Leave	10
Public Holidays	9
Paid Public Holidays	9

Figure C.1 — Completed WS 1 — Lookup Tables

(Example of a lookup table used to support consistent data entry across worksheets.)

Income

Base Pay Calculator		
Hourly Rate	Super Rate	Base Rate
$ 78.19	0.1	$ 71.08

Weekly Breakdown Calculator		
Amount	Frequency (weeks)	Week
$ 591.50	12	$ 49.29

Income Source	Hours per Week	Base Pay Rate	Taxable	Tax-Free Threshold	Week	Fortnight	Month	Quarter	Year	Superannuation rate	Annual Super Amount	Package	Tax Week	Take Home Week	Take Home Annual
Main Job	38	$ 34.0000	Y	Y	$ 1,292.00	$ 2,584.00	$ 5,598.67	$ 16,796.00	$ 67,184.00	0.1	$ 6,718.40	$ 73,902.40	$ 236.28	$ 1,055.72	$ 54,897.44
Side Hustle	6	$ 40.0000	Y	N	$ 240.00	$ 480.00	$ 1,040.00	$ 3,120.00	$ 12,480.00	0	$ -	$ 12,480.00	$ 38.40	$ 201.60	$ 10,483.20
		$ -	Y	N	$ -	$ -	$ -	$ -	$ -	0	$ -	$ -	$ -	$ -	$ -
		$ -	Y	N	$ -	$ -	$ -	$ -	$ -	0	$ -	$ -	$ -	$ -	$ -
		$ -	Y	N	$ -	$ -	$ -	$ -	$ -	0	$ -	$ -	$ -	$ -	$ -
		$ -	Y	N	$ -	$ -	$ -	$ -	$ -	0	$ -	$ -	$ -	$ -	$ -
		$ -	Y	N	$ -	$ -	$ -	$ -	$ -	0	$ -	$ -	$ -	$ -	$ -
		$ -	Y	N	$ -	$ -	$ -	$ -	$ -	0	$ -	$ -	$ -	$ -	$ -
		$ -	Y	N	$ -	$ -	$ -	$ -	$ -	0	$ -	$ -	$ -	$ -	$ -
		$ -	Y	N	$ -	$ -	$ -	$ -	$ -	0	$ -	$ -	$ -	$ -	$ -
		$ -	Y	N	$ -	$ -	$ -	$ -	$ -	0	$ -	$ -	$ -	$ -	$ -
		$ -	Y	N	$ -	$ -	$ -	$ -	$ -	0	$ -	$ -	$ -	$ -	$ -
		$ -	Y	N	$ -	$ -	$ -	$ -	$ -	0	$ -	$ -	$ -	$ -	$ -
		$ -	Y	N	$ -	$ -	$ -	$ -	$ -	0	$ -	$ -	$ -	$ -	$ -
		$ -	Y	N	$ -	$ -	$ -	$ -	$ -	0	$ -	$ -	$ -	$ -	$ -
				Total	$ 1,532.00	$ 3,064.00	$ 6,638.67	$ 19,916.00	$ 79,664.00		$ 6,718.40	$ 86,382.40	$ 274.68	$ 1,257.32	$ 65,380.64

Figure C.2 — Completed WS 2 — Income

(Completed Income worksheet showing earnings from primary employment and side hustle income.)

Expenses - Budget

Work days
5

Set your pay period below	
Pay Period	Annual Payments
Month	12

Expense	Provider/Payee	Workday Expenses	Week	Fortnight	Month	Bi Month	Quarterly	Annually	Totals	% of Expenses	% of Total Income	Budget
									$ -	0.00	0.00	$ -
Groceries	Supermarket		$ 200.00						$ 10,400.00	0.17	15.91	$ 366.67
Fruit/Vegetables	Supermarket		$ 50.00						$ 2,600.00	0.04	3.98	$ 216.67
Meat	Supermarket		$ 50.00						$ 2,600.00	0.04	3.98	$ 216.67
									$ -	0.00	0.00	$ -
Electricity	Electric Company				$ 210.00				$ 2,520.00	0.04	3.85	$ 210.00
Council Rates	Local Council						$ 525.00		$ 2,100.00	0.04	3.21	$ 175.00
									$ -	0.00	0.00	$ -
Internet/Phone	Telco								$ -	0.00	0.00	$ -
Home Insurance	Insure You				$ 90.00				$ 1,080.00	0.02	1.65	$ 90.00
Health Insurance	Insure Sick You				$ 243.00				$ 2,916.00	0.05	4.46	$ 243.00
									$ -	0.00	0.00	$ -
									$ -	0.00	0.00	$ -
Fuel				$ 100.00					$ 2,600.00	0.04	3.98	$ 216.67
Car Insurance	Insure You				$ 100.00				$ 1,200.00	0.02	1.84	$ 100.00
									$ -	0.00	0.00	$ -
ChildCare	ABC Kids				$ 300.00				$ 3,600.00	0.06	5.51	$ 300.00
									$ -	0.00	0.00	$ -
									$ -	0.00	0.00	$ -
									$ -	0.00	0.00	$ -
									$ -	0.00	0.00	$ -
									$ -	0.00	0.00	$ -
									$ -	0.00	0.00	$ -
									$ -	0.00	0.00	$ -
Holiday Saving	Savings Account		$ 140.90						$ 1,350.00	0.02	2.06	$ 610.57
Misc. Costs	Savings Account		$ 11.54						$ 600.00	0.01	0.92	$ 50.00
Mortgage	Bank		$ 390.18						$ 20,289.36	0.34	31.03	$ 1,690.78
Loans	Various		$ 115.34						$ 5,997.84	0.10	9.17	$ 499.82
	Total	$ -	$ 957.96	$ 100.00	$ 943.00	$ -	$ 525.00	$ -	$ 59,853.20	1.00	91.55	$ 5,485.83

Budget Income	$ 5,448.39
Budget Total	$ 5,485.83
Remaining Cash	-$ 37.45

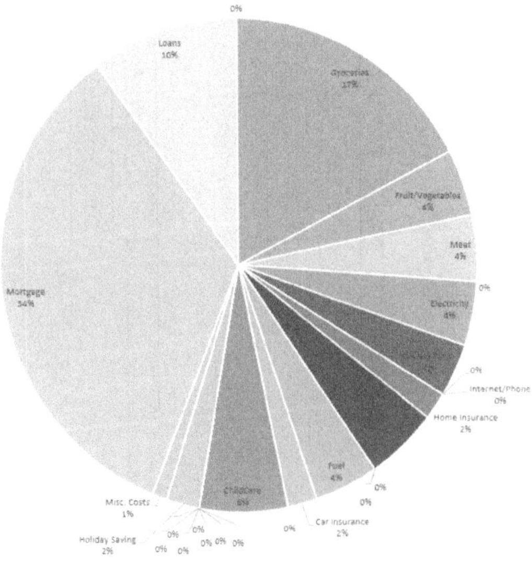

Figure C.3 — Completed WS 3 — Expenses — Budget

(Completed Expenses — Budget worksheet with planned monthly expenses.)

Expenses - Actuals

Archive this worksheet

Expense	Provider/Payee	Budget	Actual	Variance	Comment
		$ -	$ -	$ -	
Groceries	Supermarket	$ 866.67	$ 880.00	$ (13.33)	
Fruit/Vegetables	Supermarket	$ 216.67	$ 300.00	$ (83.33)	
Meat	Supermarket	$ 216.67	$ 216.67	$ -	
		$ -	$ -	$ -	
Electricity	Electric Company	$ 210.00	$ 250.00	$ (40.00)	
Council Rates	Local Council	$ 175.00	$ -	$ 175.00	
		$ -	$ -	$ -	
Internet/Phone	Telco	$ -	$ -	$ -	
Home Insurance	Insure You	$ 90.00	$ -	$ 90.00	
Health Insurance	Insure Sick You	$ 243.00	$ -	$ 243.00	
		$ -	$ -	$ -	
		$ -	$ -	$ -	
Fuel		$ 216.67	$ 185.00	$ 31.67	
Car Insurance	Insure You	$ 100.00	$ 100.00	$ -	
		$ -	$ -	$ -	
ChildCare	ABC Kids	$ 300.00	$ -	$ 300.00	
		$ -	$ -	$ -	
		$ -	$ -	$ -	
		$ -	$ -	$ -	
		$ -	$ -	$ -	
		$ -	$ -	$ -	
		$ -	$ -	$ -	
		$ -	$ -	$ -	
Holiday Saving	Savings Account	$ 610.57	$ -	$ 610.57	
Misc. Costs	Savings Account	$ 50.00	$ -	$ 50.00	
Mortgage	Bank	$ 1,690.78	$ -	$ 1,690.78	
Loans	Various	$ 499.82	$ -	$ 499.82	

Figure C.4 — Completed WS 4 — Expenses — Actuals

(Completed Expenses — Actuals worksheet showing actual spending and variances.)

Loans

Purpose of loan	Week	Fortnight	Month	BiMonth	Quarterly	Annually	Annualized Total
Car			$ 499.82				$ 5,997.84
							$ -
							$ -
							$ -
							$ -
							$ -
							$ -
							$ -
							$ -
							$ -
							$ -
							$ -
							$ -
							$ -
							$ -
							$ -
							$ -
							$ -
Totals	$ -	$ -	$ 499.82	$ -	$ -	$ -	**$ 5,997.84**

Loan Calculator	
Loan Amount	$ 28,516.00
Interest Rate (annual)	2.00
Term (years)	5.00
Total Payments	60
Monthly Interest	0.001666667
Monthly Payment	**$ 499.82**
Total Payment	$ 29,989.30
Total Interest	$ 1,473.30
Loan Repayment - Frequency	
Week	$ 124.96
Fortnight	$ 249.91
Month	$ 499.82

Divide your monthly payment in half for fortnightly payments or 4 for weekly, this will maintain the required monthly payment and result in an extra months payment per year	**Repayment**	**Frequency**	**Total**
	$1,000.00	$ 12.00	$12,000.00
	$ 500.00	$ 26.00	$13,000.00
	$ 250.00	$ 52.00	$13,000.00

Figure C.5 — Completed WS 5 — Loans

(Completed Loans worksheet calculating payments and balances for personal loans.)

Mortgage

NOTE: This worksheet is for mortgages only, if you are renting, put the rent in 'Expenses - Budget' as an expense

Mortgage for	Original Loan Date	Original Term (Years)	Remaining Term	Week	Fortnight	Month	BiMonth	Quarterly	Annually	Totals
My House	2008-07-01	30	13.05	$ 390.18						$ 20,289.36
			0.00							$ -
			0.00							$ -
			0.00							$ -
			0.00							$ -
			0.00							$ -
			0.00							$ -
			0.00							$ -
			0.00							$ -
			0.00							$ -
			0.00							$ -
			0.00							$ -
			0.00							$ -
			0.00							$ -
			0.00							$ -
			0.00							$ -
			0.00							$ -
			0.00							$ -
Totals				$ 390.18	$ -	$ -	$ -	$ -	$ -	$ 20,289.36

Divide your monthly payment by 2 for fortnightly payments or 4 for weekly, this will maintain the required monthly payment and result in an extra months payment per year for weekly and fortnightly payments

Repayment	Frequency	Total
$ 1,000.00	12	$ 12,000.00
$ 500.00	26	$ 13,000.00
$ 250.00	52	$ 13,000.00

Mortgage Calculator	
Loan Amount	$ 212,000.00
Interest Rate (annual)	6.34
Term (months)	240
Total Payments	240
Monthly Interest	0.5283%
Monthly Payment	**$ 1,560.71**
Total Payments	$ 374,570.14
Total Interest	$ 162,570.14
Mortgage Repayment - Frequency	
Week	$ 390.18
Fortnight	$ 780.35
Month	$ 1,560.71

What to enter when refinancing
Current balance of loan
New interest rate
Remainder of Original Term in months

Figure C.6 — Completed WS 6 — Mortgage

(Completed Mortgage worksheet tracking payments and remaining balance.)

Holiday Plan

Destination	Start Saving Date	Depart Date	Return Date	Total Days	Saving Weeks
Byron Bay	01-06-25	07-11-25	10-11-25	3	22

Expense	Cost	Note	
Fuel	$ 150.00		
Accomodation	$ 600.00		
Food/Dining	$ 300.00		
Activities	$ 200.00		
Misc	$ 100.00		
	$ -		
	$ -		
	$ -		
	$ -		
	$ -		
	$ -		
	$ -		
	$ -		
	$ -		
	$ -		
	$ -		
Total Cost	**$ 1,350.00**	$ 62.17	Save each week to reach goal
		$ **62.17**	Current budget amount

Destination	Start Saving Date	Depart Date	Return Date	Total Days	Saving Weeks
Sunshine Coast	01-06-25	22-07-26	29-07-26	7	58

Expense	Cost	Note	
Plane Tickets	$ 800.00		
Accomodation	$ 1,800.00		
Food/Dining	$ 800.00		
Car Hire	$ 400.00		
Activities	$ 600.00		
Souvenirs	$ 200.00		
	$ -		
	$ -		
	$ -		
	$ -		
	$ -		
	$ -		
	$ -		
	$ -		
	$ -		
	$ -		
Total Cost	**$ 4,600.00**	$ 78.73	Save each week to reach goal
		$ **78.73**	Current budget amount

Figure C.7 — Completed WS 7 — Holiday Planning

(Completed Holiday Planning worksheet showing savings targets and progress for upcoming holidays.)

Misc. Costs

Expense	Cost	Note
Car Maintenance / Repairs	$ 600.00	Car maintenance per year
Total	**$ 600.00**	

These can be any random costs that come up and will appear in expenses averaged out to a weekly value

Figure C.8 — Completed WS 8 — Miscellaneous Costs

(Completed Miscellaneous Costs worksheet tracking irregular or annual expenses.)

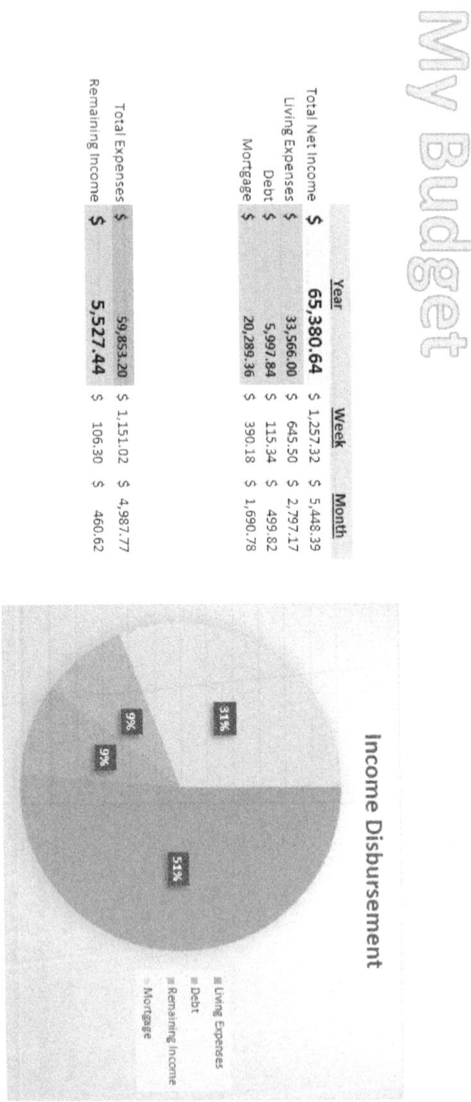

Figure C.9 — Completed WS 9 — Home Dashboard

(Completed Home Dashboard summarising income, expenses, debt, and available funds.)

Comparison - Current income with new job

All calculations taken to MONTHLY value

	Current Job Income			New Job Income			Difference (Month)	
Income	Week			Hours per week		40		
	Fortnight			Rate per hour	$	35.00		
	Month	$	5,598.00					
Income Totals	Month Gross	$	5,598.00	Month Gross	$	6,066.67	$	468.67
	Tax (Month)	$	1,023.88	Tax (Month)	$	1,173.64	$	149.76
	Month Net	$	4,574.12	Month Net	$	4,893.03	$	318.91
	Monthly Estimate values for these values							
Expenses	Transport or Tolls	$	-	Transport or Tolls	$	223.00	$	223.00
	Fuel	$	-	Fuel	$	120.00	$	120.00
	Food	$	-	Food	$	-	$	-
	Coffee	$	-	Coffee	$	-	$	-
	Total	$	-	Total	$	343.00	$	343.00
Income after expenses		**$**	**4,574.12**		**$**	**4,550.03**	**-$**	**24.09**

Unemployment Benefit with job calculated over a month -- Only relevant if the above Current income is from a benefit payment			
Calculate sliding scale to reduce current benefit payments, these calculations are done pre tax			
Non affected amount (week)	$	65.00	The weekly amount you can earn before your benefit payments are affected
Non affected amount (month)	$	281.67	per month
Amount reduced per $	$	0.50	How much is your benefit payment reduced per $1.00 earned
Income less free earnings	$	5,785.00	This amount will be subject to sliding reduction scale on earnings
benefit amount reduced by	$	2,892.50	This amount will be deducted from the benefit payment
benefit amount retained	**$**	**2,705.50**	
Job Earnings after tax	$	4,550.03	What you take home after tax and after paying your estimated monthly expenses.
Total Income	**$**	**7,255.53**	Total take home pay from job plus adjusted benefit payment
Difference	**$**	**2,681.41**	This is how much you will be in front/behind after all calulations are taken into consideration

Figure C.10 — Completed WS 10 — New Job Pay Comparison

(Completed New Job Pay Comparison worksheet comparing current income with potential new job income and benefit impacts.)

Discover More from PetiteKat Press!

Thank you for reading! If you enjoyed this book, you may also like our other titles. Click or scan the QR codes to learn more.

The MySQL Workshop
(Published by Packt Publishing)
(Training Guide)
A hands-on guide to mastering MySQL database development and administration.

Australian Slang Word Search
(Puzzle Book)
Find Aussie slang hidden in fun and challenging word search puzzles!

Periodic Table Word Search Puzzles
(Puzzle Book)
Learn elements and chemical symbols while solving puzzles built around the periodic table.

Visit us online at www.petitekatpress.com.au or scan the QRCode
Discover more books, bonus downloads, and updates.

Made in the USA
Monee, IL
04 November 2026

67384324R00236